Cities
of
Gods

Recent Titles in
Contributions to the Study of Religion
Series Editor: Henry W. Bowden

Southern Anglicanism: The Church of England in Colonial South Carolina
S. Charles Bolton

The Cult Experience
Andrew J. Pavlos

Southern Enterprize: The Work of National Evangelical Societies in the Antebellum South
John W. Kuykendall

Facing the Enlightenment and Pietism: Archibald Alexander and the Founding of Princeton Theological Seminary
Lefferts A. Loetscher

Presbyterian Women in America: Two Centuries of a Quest for Status
Lois A. Boyd and R. Douglas Brackenridge

Marchin' the Pilgrims Home: Leadership and Decision-Making in an Afro-Caribbean Faith
Stephen D. Glazier

Exorcising the Trouble Makers: Magic, Science, and Culture
Francis L. K. Hsu

The Cross, The Flag, and The Bomb: American Catholics Debate War and Peace, 1960–1983
William A. Au

Religious Conflict in Social Context: The Resurgence of Orthodox Judaism in Frankfurt Am Main, 1838–1877
Robert Liberles

Triumph over Silence: Women in Protestant History
Richard L. Greaves, editor

Neighbors, Friends, or Madmen: The Puritan Adjustment to Quakerism in Seventeenth-Century Massachusetts Bay
Jonathan M. Chu

CITIES
OF
GODS

Faith, Politics and
Pluralism in Judaism,
Christianity and
Islam

EDITED BY
NIGEL BIGGAR,
JAMIE S. SCOTT,
AND **WILLIAM SCHWEIKER**

CONTRIBUTIONS TO THE STUDY OF
RELIGION, NUMBER 16

GREENWOOD PRESS
NEW YORK • WESTPORT, CONNECTICUT • LONDON

Library of Congress Cataloging in Publication Data

Main entry under title:

Cities of gods.

(Contributions to the study of religion,
ISSN 0196-7053; no. 16)
Bibliography: p.
Includes index.
1. Religion and politics— Addresses, essays,
lectures. 2. Judaism— 20th century— Addresses,
essays, lectures. 3. Christianity— 20th century—
Addresses, essays, lectures. 4. Islam— 20th
century— Addresses, essays, lectures. I. Biggar,
Nigel. II. Scott, Jamie S. III. Schweiker,
William. IV. Series.
BL65.P7C57   1986   291.1'77   85-9879
ISBN 0-313-24944-X (lib. bdg. : alk. paper)

Library of Congress Catalog Card Number: 85-9879
ISBN: 0-313-24944-X
ISSN: 0196-7053

First published in 1986

Greenwood Press, Inc.
88 Post Road West
Westport, Connecticut 06881

Printed in the United States of America

∞

The paper used in this book complies with the
Permanent Paper Standard issued by the National
Information Standards Organization (Z39.48-1984).

10 9 8 7 6 5 4 3 2 1

Copyright Acknowledgments

Grateful acknowledgment is given for permission to reprint "Islamic Values and Radicalism
in the Islamic Near East," by Khalid Bin Sayeed, which appeared in *Orient* 25 (1984), published by Deutsches Orient-Institut, Hamburg, West Germany; and extracts from *The Poems
of Iqbal,* translated by V. G. Kierman (London: John Murray Publishers, Ltd., 1955).

Contents

Series Foreword   vii

Acknowledgments   ix

Introduction   1
NIGEL BIGGAR, JAMIE S. SCOTT AND WILLIAM SCHWEIKER

PART I.   **JUDAISM**

1.   The State as Essential Expression of the Faith of Judaism   11
      MANFRED H. VOGEL

2.   Judaism and Liberal Causes: A Severed Covenant?   21
      ROBERT M. SELTZER

3.   Pluralism and Theocrats: The Conflict Between Religion
      and State in Israel   35
      MITCHELL COHEN

4.   Jewish Approaches to Pluralism: Reflections of a
      Sympathetic Observer   55
      JOHN T. PAWLIKOWSKI, O.S.M.

PART II.   CHRISTIANITY

  5.   Christianity Within the Political Dialectics of
       Community and Empire   73
       MATTHEW L. LAMB

  6.   The Protestant Principle: Between Theocracy
       and Propheticism   101
       MARTIN E. MARTY

  7.   Human Rights Theory: A Basis for Pluralism Open
       to Christian Ethics   119
       JOHN P. LANGAN, S.J.

  8.   The Limits of Politics: The Christian Clash
       with Radicalism   143
       CHARLES DAVIS

PART III. ISLAM

  9.   Islam and Political Action: Politics in the Service
       of Religion   153
       FAZLUR RAHMAN

 10.   Islamic Resurgence: Religion and Politics in the Muslim
       World   167
       CHARLES J. ADAMS

 11.   How Useful Is "Islam" as an Explanation of the Politics
       of the Middle East?   193
       MARVIN ZONIS

 12.   Islamic Values and Radicalism in the Islamic Near East 211
       KHALID BIN SAYEED

       Bibliography: For Further Reading   231

       About the Contributors   235

       Index   237

Series Foreword

It has been a common observation since the days of Aristotle that human beings are political animals. Their social organizations take different shapes and allocate authority along varying lines, but forms of political management are distinctive to human cultures. Another quality, noted with perhaps less frequency and appreciation, is that people are religious, too. Different bases and emphases characteristically abound in this area, but religiosity of some sort appears endemic to human expressions. Components of religious perception and political action are naturally and inevitably intertwined at every level of social sophistication, in every age, on every section of the map. Recent events from presidential elections in the United States to popular movements in the Near East have reminded us that vital connections between spiritual values and political programs have important consequences. This book analyzes fundamental aspects of the continuing interaction between transcendental ideals and practical attempts at social implementation.

Half of this book took shape in the form of addresses originally delivered at a conference on religion and politics in 1982. Since then, those early papers have been revised and updated to include the most recent data on their respective topics. Six more essays on related subjects have been added to round out the spectrum of viewpoints and critical insights needed to cover the field more adequately. They shed light on the general relationship between religious values and governmental policy from a range of academic perspectives including philosophy, history, theology, ethics and political science. While many of these chapters take the long view and suggest a range of procedures, each of them focuses on basic qualities in Western religions as these three faiths (Judaism, Christianity and Islam) have actually been practiced. Similarly they concentrate on the concrete expressions of political policies, treating the field from a humanistic point of view rather than from the rarified abstractions of social science.

Jewish topics afford an investigation into the relation between "vertical" standards drawn from biblical prophets and the "horizontal" dimensions of human collectivities. They also invite analysis of shifting bases and agendas for a commitment to liberal principles. Another chapter concentrates on fundamentals such as peoplehood, nationality, religion and land in Zionism up to 1948, through the 1967 war, and after the 1984 elections in Israel. Another chapter probes questions of pluralism and toleration for Oriental Jews in a state where European Jews have dominated its ideas about existence and security. Christian topics include an overview of ambiguous legacies that can either sustain or destroy human life. Another surveys relationships between sacred realities and society, exploring stances from conservatism to radical revisionism. A third chapter probes tensions between Christian ethics and secular theories of human rights, seeking ways in which they challenge and possibly complement each other. Finally there is a consideration of whether radical perfectionist politics is compatible with Christian beliefs. Topics on Islam begin with a study of the ideal Muslim state as an entity that exists to serve spiritual values and moral principles, as an instrument where religion directs all spheres of human life. Another analyzes fundamentalist protest movements against modern regimes, clashes that often exhibit contrasting kinds of authoritarianism. A third chapter pursues the same theme where data from Iran, Egypt and Syria point to recurrent ethical mandates and political action. Finally there is a case study of how lower-class expectations in Pakistan and Iran contrast with capitalists and landowners in those countries.

All of these essays come into sharp focus against the backdrop of modern pluralism. There are multiple choices in different cultural spheres, and these various political options exist beside versions of Judaism, Christianity and Islam. Such plurality is historical fact. This book explores the ramifications of pluralism: philosophical acceptance of that fact. It asks how religion affects political progressivism, exploring mutual acceptance in our modern global village. It asks whether religious toleration is derived from political differentiation or if political exigencies contribute to a spectrum of theological expressions. It ponders this as a question basic to all three Western faiths and wonders if it pertains differently in the separate traditions. While not producing formulaic solutions that are quickly dated, this volume addresses vital questions that go to the heart of peace, harmony and justice as issues of common concern to religious and political leaders in modern societies.

Henry W. Bowden

Acknowledgments

No work of this length comes into being without the help and support of many people. This one is no exception. Since *Cities of Gods* had it beginnings in the 1982 Spring Conference, "Religious Conviction and Public Action: The Life of Faith in a Pluralistic World," at the Divinity School of the University of Chicago, thanks are due first to all those who made that possible. These include Dean Franklin Gamwell and the staff of the dean's office, especially Dolores Smith; and those who participated in the conference but who are only tacitly represented in the book, notably Rabbi Arnold Wolf and Professors Anne Carr and John O. Hunwick. We would also like to thank the Divinity School Association, the Divinity School and the University of Chicago for sharing the funding of the conference, and Deutsches Orient-Institut for allowing Professor Bin Sayeed's essay, "Islamic Values and Radicalism in the Islamic Near East," which appeared in the journal *Orient*, volume 25 (1984), to be reprinted here. Of course, no one deserves more gratitude than the contributors themselves, without whose industry and patience this volume would never have seen the light of day. Finally, we would like to extend a warm word of appreciation to Elizabeth Barrett Scott, Virginia Dunn-Biggar and Barbara Shenk for their support and help, which has been characteristically generous and unstinting.

Cities
of
Gods

Introduction

NIGEL BIGGAR, JAMIE S. SCOTT AND WILLIAM SCHWEIKER

This is a book about religion and politics. More specifically, it is a collection of essays variously addressing the mutual entanglements between religious faith and political engagement in the three great religions of the Book—Judaism, Christianity and Islam. Anyone who glances at today's newspaper headlines or catches a few moments of the evening news on television or radio will know just how pervasive such entanglements are in the modern world. Jewish orthodox extremists stubbornly, sometimes violently, resist Israeli withdrawal from the occupied territories of the West Bank and southern Lebanon. The fact that John Paul II is a Polish pope only highlights the extent to which the Catholic Church has long exercised a decisive influence over the political destiny not only of Poland, but of several other Eastern Bloc countries as well. In North America, Catholic bishops have recently confronted governments with bold, critical statements on issues ranging from social and economic injustice to the nuclear arms race. In South Africa, an Anglican bishop won the 1984 Nobel Peace Prize for his outspoken advocacy of the civil rights of blacks over and against the oppression of *apartheid*. And in the Islamic world, religious motives lay behind the overthrow of the shah of Iran and the assassination of Egypt's President Anwar al-Sadat.

These are only a few of the many recent instances of religious faith finding expression in political statement and action, and the list might be lengthened indefinitely. Among the first questions that any observer of such things is bound to ask is this: Is it inevitable that so many of the faithful among contemporary Jews, Christians and Muslims must become involved in politics? There are, of course, almost as many answers to such a question as there are incidents of religio-political controversy to illustrate it. Nevertheless, to begin with, let us hazard one broad assertion: The religious traditions of Judaism, Christianity and Islam are not merely invoked for political ends; they assign them. That is to say, as long as certain sets of religious beliefs make moral claims upon those who hold them, religious faith is bound to move faithful Jews, Christians and Muslims through political judgments to political actions with political consequences. Nor is this only so when those judgments lead to the self-conscious commission of political acts; for even if a particular kind of religious self-understanding compels a member of the faithful to withdraw from the political process, such an act of omission constitutes a political statement and carries political consequences all its own.

But this book is not simply about religious faith and political engagement. It is also about the very complex phenomenon of pluralism in contemporary religion and politics. Each of these three great traditions is without a doubt and self-avowedly monotheistic, but no longer may any of them be said in any but the weakest of senses to be monolithic—theologically or politically. Indeed, it may be the case that it has never been proper to describe any of these varied faiths as monolithic. But it is a commonplace of contemporary learning that, as the media of trade and communication have expanded through the centuries and one empire has replaced another in the name of modernity, the world has shrunk to become the now-familiar global village. And as the world has shrunk, so in practically every arena of human activity the number of choices for thought and action has multiplied—or, at least, people are aware of this multiplication of options, even if in certain societies not all options are live ones. Such are the dynamics of modern history and of the movement we broadly know as modernism, and such are the dynamics of life in our own time in particular. And to the extent that Judaism, Christianity and Islam are and strive to remain part of this modern world, Jews, Christians and Muslims cannot help but participate in these dynamics—or, at a minimum, feel their impact upon their lives.

Put another way, this means that while it was once possible for Saint Augustine to title a major treatise on relations between the religious and secular realms *De Civitate Dei* and make no apologies for so doing, in one sense at least this can no longer be the case. There are many reasons for this, and the phenomenon of pluralism in the modern world embraces several of them. First, within each of these three great religions of the Book, individual believers today face a plurality of theological options. There are several kinds of Judaism, several kinds of Christianity, and several kinds of Islam. While it is certainly not the case that every kind of Judaism, Christianity or Islam tolerates the idea of theological choice, to the extent that the historical fact of theological choice is confronted in a self-conscious, systematic and constructive way, we can talk meaningfully not simply about theological plurality, but about genuine theological pluralism in the modern world. Secondly, in a parallel fashion, life in the modern world presents

individual believers with a plurality of political options, even if in a particular
state the religious or the political authorities—or both—give no official
sanction to the idea of political choice. To the extent that the historical
fact of political choice, whether that choice is expressed in the form of a
democratic vote or in the form of outright revolution, is confronted in a
self-conscious, systematic and constructive way, we can talk meaningfully
not simply about political plurality, but about genuine political pluralism
in the modern world. Nor, third, are such competing claims upon the allegiance of the faithful restricted to alternative interpretations of their own
familiar religious traditions and political systems. Rather, the smallness of
the modern global village makes it all but impossible for any Jew, Christian
or Muslim to escape entirely more foreign religious and political visions of
the way things are and of the way things ought to be. Thus, to the extent
that this historical fact is confronted in a self-conscious, systematic and
constructive way, we can talk meaningfully not simply about the plurality
of religious traditions and political systems, but about the real possibility
of a genuine universal pluralism in both religion and politics. Not all of the
essayists would endorse such a broad schematization of the phenomenon
of pluralism in the modern world, of course, because either a particular
attitude or a particular method adopted does not allow for it. But it is clear
from the essays that follow that, whatever their theological and political
identities, contemporary believers in each of these three great religions of
the Book are faced with quite fundamental religious and political choices
among a range both of gods and of cities.

These general features of the way in which religion and politics are
entangled in the modern world give rise to a whole host of interrelated
questions. For example, given the plurality of theological expressions within
Judaism, Christianity and Islam alike, what does any individual Jew, Christian
or Muslim conceive to be the *appropriate* political expression of his or her
tradition? How does he or she select from his or her own diverse religious
tradition a specific and coherent political stance or identity? On a more
theoretical level, how does each of these three great religious traditions
evaluate the question of genuine political pluralism on the one hand and
on the other, the question of proper religious and political relations to other
traditions within the modern global village? How does each of these religious
traditions maintain a coherent theological identity among the plurality of
theological and political options within its own history on the one hand
and on the other, in the fact of those rival religious and political visions to
which the faithful are increasingly exposed? What kind and degree of religious and political pluralism does Judaism endorse—or Christianity, or Islam? What are the conditions and limits of this pluralism, and how and why
are they decided? Finally, in their approaches to the phenomenon of pluralism in the contemporary world, how similar and how different are the
problems and responses of Judaism, Christianity and Islam compared one

with another? And what determines the reactions of each of these three great traditions of the Book both to the plurality of theological and political options and to the questions of self-conscious, systematic and constructive religious and political pluralism which encroach increasingly upon them as each enters more deeply into contact and, one hopes, into meaningful conversation with the others?

These are large issues, and individual Jews, Christians and Muslims may and do react in many different ways when faced with such an array of challenges. If we were to schematize these reactions in terms of ideal types, we would find at one extreme, those for whom either a religious symbol or a memory of some historical experience fraught with religious signifi-cance—the prophetic tradition of the Hebrew scriptures, let us say, or the career of the Prophet Muhammad—is predominantly determinative what-ever other claims the modern world may make upon them and whether those claims take a religious or a political form, or both. In such cases, competing visions of the way things are or of the way things should be, either theologically or politically, will be rejected as alien and aberrant, whether they originate from within the religious tradition or impose them-selves from without. At the other extreme, we would find those for whom some aspect of the contemporary political situation—the social injustice of gross economic disparities, for instance, or the threat of nuclear extinction—so commands attention as to bring to the fore of awareness apparently pertinent themes or symbols in classic religious sources and particular re-ligiously significant historical memories. Thus educed, such religious motifs and memories are reinterpreted so as to address the contemporary political situation. Moreover, it is in cases both where current economic, social or political concerns—such as human rights, for example—predominate and determine the reinterpretation of classic religious themes and symbols and the re-evaluation of the religiously significant past, and where such concerns are held in common, that we are most likely to find numbers of the faithful, whether Jews, Christians or Muslims, who are willing to turn a sympathetic eye to alternative religious visions expressed within their own religious tradition—or even outside it. Here, then, lies one set of grounds for genuine religious and political pluralism within a religious tradition, and perhaps the first stirrings of a diverse but nonetheless valid universal pluralism.

The extreme case, of course, almost never occurs. Rather, every religious adherent's decision—even the martyr's—for or against a particular religio-political statement or course of action will arise out of a mixture of motives and influences. Where a classic religious theme or symbol is taken as uner-ringly normative, or a period of historical experience is taken as especially significant, it may fairly be supposed that the selection of one traditional source or period of history over another is itself a function of certain latent concerns about the current religio-political situation. Conversely, in cases where the specific demands of the contemporary situation appear to dominate the believer's decision making, it may also fairly be assumed that the moral exigencies of the moment only command the attention they do because, no matter how remotely, his or her modern political and religious consciousness is informed both by certain classic religious themes and symbols, and by a particular painful or liberating historical memory. In other words, a dialectic is at work in the religio-political judgments and actions of those faithful who, whether by accident or by intent, find themselves caught up in the complexities of contemporary politics. Sometimes, it is the traditional authority of some classic religious source or of some religiously significant historical experience which predominates; at others, the sheer immediacy of the demands placed upon the believer's attention by the current social, economic and political situation. But whichever aspect looms larger, today neither Jew nor Christian nor Muslim may make religio-political decisions which are not a balancing—albeit a biased balancing—of religious tradition colored by contemporary political conditions over and against political exigencies informed by received religious belief.

It would be quite possible to write Western history in terms of the conflicts and accommodations between faith and politics. If such entanglements seem to be forever with us, it is perhaps because of the equal power of religion and the state to inspire the deepest loyalties of mind, heart and will on the one hand, and on the other, because of the rival claims each makes upon those loyalties. Life in the modern world is without a doubt characterized by an increasing awareness of the seriousness and ubiquity of religio-political controversy. This is something of a contrast with our more recent past, for we no longer one-sidedly assume without question that such entanglements between religion and politics result from the emotionalism and fanaticism of the faithful. A fresh assessment is called for. The prophets of seventeenth-century rationalism and eighteenth-century Enlightenment in the West proclaimed the passing of historical religions and with their demise the end of ignorance and barbarism. Modernity, they liked to think, meant the dawn of universal civility and the emergence of a mature humanity from the dark ages of superstition. But today, in an ironic and often disturbing way, we see what looks like the pre-rational religion of our forefathers once again at work upon the rational structures of contemporary social, economic and political life. Western sociologists, economic historians and political theorists, as well as religious thinkers, are bemused by the picture of a Polish shipyard worker praying to the Virgin Mary, by the steely confidence of the Ayatollah Khomaini's stare—a medieval image, it seems to some, projected by televisual technology into our twentieth-century living rooms—or by the bizarre and bloody mismatching of age-old religious convictions and efficient modern weaponry in Israel or Ireland. Such sights jar popular assumptions about the eclipse of religion in the modern world.

Modern political theorists have tended either to discount religion as a social and economic force in a technological world or to reduce it to social and psychological functioning. All of this neglects the specific content of each of these great religions of the Book. On the other hand, many recent religious thinkers in each of these traditions have understood the task of religious reflection as in the main involving the business of making archaic and outdated faiths somehow intelligible and relevant to the modern world. This conception does attend to the content of Judaism, Christianity or Islam, but fails to account for the role that certain traditional expressions of each of these faiths now seems to play in the daily social, economic and political decision making of large numbers of the faithful. Religion and politics are entangled in questions of both matter and method in the modern world, whether one looks at things from a religious perspective or from that of a social, economic or political theorist. Recent history testifies all too vividly to this fact. To neglect the content of a religious tradition by concentrating only on its social, economic and political functions is to misinterpret the phenomena we daily witness; it is to associate Gdansk and Tehran without distinction. Conversely, to focus only upon the continuity within a religious tradition that the re-emergence of a classical theme or symbol in a modern political situation seems to imply is to overlook the very real social, economic and political issues which have drawn the attention of the faithful so forcefully to that traditional religious source; it is to reduce the concrete vitality of Gdansk or Tehran to hollow theological formulae. Today we must deal with religio-political phenomena on the levels both of reflection and of action, and we must resist the temptation to reduce political action to religious reflection, or to reduce religious expression to social, economic or political functioning. To this extent, the three great religions of the Book are perhaps better understood, at least to begin with, as each offering in different ways and to different degrees possibilities for the reintegration of human aspiration and action in a world fragmented by modern technological reason and bureaucratic indifference. The images which challenge us daily from the front pages of our newspapers and from the evening news on our televisions demand our fullest powers of religio-political interpretation. The resurgence of certain traditional aspects of each of these three faiths is part of a piercing criticism of those modern assumptions which both inform and support the way we understand and organize our world. As at once a problem for religio-political reflection and action today and a possible source of solutions for religio-political controversy in the modern world, the complex phenomenon of pluralism provides a suitable focus for the essays that follow.

It was to such considerations as these that the essayists represented here were asked to address themselves. Six of their essays appeared in earlier versions as the principal papers presented at a conference sponsored by the Divinity School Association (DSA) of the University of Chicago. The conference held at the Divinity School from March 31 to April 2, 1982, was entitled, "Religious Conviction and Public Action: The Life of Faith in a

Pluralistic World." Those who participated, and whose work now appears here in revised and updated form, included a philosopher of religion (Manfred H. Vogel), three historians of religion and religious thought (Robert M. Seltzer, Martin E. Marty and Fazlur Rahman), a theologian and student of modern Critical Theory (Matthew L. Lamb), and a political scientist (Marvin Zonis). To their contributions have been added a further six, authored by another theologian and student of Critical Theory (Charles Davis), by two theologians and ethical theorists (John Pawlikowski and John P. Langan), by another historian of religion (Charles J. Adams), and by two more political scientists (Mitchell Cohen and Khalid Bin Sayeed). To the religious and political pluralities which the essays address, therefore, we may add another plurality—the plurality of methods.

This collection represents a variety of ways of approaching the questions raised in and for Judaism, Christianity and Islam by and for Jews, Christians and Muslims who, willingly or not so willingly, are involved in religio-political conflict in the modern world. It is in such a world that we all live, a world in which religious and political conflicts daily threaten our lives and livelihoods, and in which, pre-eminently, we fear the menace of nuclear arms and the threat they pose to our very survival as a race. If in such a world, therefore, there are some who claim for their political convictions an absolute, religious sanction, and who would put the rest of us at fatal risk in order to realize those convictions, it behooves us to try to understand how and why such politics may be derived from such religion, and how and why such religion may be interpreted to support such politics. True understanding can only come through open and considered communications; and here, straight away, we are met by a large and fundamental problem. How is a pluralist, whether Jew or Christian or Muslim, to embrace a mon-archist? How is he or she to communicate with a propagandist? How enter into meaningful dialogue with a militant ideologue? How remain open to one who would dominate by force, perhaps destroy, what differs or whosoever disagrees? These are not idle, rhetorical questions; they bear heavily and all too immediately upon us. Yet each of these three great Western traditions—Judaism, Christianity and Islam—offers possibilities for transcending religious and political conflicts, for transforming the alien and outsider, be he or she of the same tradition or of another, into a member of a genuine religious and political pluralism. The essays that follow discuss several such possibilities for transcendence and transformation, the problems they entail and the promises they suggest.

PART I

JUDAISM

1

The State as Essential Expression of the Faith of Judaism

MANFRED H. VOGEL

The purpose of this essay is to examine the stance that Judaism takes with respect to the political dimension in life. We should note, therefore, at the very start that we are concerned here with the stance that *Judaism* takes rather than with the stance that *Jews* may or may not take toward the political dimension. It is important to note this, as it is by no means the case that the stance that Jews may take is always and necessarily the same as the stance that Judaism may dictate. The needs and requirements of the former are by no means always and necessarily identical with those of the latter. Indeed, the whole history of Judaism and of the Jewish people—and it is rather a long history—bears witness to the continuous tension between the two. What Jews as human beings wish and require is not necessarily what Judaism wishes and requires for them. Conversely, therefore, it also follows that what is good for Jews is not necessarily good for Judaism, and vice versa, what is good for Judaism is not necessarily good for the Jews.

As stated, this ironic discrepancy characterizes the situation throughout Jewish history, but it certainly comes to the fore and is most pronounced in the modern era in the context of the Emancipation. There can be no denying that in this context the interests and needs of the emancipated Jew often collide head-on with the interests and needs of Judaism. Thus, what we may claim on behalf of Judaism may not be at all what emancipated Jews would want to claim as their position. But be this as it may, our concern is with the position of Judaism and not with the position of Jewry, specifically emancipated Jewry. Namely, we are not concerned with the historical, sociological or psychological analysis of the attitude taken by a certain collectivity of people but rather with the philosophical analysis of a certain *Weltanschauung* or view of the world and the human place and vocation in it, which we call Judaism; that is, as we would be inclined to say, we are concerned with a philosophical analysis of the structure of faith which constitutes Judaism.

We must realize, however, that Judaism in its historical manifestation—as, indeed, all other historical religions—encompasses a number of structures of faith. It is not monolithic; rather, it is a mixture of different structures of faith held together by shared symbols, rituals and institutions. Thus, we should specify that our intention is to deal exclusively with those structures of faith that can be encountered in the prophetic strand of the Bible and in the non-mystical halakhic strand of rabbinic Judaism; and that we do not propose to deal here with those structures of faith which may manifest themselves, for example, in the priestly strand or the wisdom strand of the Bible or in the mystical or hasidic strand of rabbinic Judaism. Had we dealt with these latter strands the picture that would have emerged regarding our topic would have been quite different.

Our decision to deal with the former prophetic and non-mystical halakhic strands is not, however, completely arbitrary. For we would want to argue that these strands represent the mainstream expression in the historical manifestation of Judaism, and what is even more significant, that they represent the *distinctive* expression of Judaism. Indeed, no less significantly, though on a different level, a case can be made that it is by virtue of the structures of faith encountered in these strands that Judaism has been able to survive through millennia of years of diaspora-existence. But whether or not one accepts the validity of these justifications, it is important that we are clear about the parameters of our investigation; namely, that when we refer to Judaism in this essay we have in mind its prophetic and non-mystical halakhic strands.

Last, by way of clarification, we should specify that the notion of "political dimension" involved in our discussion here is used in its broadest sense as that dimension which encompasses social and economic, as well as narrowly "political," relations. In short, "political dimension" is used here to signify what we may call the "horizontal dimension" of life in its totality.

Thus, the task before us in this essay is to examine in what way—and if at all—the structure of faith of Judaism, and specifically of the prophetic and halakhic strands, implicates involvement in the horizontal dimensions of life. That is to say, is involvement in the horizontal dimension of life a necessary, essential and inextricable aspect of the religious life or is it of no real consequence? And if the former, in what sense does it constitute the religious vocation for Judaism?

We can answer this central question in a very straightforward and unqualified way: Our thesis is that the structure of faith of Judaism necessarily implicates, as an essential and inextricable act, its involvement within the horizontal dimension of life in all its aspects—the social, economic and political. Take away the possibility of involvement in the horizontal dimension of life and the very structure of faith of Judaism disintegrates. The task before us now, of course, is to justify and explain this claim.

To justify it should not, in our judgment, be too difficult. For it can hardly be denied that biblical prophecy by its very essence is deeply involved in the horizontal dimension of life. Apart from its critique of social injustice and of economic oppression and its concern for international politics what is biblical prophecy? And is not the distinctive and imposing feature of the Halakhah the fact that, in addition to the ritual law, it encompasses a comprehensive civil, political and criminal law and so the totality of the horizontal dimension of life? The point, I think, needs no further elaboration. Indeed, biblical and rabbinic scholarship has almost universally recognized and acknowledged this point. To quote at random only a few sources: "the justice of the prophets is social justice. They demand not only a pure heart but also just institutions. They are concerned for the improvement of society even more than for the welfare for the individual. . . . "[1]; "the Hebrews were the first who rebelled against the injustice of the world. . . . Israel demanded social justice"[2]; "our social legislation is derived from the spirit of the prophets. Also in the future will the spirit of Israel remain the instigator and awakener of social reforms"[3]; "the basis of Judaism is ethics"[4]; "the idea of the inseparateness between religion and ethical life arose for the first time in Judaism. . . . This idea of the unity of ethics and religion passes through the whole Bible . . . and this applies equally to rabbinic literature"[5]; "in any reading of Judaism the ethical dimension is of supreme importance. Judaism has always taught that God wishes man to pursue justice . . . to make his contribution towards the emergence of a better social order."[6] This is the intriguing and challenging task which we will try to pursue in the remainder of this essay.

We would submit that the key to the understanding of why the structure of faith in these strands of Judaism necessarily and essentially implicates involvement in the horizontal dimension of life lies in the fact that the very structure of faith here formulates itself from an ethical perspective rather that from an ontological one. What do we mean by this? We mean that the fundamental human predicament is not perceived here to consist in the way people are constituted but rather in the way in which they express and realize themselves within the possibilities and limitations of their given ontological constitution. The fact that people are constituted, to use Buberian terms, as an It-Thou being, as body and soul, as material and spiritual, as divine and earthly—as the bearer of the divine image and a being of nature, a member of the animal kingdom—is not perceived to constitute the fundamental predicament. There is nothing wrong with the way people were created. By and large, the structure of faith of Judaism is not pessimistic or desperate about creation; on the contrary, it judges it to be good. Rather, it perceives the fundamental predicament, the problematic, to lie in the balance which people all too often strike between these two dimensions in the way they express and realize themselves. The problematic lies in the fact that people all too often realize and express themselves as beasts—albeit sophisticated beasts but therefore also very mischievous ones—rather than as bearers of the divine image. To use Buberian terms again, the predicament lies in the fact that people all too often act and relate to others in the I-It rather than in the I-Thou context. Commensurately, therefore, the salvation that is envisioned and yearned for does not involve the ontological transformation of people, their new creation as "new beings," but rather their steadfastness in striking and maintaining the proper balance between the two dimensions constituting their being. Indeed, redemption rather than salvation is envisaged. It should be clear that as such the perceived predicament and the envisaged redemption are centered here not on the way people are constituted—their ontological makeup—but on their actions and relations with others. Consequently, the perspective involved here and in terms of which the structure of faith formulates itself, is evidently an ethical perspective. For the evaluation of actions and relations, specifically of *human* actions and relations, is precisely what constitutes the business of ethics.

Further, a structure of faith that formulates itself from the ethical perspective necessarily implicates involvement in the horizontal dimension of life. For in being concerned with the proper balancing between the It- and the Thou-dimension in people's expression and realization of themselves in their actions and relations, it must of necessity encompass human action and relations with respect to the world, the human world, the human horizontal dimension of life. The horizontal dimension of life cannot be left out of the picture as inconsequential precisely because the perceived predicament and corresponding redemption necessarily involve here, at least in part, the human actions and relations which impinge upon the horizontal dimension of life. Thus, people's actions and relations with respect to that dimension play here an essential part in the formulation of the two basic categories of the structure of faith; that is, the category of the fundamental predicament and that of redemption.

But even more to our point—and this, indeed, is the very crux of the matter—the very actions and relations of people with respect to God and, conversely, God's actions and relations with respect to people must be refracted or mediated through the horizontal dimension of life. For we must not overlook or forget that the It-dimension in people is not to be extirpated. People remain this-worldly beings.[7] But this, in turn, means that all actions involving people and thus including the actions and relations which express the Thou-dimension, must inevitably be refracted through the It-dimension. Thus, even human actions and relations with respect to God, which belong exclusively to the pure Thou-dimension because God is a pure Thou being—the Eternal Thou—must be refracted here through the horizontal It-dimension because of the inextricable presence of that dimension in the human constitution. This, of course, means that the most fundamental and central aspect of the religious life, the relation between the human and the divine, is required here to be mediated through the horizontal dimension. Indeed, in the prophetic and non-mystical halakhic strands of Judaism the burden of the expression of the relationship of people to God—the burden of the expression of faith and of worship—is not expressed in direct vertical relationships but rather in indirect relationships; that is, in relationships which go through the horizontal dimension, specifically the human horizontal dimension, since people are the only beings in nature endowed with the Thou-dimension.[8]

Or, to make the same point, but this time not with respect to people but rather with respect to the divine: it is indeed the case that, in the structure of faith of the prophetic and non-mystical halakhic strands of Judaism, God, who is constituted as a pure Thou and as transcending the world, is nonetheless represented as deeply and essentially involved in the relations of people to the world—again, specifically the human social world. God, the pure Thou, the transcending God, is affected in the most real and profound sense by what people do or do not do with respect to the world, especially with respect to fellow humans.[9] Thus, in the prophetic and in the non-mystical halakhic strands of Judaism, people can fully witness to God in the last analysis only through the world; they can fully establish their relationship to God only through and in the world. Take away people's involvement in the horizontal dimension of life, and the whole structure of faith collapses. Thus, in the strands of Judaism represented here one cannot separate the vertical from the horizontal, the sacred from the profane, relegating the religious concern—that is, faith—exclusively to the former. The religious concern that, of course, must ultimately come to rest in the vertical, is nonetheless inextricably intertwined with the horizontal.

But let us be clear about the precise meaning of the relationship that exists here between faith and the horizontal dimension of life. Clearly, it is diametrically opposed to the model whereby faith as the direct vertical relating of people to the divine is completely (one is tempted to say hermetically) separated from the horizontal dimension—a model that may be found, for example, in some formulations of German Lutheranism. But let us note what may not at first sight appear so clear, that it also differs from the model whereby faith, still conceived here as the direct vertical relating of people to the divine, is secondarily connected with the horizontal dimension; where it is brought to bear upon the horizontal dimension, for example, by molding and guiding it or by manifesting its fruit within it, a model that may be encountered, perhaps, in Calvinism or in Catholicism. For in Judaism the very constitution of faith is effected through the horizontal dimension. It is not that faith is constituted here independently as a direct vertical mode of relating which is then brought into relation with the horizontal dimension of life. Rather, faith is constituted from the very beginning as an indirect mode of relating, which is refracted through the horizontal dimension of life. Without relating through the horizontal dimension of life there can be no faith. Perhaps we can put the matter thus: the relation of faith to the horizontal dimension of life is not established in the context of sanctification; it is established in the very context of justification.

But to return to our main line of argument, there is an all-important aspect which the formulation of the structure of faith from the ethical perspective further implicates for the prophetic and non-mystical halakhic strands of Judaism. For, in implicating the involvement of religion in the horizontal dimension, it also implicates an inextricable bond between religion and the category of the ethnic-national entity. This is to say, it establishes religion as being primarily the affair not of the individual but rather of the collectivity, specifically, of the ethnic-national collectivity. Religion expresses itself primarily in the context of the ethnic-national entity, impinging upon the individual secondarily and then only by virtue of his membership in the ethnic-national entity. It is not surprising, therefore, that the human pole in the divine-human relation, both when it is the active agent and when it is the receiving object in the relation, is represented here primarily by the ethnic-national collectivity and not by the individual.

The claim that religion must implicate the collectivity rather than the individual as the primary context of its expression is implicit in the fact that religion here formulates itself from the ethical perspective, and therefore impinges on questions concerning human actions and relations and not human being. As such, it cannot impinge exclusively on the individual person but must impinge on people and the object of their actions or their partners in relation. For a number of reasons that cannot be elaborated upon here, this partner—this "other"—must be a fellow human. That is to say, inasmuch as the ethical perspective involved here represents an ethics that is grounded in accountability and responsibility, it must impinge on actions and relations that arise exclusively between people and their fellow-humans and not between people and the inanimate objects of nature. Thus, religion here impinges, not upon people in their monadic individuality, but upon both people and their fellow humans, and a twosome, a person and a fellow-human, constitutes a collectivity, a human community.

Furthermore, that the collectivity implicated here cannot be just any collectivity but must be specifically that of the ethnic-national entity can be seen from the fact that only the latter can encompass the full gamut of horizontal relations on which a religion formulating itself from the ethical perspective should optimally impinge. All other subnational or extranational collectivities such as, for example, the family, the clan, or any social, cultural, professional, ideological or political association, can present only some of these relations, never all of them. Thus, if the horizontal dimension of life is to be made available to religion in all its relations—the social, economic and political—the collectivity implicated here must be specifically the ethnic-national collectivity.

It must be clear, however, that this collectivity alone cannot really fulfill its function with respect to religion—that is, that it cannot make the horizontal dimension of life fully available—unless it has sovereignty. In other words, the ethnic-national entity must have the power to shape, regulate and determine the relations constituting the horizontal dimension of life. It must have the power to impose its wishes and judgments in regard to these relations. In other words, it must possess the horizontal dimension. It must have it at its disposal and be free to determine its destiny.

We have argued thus far, therefore, that in formulating themselves in ethical terms the prophetic and non-mystical halakhic strands of Judaism implicate an indirect relating to the divine, a relating that is refracted through the horizontal dimension of life and thus involves Judaism fundamentally and essentially in all the aspects of the matrix of the horizontal dimension without exception. We have further argued that this implicates an inextricable bond between Judaism and an ethnic-national entity. And finally, we have argued that for Judaism to express and realize itself optimally, that ethnic-national entity must possess sovereignty.

Indeed, in light of these considerations one can come to understand and evaluate the major developments in Jewish history not only from the vantage point of the fortunes or the suffering of Jewry, but also from that of the exigencies of the structure of faith of Judaism. In other words, we can gain fresh insights into the strengths and weaknesses of the major periods of Jewish history, strengths and weaknesses that will be judged now not in terms of how they impinged on the well-being of Jewry, but rather in terms of how they impinged on the viability of the structure of faith of Judaism.

Accordingly, from this vantage point the essential virtue of the biblical period lies in the fact of sovereignty and in the consequent putting of the horizontal dimension in all its relations at the disposal of Judaism. Such a context enabled Judaism to express itself fully, and in this sense it was the fulfillment of the promise. Indeed, the tradition acknowledged this in its continual yearning for a restoration that signified for it not only liberation from the physical suffering of exile, but the renewal of the opportunity for Judaism to express itself *fully*, that is, to use its own language, the renewal of the opportunity to observe *all* of God's commandments. It is no coincidence that the tradition ties its messianic hope to this restoration, making the former contingent upon the latter.

Conversely, the essential predicament and problematic which diaspora-existence poses must be understood to lie principally in its significance as the abrogation of sovereignty. But more specifically, the problematic of the abrogation of sovereignty must be seen here to consist not so much in the scattering of the Jews or in their dependence for their very physical survival on the good graces of others, but in the fact that the abrogation of sovereignty threatened the availabilty to Judaism of the horizontal dimension of life. For without a horizontal dimension at its disposal Judaism cannot survive.[10] Indeed, Judaism managed to survive in diaspora-existence only because it succeeded, partly due to fortuitous circumstances, in establishing what has been called "a state within a state"; that is to say, only because it succeeded in creating in diaspora, and thus without sovereignty, a portable horizontal dimension that was at its disposal. Certainly, this horizontal dimension provided by "ghettoized" existence was limited, and consequently the expression of the structure of faith of Judaism in these circumstances could only be truncated. Still, it was evidently sufficient to allow the survival of Judaism.

Correlatively, by the very same logic of viewing matters from the vantage point of the interests and requirements of the structure of faith of Judaism, the crisis which the Emancipation has precipitated in modern Jewish life must be seen to lie essentially in the fact of its abrogation of the limited horizontal dimension which Judaism had managed to establish for itself in the context of diaspora-existence. For what the Emancipation really signifies is the exit of Jewry from its "ghettoized" existence and its entry into the life stream of the host nation, and the real crisis that this represents, when viewed from the vantage point of the structure of faith of Judaism, is the loss of the horizontal dimension to Judaism. For the horizontal dimension— albeit limited and truncated—that Judaism managed to constitute for itself in the context of "ghettoized" existence could not be transferred into the life stream of the host nation. This meant that to the extent that Judaism did manage to accompany emancipated Jewry, albeit in a restricted and mitigated way, into the life stream of the host nation, it was nonetheless, in terms of its own structure, made impotent in the process. Thus, from the vantage point of the structure of faith of Judaism, the real crisis which the Emancipation precipitates for Judaism must be seen to lie in the fact that it abrogates the horizontal dimension that was at the disposal of Judaism, and that it consequently and necessarily emasculates Judaism and renders it impotent.[11]

Finally, the real significance of the re-establishment of the State of Israel from the vantage point of the structure of faith of Judaism lies in its recovery for Judaism of the horizontal dimension in terms of emancipated Jewry, that is, no longer in a truncated form, but to its full extent. For only in the context of the re-established State of Israel can Jewry re-enter the life stream of history, can Jewry be emancipated from its "ghettoized" existence, in a way that allows Judaism to accompany it fully and in a viable manner. If Judaism is to survive in the context of the Emancipation, therefore, the re-establishment of the State of Israel becomes a condition sine qua non. For only in the context of the re-established state can the horizontal dimension in terms of emancipated Jewry be placed at the disposal of Judaism. And what is more, because the horizontal dimension is endowed here with sovereignty, it allows Judaism not only to survive—to hold the fort and mark time as did the horizontal dimension in the context of "ghettoized" existence—but also to pursue its vocation once more in full force.

Thus, we have argued that insofar as its very structure of faith formulates itself from the ethical perspective, Judaism must express itself in the horizontal dimension. It must impinge upon the horizontal dimension in all of its aspects. The availability, therefore, of the horizontal dimension is essential to Judaism. Without a horizontal dimension at its disposal, Judaism would disintegrate. In no other religion is this requirement to be involved in the horizontal dimension, to impinge upon it in all its aspects, more central or essential than in Judaism. Moreover, we have also argued that Judaism can impinge upon the horizontal dimension only if the horizontal dimension legitimately belongs to it, only if it possesses sovereignty over it. Otherwise put, it can impinge upon the horizontal dimension only in its own "back yard," in its own "home." But this means that the most that Judaism can do in the context of diaspora-existence is to constitute, if allowed, a limited horizontal dimension, separated and isolated from the life stream of the host nation. Clearly, it cannot impinge upon the horizontal dimension of the host nation. No host would allow it to do so, and quite rightly.

But one might contend that while this argument is valid with respect to host nations that are homogeneous, it would be far less so with respect to host nations that constitute pluralistic societies. For would not Judaism in these circumstances have a rightful claim upon part of the horizontal dimension of life, and would it not, therefore, be allowed to impinge, at least in part, upon it? Thus, if the Emancipation were to take place in the context of a pluralistic society, would not the problematic which it precipitates for Judaism be greatly mitigated? There is no question that at first sight the pluralistic alternative appears very attractive. But on a closer look, we would submit, its attractiveness is greatly diminished.

First, there are several very difficult practical problems which a pluralistic situation would pose. How, for example, would such an arrangement work when there are any number of religions claiming the right to impinge upon the horizontal dimension? Would it work by finding the least offensive common denominator of these religions and allowing only that to impinge upon the horizontal dimension, or would the horizontal dimension be partitioned among the various religions allowing each to impinge on only part of it? Clearly, neither of these alternatives would be satisfactory to Judaism nor, I dare say, to any other religion. But as far as Judaism is concerned, there is an even more serious problem, a problem not of mere practicality, but of substance. It presents itself when we ask what kind of pluralism are we talking about? Are we talking of a pluralism that is merely religious, or are we talking of one that is actually ethnic? If it is the former, then Judaism, unlike other religions, may well be unable to avail itself of the opportunities that it affords. For, as we have seen above, Judaism is inextricably bound to a specific ethnic-national entity and it would perforce be excluded from such pluralism by virtue of this ethnic bond. Thus, for pluralism to present meaningful possibilities to Judaism in diaspora-existence, it would have to be specifically ethnic. But given the way the world is, I am not at all sanguine that such an ethnic pluralism is feasible. I certainly do not know of any instance of ethnic pluralism which is stable and viable and even apparently permanent, let alone any instance which would also incorporate Judaism as a fully fledged ethic partner.[12]

Therefore, we must conclude that as far as diaspora-existence is concerned, Judaism in the context of the Emancipation is not really in a position to impinge upon the horizontal dimension of life, even if *emancipated* Jewry does. This is somewhat ironic because Judaism, perhaps more than any other religion, is a religion whose very essence requires it to impinge upon the horizontal dimension of life. But, then, this is part of the price which diaspora-existence exacts.

NOTES

1. Julius Wellhausen, *Israelitische und Judische Geschichte* (Berlin: Reimer Publishing House, 1895), p. 114.

2. Ernest Renan, *Histoire de peuple d'Israel*, 5 vols. (Paris: Calmann-Levy, 1894–95), 3:vi-vii.

3. Herman Gunkel, *Deutsche Rundschau*, 11 (1928): 231.

4. K. Kohler, *The Ethical Basis of Judaism* (New York: Young Men's Hebrew Association, 1887), p. 143.

5. I. Epstein, *Emunat Ha-Yahadut* (Jerusalem: Mosad Harav Kook, 1965), pp. 18–19.

6. L. Jacobs, *A Jewish Theology* (New York: Behrman House, 1973), p. 231.

7. See, for example, Martin Buber, *I and Thou*, 2d ed., trans. Ronald Gregor Smith (New York: Charles Scribner's Sons, 1958), pp. 11, 34.

8. Manfred H. Vogel, "The Distinctive Expression of the Category of Worship in Judaism," *Bijdragen* 43, no. 4 (October 1982): 350–82.

9. For a striking description of this aspect of the divine in prophetic literature, see A. J. Heschel, *The Prophets*, 2 vols. (New York: Harper & Row, 1969), particularly vol. 2, chapters 1, 3 and 4.

10. For a penetrating analysis of this point, see Max Wiener, *Judische Religion in Zeitalter der Emanzipation* (Berlin: Philo Verlag und Buchhandlung, 1933).

11. For a fuller analysis of the problematic which the Emancipation precipitates for Judaism, see Manfred H. Vogel, "The Dilemma of Identity for the Emancipated Jew," reprinted in *New Theology, No. 4*, ed. Martin E. Marty and Dean G. Peerman (New York: Macmillan, 1967), pp. 162–77.

12. For a fuller critique of the notion of pluralism as it impinges upon the state of Judaism and Jewry in diaspora, see Manfred H. Vogel, "The Impact of the Emancipation on Continuity and Change in Judaism," *Journal of Religion* 59, no. 4 (October 1979): 464–71.

2

Judaism and Liberal Causes: A Severed Covenant?

ROBERT M. SELTZER

Of all the political philosophies, liberalism has the greatest openness to genuine pluralism. Committed to limited government and the essential separation of the public from the private realms, liberalism is concerned with arrangements protecting the individual's rights against invasion by a despotic sovereign power. Liberalism takes as its starting point the liberty of the citizenry, each of whom is endowed with rights (including the freedom of religion) which are held to exist prior to and independent of the state. Liberals often find it more difficult to establish a clear position with respect to communal pluralism—pluralism of group rights within the body politic. This is most problematic where certain religions insist on maintaining an especially sharp boundary between the faithful and the gentiles, or where certain ethnic minorities insist on the primacy of their group identities within the nation-state. The problem then arises as to how the common good of society can be assured if the divisions within it are too occupied with their own interests.[1]

Traditional Judaism survived in the Diaspora because there were societies which allowed the Jewish collective sufficient social autonomy to maintain itself as a legitimate, self-perpetuating corporate minority and which were more or less willing to tolerate the ritual and theological boundaries which defined Jewish existence. Liberalism's individualistic pluralism would seem to deny the conditions that facilitated Jewish survival for so many centuries; yet, modern Jews have been quite favorably disposed to liberalism and liberal causes.

Not all Jews have been liberals, of course, but enough to have attracted attention from admirers and from those who have found this propensity disturbing. The young Reinhold Niebuhr wrote in 1928, when minister to a Detroit church, "The more I make contact with the Jews the more I am impressed with the superior sensitiveness of the Jewish conscience in social problems."[2] T. S. Eliot, speaking in 1933 against liberalism as destructive of a stable, creative tradition, remarked that in a nation concerned to preserve that tradition, "reasons of race and religion combine to make any large number of free-thinking Jews undesireable."[3] The question of "why Jewish liberalism" has taken a new turn since the mid-1970s, when an articulate group of American Jewish intellectuals began in earnest to argue for the Jewish stake in a modern conservative position. Not long ago one would have included only friends among the admirers of Jewish liberalism and anti-Semites among those who were disturbed by Jewish liberalism. Times change. Now, the past association of Jews with liberalism is cited by those who do not approve of our particularistic Jewish loyalties, while among the most severe critics of Jewish liberalism are loyal Jews who insist that our natural allies are to be found toward the right rather than the left wing of the American political spectrum, and that Jews must adopt a more hard-headed, less utopian, certainly less moralistic stance in issues of public policy affecting vital Jewish interests.[4]

In this chapter I will examine as a historian the modern Jewish attraction to liberal (and to some extent radical) positions. I am also a Jew looking for a Jewish liberalism not rendered nugatory by changed circumstances. Jewish liberalism can refer to the liberalism of Jews as an empirical fact, or to the conviction that liberalism is a valid, even compelling expression of the Jewish tradition. The first is well documented and subject to a variety of causal analyses. The second implies that Jews *should* be sympathetic to a liberalism informed by one's Jewish religious commitment and that a Jewish religious commitment should spur one to universal humanitarian concerns. A scholarly defense of this view raises the further question of the role of modern Jewish history in defining a modern Jewish theology. To those for whom Judaism is a living faith, the lessons which history can teach theology is a matter of considerable importance.

The question of Jewish liberalism, therefore, is a whole agenda of questions. First, there is the issue of which methodologies should be used. Then there is the question of whether there are elements in the Jewish tradition that bear directly on modern liberalism. Next, there is the changing character of Jewish liberalism from classical nineteenth-century formulations to twentieth-century welfare-state liberalism. Further, there is the question of whether a future Jewish liberalism will require a more explicit theological grounding. Finally, the question of whether Jews *should* be liberal directs us to the hoary issue of the relation of the particularistic to the universalistic in Judaism, that is, to the relationship between a primal concern of Jews with their own people and an outward-facing Jewish social responsibility. An ongoing Jewish liberalism rooted in religious faith should be able to cope with both Jewish and general needs—not to abolish all tension between them (we will always have to make specific choices in this world) but to show the logical congruence of the particular and the universal in any Jewish political philosophy which can claim a reasonable degree of Jewish authenticity.

Some recent approaches to the political behavior of Jews explain Jewish liberalism and radicalism as a compensatory mechanism for powerlessness and insecurity, a psychology stemming from the marginal social position of the Jew seeking acceptance in modern society. Stanley Rothman and S. Robert Lichter in their recent *Roots of Radicalism: Jews, Christians, and the New Left* suggest that Jewish attraction to universalistic ideas of a liberal or a radical kind is a means for ending a felt marginality through undermining the very concepts that define the Jews as subordinate and different. Radical Jews search for (or invent) a new brotherhood to join, and they lose (or sublimate) their Jewishness in a struggle against a common enemy—say, against all capitalists or imperialist exploiters. Liberal Jews retain a measure of Jewishness but prefer to deny the reality of the cultural or religious differences between them and Christians: they are portrayed as having a powerful need to assume that Jews and non-Jews are brothers under the skin and in the harmony of their civic good intentions.[5] Jewish liberalism may be a result of the modern social situation of the Jews in certain countries, but is it then only a form of acculturation or assimilation?

Charles Liebman in his provocative *The Ambivalent American Jew* has proposed that American Jewish political liberalism attempts to bring America into harmony with the basic values of acculturated American Jews, but not necessarily of traditional Judaism. Liebman argues that those Jews who are closest to traditional beliefs and most immersed in traditional practice are often the least prone to liberalism.[6] We will return to this problem of defining the relationship of Jewish liberalism to the Jewish heritage later in this essay. Steven M. Cohen in *American Modernity and Jewish Identity* suggests, first, that Jewish liberalism, especially in America, expresses an insecure minority's tendency to identify with groups more predisposed to intergroup tolerance. Second, far from undermining this long-standing liberal commitment, the changing economic profile of American Jews has harmonized with the changing character of liberalism. Third, Jewish insecurities and anxieties conditioned Jews to liberalism as a sign of acceptance into the most "progressive" and prestigious segments of the larger society.[7] This multifactored analysis, for all its suggestiveness, shows no interest in the morally sensitive person who asks how Judaism would conceive of the ideal modern polity. Even the most perceptive and refined sociology can hardly provide a sufficient explanation of Jewish liberalism. At best it provides partial insights that must be complemented by the other part.

The supposed burden of marginality may indeed explain some of the psychological motivations of Jews, especially of some radical Jews. But can there not be a Jewishly affirmative liberalism as well as a self-denying liberalism? Marginality as a sociohistorical explanation brackets two questions that remain on the existential agenda regardless of the historical or socio-psychological etiology of Jewish liberalism. First, What public policy is most ethical? Second, What Jewish sources lie behind the Jewish attraction to certain conceptions of an ideal society? Marginality is a condition. Responses to a condition draw on one's cultural resources. Not long ago, Jacob Katz wrote,

In seeking the reasons for the historically established affinity between Judaism and liberal ideas, . . . one must have recourse to the basic assumptions of the belief system, the far-reaching accountability of man for his deeds and destiny, . . . the emphasis on this world as the main scene of individual human endeavor as well as the scene of history's course and consummation, to [a] concomitant absolute evaluation of human life, and the high premium set upon securing the means to sustain it.[8]

We would like to push Katz's suggestion at least one step further in ex-plaining the attraction of Jews to liberal causes.

No historian would deny the heuristic principle that social conditions shape a historic phenomenon such as Jewish liberalism. Yet there are other shaping elements that may be at work, specifically, that body of historical Jewish injunctions, beliefs and values that have acted to censor, to condemn, to reject, to inhibit, to channel certain universal urges and impulses. The impact of Judaism on the real-life choices and attitudes of Jews throughout history is not invariable nor does it always possess the same salience. Not all Jews practice what Judaism teaches. Not all Jews agree to what Judaism teaches. Not all Jewish commentators, thinkers or communal leaders have interpreted the classic texts in the same way and agree as to what Judaism teaches. But Jewish values can insinuate themselves into all but the most assimilated or attenuated Jewish super ego, sharpening the conscience, fo-cusing attention on certain conditions, recalling what was said about certain priorities.

There are certain historical constituents of the Jewish tradition that are relevant to any modern theology of Jewish liberalism. First is the classical prophecy of ancient Israel as it developed out of the covenantal law of the Torah. Covenantal law already possessed a decided ethical component, as in its concern for the claim on society's attention by the widow, orphan and resident alien. Classical prophecy carried this to the point where the future destiny of the people of Israel was held to depend on fulfillment of its duties to the poor and powerless. We recall, for example, Amos 5:10– 25, Micah, chapter 3, Isaiah 1:1–17, Jeremiah 22:13–17, Isaiah, chapter 58. The use of these and similar prophetic passages by modern preachers in their homilies on social justice is not without some justification in the original context, where the Holy God of Israel issued unambiguous instruc-tions for the pursuit of justice among his people and gave that pursuit absolute priority. One does not assert that this is the only message of the Hebrew Bible if one observes that these passages of warning and condemnation are imbedded in the Scriptures to reawaken to life in many an anguished historical situation in subsequent centuries.

A second element of traditional Judaism relevant to Jewish liberalism is the utopian stream in Jewish messianism, which built on the eschatology of classical prophecy. Gershom Scholem reminds us in his essay on the messianic idea in Judaism that Jewish messianism, especially its apocalyptic mode, contains restorative, as well as utopian themes.[9] The particular redemption of the people of Israel from dispersion, oppression and subjugation to idolatrous powers was vividly and ardently hoped for: "Sound the great shofar for our freedom; lift up the banner to gather our exiles, and gather us from the four corners of the earth. Blessed art thou, O Lord, who gatherests the dispersed of thy people Israel" (from the daily worship service). The utopian dimension is reflected in the formulations that a time will come "when the world will be perfected under the kingdom of the Almighty" (in the *Alenu* passage of the worship service). As noted by Scholem, a philosophical fusion of the universal and particular can be seen in Maimonides' remarks at the end of the eleventh and twelfth paragraphs of the Laws Concerning the Installation of Kings in the *Mishneh Torah*:

In that age there will be neither famine nor war, nor envy nor strife, for there will be an abundance of worldly goods. The whole world will be occupied solely with the knowledge of God. Therefore, the children of Israel will be great sages; they will know hidden things and attain an understanding of their Creator to the extent of human capability, as it is said, "For the earth shall be full of the knowledge of God as the waters cover the sea" (Isaiah 11:9).

Together, the restorative and utopian elements in Jewish messianism oriented the believer to the longed-for climax of universal history and the central Jewish share in it. The messianic horizon gave ultimate meaning to the rise and fall of empires, the catastrophes of violence and expulsion, the glorious moments of temporal salvation. Periodically this vision erupted in excited, sometimes fantastical episodes of revolt against Jewish exile and humiliation that were fueled by the conviction that the generation stood at the very horizon of history. The notion of collective redemption was variously developed by medieval Jewish philosophers, preachers and mystics into a gamut of views that are not to be read as preternaturally modern. But neither can one ignore the power of this ideal of collective redemption which, taken out of its original religious context, has proven to be one of the most vehement forces in modern ideology.

A third traditional element that feeds into modern Jewish liberalism is the motif of the welfare and harmony of the community in rabbinic law and Jewish communal enactment, the roots of which are to be found in the biblical social ideal of a covenantal people. In a discussion on the features of Talmudic law which distinguish it from Roman law of late antiquity, Samuel Atlas observes that Roman law is rarely concerned with the duties of the owner of property, because in Roman law property ownership is derived from occupancy and power. Talmudic law limits property rights because ownership is not an expression of the will and power of the individual, but of rights that can be qualified according to an ideal of the common good. In illustrating his point Atlas writes:

In case of the court's exacting payment of a debt from the debtor's property, the debtor has the right to redeem his former property by paying off the debt whenever he is in a position to do so. The reason given for ths law in the Talmud (Baba Metsia 35a) is the biblical passage, "And thou shalt do that which is right and good," which is a moral duty interfering with the rights of the creditor. Indeed, this duty, imposed out of moral considerations, became a part of the law of property.[10]

Atlas goes on to observe that the Talmud respected human beings' inclination to strive for economic security and condoned economic pursuits so long as they were in harmony with the general good. However, "where strict ownership interferes with justice, property rights had to be accommodated and changed accordingly." In this and other ways, rabbinic law defended the common good of the community and sought ways to protect the poor and vulnerable from the arbitrary rapacities of social existence in order to fulfill what could, in those given conditions, be fulfilled of the covenantal ideal.

There were in traditional Judaism, Christianity and Islam none of the fundamental separations that made for liberal pluralism. There was no separation of church and state in the *anciens régimes* of Christian Europe or in the ghettos. Jewish law, like Islamic law, is theocratic, the articulation of transcendent ends but also of time-bound rigidities. Theocratic law shows little pluralism in its lack of a clearly defined boundary between the authority of the law and the private sphere of the individuals that make up the community. Rabbinic law sought to regulate relations within the Jewish community, not to project their concept of justice and the common good outward. The social ideal in the tradition as it related to the larger community remained implicit and general.

Except for sporadic outbursts of messianic enthusiasm, the Jewish End of Days remained a passive vision, not an idealized blueprint that could be applied, actively if imperfectly, to the societies within which Jews lived. This was the case not only because of the recalcitrance of all existing social arrangements but also because of Jewish social and political isolation. Throughout its diaspora history, the Jewish people conducted their political affairs within their own framework, in exilarchic courts, geonic yeshivot, aljamas and kahals. From late antiquity to the early modern period a fundamental premise of Jewish diaspora survival was that the Jews were not to assume positions of authority over Christians in Christian lands or Muslims in Muslim lands. They were not to participate in gentile politics, except as official representatives of a subordinated Jewry. (We put aside the well-known exceptions, of course, of Court Jews, valued for their expertise and loyalty by Muslim and Christian princes.) Therefore, under conditions of political subordination and semi-autonomy, the accumulated wisdom and shrewd judgment of the Jewish leadership consisted of the management of the Jewish polity and of rules of thumb on how to cope with gentile governments through persuasion, diplomacy and pointing to the putative financial advantages of having Jews around.

Jewish emancipation changed all that. Piecemeal or in a sweeping fashion, by parliamentary legislation, revolutionary proclamation, or royal edict, the venerable system of legal disabilities, humiliating restrictions and carefully circumscribed privileges that defined the status of Jewry and other orders and estates crumbled. Not just the Jews but many groups before emancipation had had special status defined by the particular freedoms and disabilities they were awarded. Liberalism was born in the dismantling of these systems of particular freedoms and disabilities, Jewish liberalism included.

The first pronounced identification of Jews with liberalism occurred in Germany in the decades after the post-Napoleonic restoration, when conservative circles continued to insist on the Christian nature of the state. Only a limited number of Jews accepted the offer to demonstrate their loyalty to the German nation by baptism. It was the German liberals who stood for Jewish emancipation, as part of a classical liberal program: sovereignty of the people, a parliamentary government, a bill of rights, and so forth. The liberal-conservative bifurcation on secularizing the state and admission of the Jews to full citizenship clearly limited Jewish political options. During the revolutionary year of 1848, an Orthodox rabbi (Dov Berush ben Isaac Meisels) took his seat on the left side of the provisional Austrian Reichsrat. When asked why, he replied, "*Juden haben keine Recht*" (Jews have no right).[11] As Michael A. Meyer has noted of mid-nineteenth-century German Jewry, "If most liberals were not Jews, most Jews were liberals."[12]

There was a streak of high-flown political idealism in the universalistic enthusiasm of liberally inclined German Jews of that time. In the 1820s Heinrich Heine exclaimed that the great task of the day was "not simply [the emancipation] of the Irish, the Greeks, the Frankfurt Jews, and West Indian blacks, and all such oppressed people, but the emancipation of the whole world."[13] An extreme formulation of this universalism, stripped of any particularism, was the proud insistence during the euphoric days of 1848 of the Jewish socialist J. L. Bernays that "the Jews have reduced men from the narrow idea of an exclusive fatherland.... The Jew is a cosmopolitan...he has made man only a free citizen of the world."[14] For most Jews, universalism meant loyalty to the idea of the German nation as well as to the idea of universal humanity. The constellation of circumstances that gave rise to German Jewish liberalism brought forth theological apologies for Judaism based on the principles that the living kernel of Judaism was pure ethical monotheism and the mission of Jewish existence was only to give the message to the world. A well-known spokesman for the Jewish Reform tendency in Germany, Ludwig Philipson, wrote, "It was the task of the new age to form a general human society which would encompass all the peoples organically. In the same way it was the task of the Jews not to create...a separate political entity, but rather to obtain from the other nations full acceptance into their society and thereby attain to participation in the general body social."[15] For all its ethnically self-abnegating tone and one-sided analysis, however, this German Jewish religious universalism should not be dismissed merely as false consciousness. To a generation for whom the only particularly Jewish political interest was emancipation (and emancipation itself was a universal ideal), the theology of monotheistic mission represented a serious effort to reorient the Jewish heritage outwardly to its new context.

Jewish liberals in the late nineteenth century in eastern Europe moved away from this approach in their effort to recover a much greater range of Jewish authenticity. The Zionist essayist Ahad Ha'am labeled Western Jewish universalism "slavery in the midst of freedom"—a defensive strategy that rationalized a natural identification with one's people by means of a forced, overly idealized conception of its universal mission. Early in the twentieth century the Russian Jewish historian and diaspora nationalist Simon Dubnow wrote that "in rejecting their own nationality, [the Jewish cosmopolitans] believed they were carrying out the commandments of mankind as a whole, until bitter experience taught them that individuality is respected by others only if it respects itself, if it does not efface itself before others and if it does not allow others to blot out its own character."[16] The individuality he had in mind was the Jewish collective as a modern secular culture, which does not need any theological or idealist self-justification other than the individualistic pluralism of liberalism suitably widened to apply to ethnic collectivities.

Toward the end of the nineteenth century in eastern Europe there appeared a spectrum of secular Jewish parties based on ethnic self-affirmation and self-concern. General Zionism was a liberal movement with the Jewish agenda of auto-emancipation and a Jewish national homeland. But classical liberalism was under attack almost everywhere in Europe. For the youth, the compelling intellectual fashion was populist, Marxist and other socialist ideologies sometimes compatible with classical liberal freedoms and sometimes not. The extent of this fervor can perhaps be gauged by the remark of Count Sergei Witte, a prominent minister to the Tsar, to Theodor Herzl in 1903 that, while the Jews formed only 7 million out of a Russian population of 136 million, about half the membership of the revolutionary parties were Jews.[17]

For all the ethnic particularism of the Jewish Workers Bund of Russia, Poland and Lithuania (which came to advocate Jewish minority rights in the Russian empire) and the nationalist particularism of the Zionist movement (which called for a modern Jewish homeland in Erets Yisrael), the ideologies of the Jewish left contained a decided neo-messianic vision of the new world that the revolutionary struggle and the new proletarian Jewry were to bring into being. While undertaking to defend the dignity of Jews against anti-Semites, to fight for the revolution under a Jewish banner, to found a modern Jewish commonwealth as a refuge for the persecuted and a home for Jewish values and culture, this Jewish particularism was not unmindful of its exemplary significance. "The flag of Jewish renascence must be raised—the banner of messiah, world-judgment, and world liberation, the symbol of a future free humanity," wrote the Yiddish writer Y. L. Peretz in a burst of enthusiasm for the utopian face of Jewish socialism.[18]

No one can mistake in Zionism a reawakening, in a modern guise, of the traditional Jewish concept of redemption. Zionism is a rereading of the restorative side of Jewish messianism from the perspective of modern cultural and political nationalism. With all due respect for differences, there are expressions of the radical utopianism of the Bundist movement and Zionist socialism that can likewise be seen to entail a reacquaintance and quickening of an old Jewish concern for social justice and the claims of the oppressed.

In the United States in the nineteenth century, there was no continental-style political conservatism. The foundational documents of the American polity are an epitome of classical liberalism, so that to be a conservative in America was to be a liberal in Europe. The radicalism that was an answer to the social traumas of industrialization and that was brought over by the Jewish and other immigrants at the turn of the century gradually moderated in the pragmatic American environment. Of course, an important offshoot of this radical generation moved further left into the Communist party and the various other radical groupings of the 1930s and 1940s. But the vast majority of Jews found their place in the "liberal-urban-ethnic" coalition that became the buttress of Franklin Delano Roosevelt's New Deal and its later incarnations.[19] Welfare-state liberalism has been called the American Jewish civil religion since the 1930s. A symptom of extent of Jewish support for New Deal welfare-state liberalism is suggested by the following estimates of Jewish voting patterns in presidential elections: 72 percent for Al Smith in 1928, 82 percent for FDR in 1932, 85 percent for FDR in 1936, 90 percent for him in 1940 and 1944, 75 percent for Truman and 15 percent for Henry Wallace's Progressive party in 1948, 64 percent for Adlai Stevenson in 1952 and 60 percent for him in 1956, 82 percent for Kennedy in

1960, 90 percent for Johnson in 1964, 81 percent for Humphrey in 1968, 65 percent for McGovern in 1972, perhaps 54 percent for Carter in 1976, perhaps 45 percent for Carter and 15 percent for Anderson in 1980, perhaps 60 percent for Mondale in 1984.[20]

For all the recent criticism of federal programs for public welfare, civil rights and social betterment, sympathy for their goals is still quite evident among most American Jews. It is still evident in spite of the shifts in rhetoric and strategy by left liberals since the late 1960s, including the introduction of affirmative action policies which raised the spectre of racial and ethnic quotas and a Third World anti-Israelism that disdained what Zionism meant in the history of the Jewish people.[21] Despite the current confusion as to what constitutes a realistic and idealistic liberalism in the face of our special perplexities and disillusions, a pronounced Jewish bias in favor of humanitarian concerns still seems to be the case.

The persistent Jewish attraction to liberal causes is overdetermined: it is traceable to various levels of motivation. Once we have specified the immediate historical context and an inertia resulting from these original historical circumstances, there remain other factors. We recall the concept of Jewish marginality as developed by the sociologists and our objection that this does not account for Jewish values. Yet Jewish sociologists have rightly observed that Judaism in and of itself does not condition Jews to liberalism, for those Jews who are closest to traditional beliefs and most immersed in traditional practice are not especially prone to liberalism.[22] Perhaps this sector of Jewry finds it most natural to put group self-interest foremost because the voluntary semi-isolation in which they live resembles the inward-facing Jewish condition before Emancipation. We have noted that the social justice element in Judaism is not invented by modern Jewish homileticians and ideologues. But Jewish social ethics must be *interpreted* in a certain context to come alive as a force. Already present in the tradition, its continued viability rests on a hermeneutic that has been supplied, willy-nilly, by modern Jewish history itself.

What is the relevant historical context that legitimates this reappropriation and extension of the universalistic elements of Judaism? The Emancipation. Emancipation liberated (or condemned, it does not matter which) Judaism to an outward orientation as a broader participant in the broader society—a drastic shift in social location from a time when attaining justice and equity was an internal matter within the Jewish community. In accepting emancipation, Judaism gave up much of its traditional self-isolation and has been forced to take a stand on what is good and just for society as a whole.[23]

What of Jewish self-interest? The modern Jewish particularism of the late nineteenth and twentieth centuries taught Jews that they cannot give up the right to look after their own needs, including the need for the State of Israel. (The Holocaust eliminated any remaining reservations on that score.) But legitimate self-interest and Jewish liberalism are two quite different matters. The outward humanitarian concern of Jewish liberalism represents a different kind of claim than the question of correct tactics in dealing with issues that may threaten Jewish security or even survival. Circumstances beyond our control may keep Jews from actualizing the utopian ideal, but it remains a Jewish ideal nevertheless.[24]

Modern Jewish particularism, for all its self-affirming stance on the Jewish presence in the modern world, is yet another passage to active participation in a larger whole—in the case of Zionism, participation in the (still utopian) society of nations. Reserving the right to look after its own needs, Judaism has taken on a covenant with the larger whole to which the title of this essay alludes. This covenant of common purpose in a pluralistic, democratic society and in a world which must in the long run take on the form of a pluralistic, democratic federation of nations is more than a marriage of convenience. It has religious dimensions in itself. It may even be a *telos*, a supreme goal of Judaism.

Fundamental to this larger covenant is that illustrious Kantian imperative to act on the maxim through which one can at the same time will that one's action becomes a universal law. This means the following: Jews have suffered in history the painful, destructive effects of oppressive structures of domination. Jews have had plenty of that experience of subordination in their history. They know how the poor can be trampled down, the defenseless exploited, the weak humiliated, the doors shut against them. What Jews, with full moral right, claim for themselves, they must claim for others: a society where authority is legitimated by rational consensus, where rewards are made available according to standards as much as possible universally accepted, where social arrangements encourage latecomers and slow starters to participate on fair and hopeful terms. This imperative is the ground from which one can begin to formulate (only begin, of course—the hard part is to be specific) an authentic modern Jewish religious position on the larger issues of public policy. No longer able to define liberalism in absolute terms, we should seek to define it in terms of a direction of social evolution—a direction toward extending the benefits and freedoms (legal, economic, cultural) of society to groups that have previously not been able to share in those benefits and freedoms.

R. J. Zwi Werblowsky, in an essay on the unique "sacral particularity" of Judaism suggests, "Judaism, with all its temptations of ethnocentrism and exclusiveness, also harbors a potential paradigm for a meaningful variation on the theme of the dialectic between particularity and universality."[25] Judaism is a religion of universal significance and contains principles pointing to a just and humane political order, not just for Jews but for all fellow humans. The Jews are a particular people caught in particular circumstances that often have prevented them from achieving that ideal and that may do so again in the future. But the Jewish heritage, as it addresses modern Jews in a modern context, reminds them of the old protest against unfairness, exclusion and domination. Such recollection nourishes the capacity to act responsibly for the common good out of a generous and open-minded concern which is itself an intrinsic feature of liberal pluralism.

NOTES

1. I am grateful to Philip Winograd and Fred Epstein for their insights and suggestions in the writing of this essay.

2. Reinhold Niebuhr, *Leaves from the Notebook of a Tamed Cynic* (1929; reprint ed., Hamden, Conn.: Shoe String Press, 1956), p. 187.

3. T. S. Eliot, *After Strange Gods: A Primer of Modern Heresy*, The Page-Barbour Lectures at the University of Virginia, 1933 (New York: Harcourt, Brace, and Co., 1934), p. 20.

4. Most recently, Irving Kristol, "The Political Dilemma of American Jews," *Commentary* (July 1984): 23–29, and the exchange of letters apropos of this article in *Commentary* (October 1984): 4–17.

5. Stanley Rothman and S. Robert Lichter, *Roots of Radicalism: Jews, Christians, and the New Left* (New York: Oxford University Press, 1982), pp. 112 ff, especially p. 118.

6. Charles S. Liebman, *The Ambivalent American Jew: Politics, Religion, and Family in American Jewish Life* (Philadelphia: Jewish Publication Society of America, 1958), p. 135.

7. Steven M. Cohen, *American Modernity and Jewish Identity* (New York: Tavistock Publications, 1983), pp. 134–53.

8. Jacob Katz, "Post-Emancipation Development of Rights: Liberalism and Universalism," in David Sidorsky, ed., *Essays on Human Rights: Contemporary Issues and Jewish Perspectives* (Philadelphia: Jewish Publication Society of America, 1979), p. 292.

9. Gershom Scholem, "Toward an Understanding of the Messianic Idea in Judaism," in *The Messianic Idea in Judaism and Other Essays on Jewish Spirituality* (New York: Schocken Books, 1971). The Maimonides quotation below is found on p. 29 of this essay.

10. Samuel Atlas, "Rights of Private Property and Private Profit," *Yearbook of the Central Conference of American Rabbis* 54 (1944): 219.

11. Werner Cohn, "The Politics of American Jews," in Marshall Sklare, ed., *The Jews: Social Patterns of an American Group* (Glencoe, Ill.: Free Press, 1958), p. 616.

12. Michael A. Meyer, "German Political Pressure and Jewish Religious Response in the Nineteenth Century," Leo Baeck Memorial Lecture 25 (New York: Leo Baeck Institute, 1981), p. 20.

13. Hugo Bieber, ed., *Heinrich Heine: A Biographical Anthology* (Philadelphia: Jewish Publication Society of America, 1956), p. 250.

14. Paul R. Mendes-Flohr, "The Throes of Assimilation: Self-Hatred and the Jewish Revolution," *European Judaism* 12, no. 1 (Spring 1978): 39.

15. W. Gunther Plaut, ed., *The Rise of Reform Judaism: A Sourcebook of its European Origins* (New York: World Union for Progressive Judaism, 1963), p. 134.

16. Simon Dubnow, "Letters on Old and New Judaism," in Koppel S. Pinson, ed.,

Nationalism and History: Essays on Old and New Judaism by Simon Dubnow (Philadelphia: Jewish Publication Society of America, 1958), p. 101.

17. Leonard Shapiro, "The Role of the Jews in the Russian Revolutionary Movement," *Slavonic and East European Review* 40 (December 1961): 148. Shapiro is quoting from Herzl's diaries.

18. Saul L. Goodman, ed., *The Faith of Secular Jews* (New York: Ktav, 1976), p. 132.

19. See Henry L. Feingold, *A Midrash on American Jewish History* (Albany: State University of New York Press, 1982), pp. 210, 241, 267.

20. Stephen D. Isaacs, *Jews and American Politics* (Garden City, N.Y.: Doubleday and Co., 1974), pp. 151–53. The figures for 1976 and 1980 are taken from the *Encyclopedia Judaica Decennial Book 1973–1982* (Jerusalem: Keter, 1982), p. 604. The figures for 1984 are taken from the *New York Times*, November 8, 1984, p. A19.

21. On the attitude of Jewish organizations toward quotas as a retrogressive step, see Arthur A. Goren, *The American Jews*, Dimensions of Ethnicity, A Series of Selections from the *Harvard Encyclopedia of American Ethnic Groups* (Cambridge, Mass.: Harvard University Press, 1982), p. 99. On anti-Semitism as mainly coming from the left rather than the right, see W. D. Rubinstein, *The Left, the Right, and the Jews* (New York: Universe Books, 1982), especially pp. 83–85.

22. Liebman, *The Ambivalent American Jew*, pp. 142–43; Cohen, *American Modernity and Jewish Identity*, p. 146 (with important qualifications).

23. Concern for the general community is not absent in the tradition, as the frequent citation of Jeremiah 19:7 indicates ("Seek the welfare of the city where I have sent you into exile, and pray to the Lord on its behalf, for in its welfare you will find your welfare.") My point is that Emancipation created a difference in degree of involvement in the general community that, for Jewish social evolution, is a difference in kind.

24. Perhaps this is the only ideal which can keep our contemporary tribalistic world from self-destruction and it is, therefore, an ideal which must be recognized by all peoples aspiring to participation in a global society—but that is beyond our subject here.

25. R. J. Zwi Werblowsky, *Beyond Tradition and Modernity: Changing Religions in a Changing World* (London: University of London Athlone Press, 1976), p. 42.

3

Pluralism and Theocrats: The Conflict Between Religion and State in Israel

MITCHELL COHEN

As conceived by its Declaration of Independence, the State of Israel was to embody not only the rebirth of Jewish sovereignty after a lapse of two thousand painful years but also the creation of a progressive, pluralistic society. The Western-style parliamentary democracy that was established has withstood the tests of time and wars. Among the many vexing problems that have beset Israeli political life during its past three and a half decades is that of the relation between religion and state. This carries its own irony as it is almost a natural outcome of Israel's self-definition as a *Jewish* state.[1]

There are few cases in which peoplehood, nationality, religion and land are as intertwined as in Israel. The balance among these elements is the source of ongoing conflict and ambiguity. Indeed, in the days before independence was declared a vigorous dispute occurred within the Zionist leadership when, to the dismay of the secularists, its religious minority insisted on the mention of God in the text proclaiming the new state. Reference to "The Rock of Israel" was finally settled on as a phrase which might be interpreted by either side as it chose. This resolved an immediate dispute. However, the issue underlying it—that of individual and collective Jewish identity—has remained a regular feature of the Israeli political agenda as an essential (if not *the* essential) source of conflict between religion and state.

This disaccord has been primarily an internal Jewish phenomenon; freedom of worship for the various Muslim and Christian minorities in the Jewish state has always been safeguarded by the Israeli authorities. The peculiarities of the conflict must be understood within the context of the development of modern Jewish nationalism, and the political structures of the Jewish community, first in Mandatory Palestine and then in the State of Israel. We aim here not at an exhaustive examination of the question of religion and state in Israel—something hardly possible within the confines of an essay—but rather at an overview of its evolution together with an analysis of some of its salient historical and contemporary features.

I

The State of Israel was the creation of a largely secular and pluralistic national movement, Zionism. The religious elements within its ranks, like the religious components of the Israeli political spectrum, always represented a vigorous and vocal minority. For the majority, be they bourgeois liberals like Theodor Herzl and Chaim Weizmann or the socialists who founded Labor Zionism, religion per se was a secondary matter. Herzl, founder of the World Zionist Organization, was willing to consider a site for a Jewish state in east Africa or Argentina, even though all Jewish religious (and, we should add, historical) sentiments focused on Palestine. The Palestinian Jewish utopia he portrayed in his 1902 novel *Altneuland* had few recognizably Jewish characteristics. Six years earlier, in his classic *Der Judenstaat* he was blunt about the role of religion in the state he proposed, clearly envisaging a pluralistic society in it:

Shall we end by having a theocracy? No, indeed. Faith unites us, knowledge gives us freedom. We shall therefore prevent any theocratic tendencies from coming to the fore on the part of our priesthood. We shall keep our priests within the confines of their temples in the same way as we shall keep our professional army within the confines of their barracks.... Every man will be as free and undisturbed in his faith or his disbelief as he is in his nationality.[2]

More than anything else, Zionism as a political movement represented a rebellion against the"Galut" (exile) conditions of Jewish life. Until the Enlightenment and the French Revolution, western European Jews had a defined and separate place in their host societies, and both Jew and Gentile knew what its perimeters were. Radically new circumstances were created by the collapse of the feudal order and its replacement by a world of individual citizens of nations. Here there was no longer a place for the corporate and closed Jewish communal entities of the past. In a debate in the French National Assembly in 1789, the Parisian delegate Count Stanislas de Clermont-Tonnerre captured the entire matter in his now famous remark that "One must refuse everything to the Jews as a nation but one must give them everything as individuals; they must become citizens."[3] Emancipation was a gateway of Janus: freedom (at least in principle) to enter society was established on one hand, the danger of assimilation into the host culture and the loss of a Jewish communal reality was posed on the other. Whereas a religious orthodoxy hardly amenable to pluralism dominated the cloistered existence of the Jewish ghetto, Jewish identity now had to confront new possibilities and new frames of reference. When combined with rising anti-Semitism—Herzl attended the degradation of Alfred Dreyfus and heard the Parisian crowd crying "Death to the Jews" more than a century after "Liberty, Equality, Fraternity" had been proclaimed—all these elements were harbingers of a profound internal Jewish crisis to which Zionism was one response.

If Herzl came from the West, the Jewish masses that carried Zionism forth came from the East, where, particularly in the tsarist empire, they had not been "emancipated" and remained restricted and persecuted. By the turn of the twentieth century, nationalism, revolution and the desire for a "modern" existence had each made enormous inroads into this Jewry. The socioeconomic foundations on which the State of Israel was built were largely laid by rebellious, youthful, eastern European Jewish "pioneers" who came to Palestine in the first decades of this century. Socialists and Zionists, they believed that the Jewish condition in the Diaspora was hopeless and that Zionism was the revolution required to recreate a Jewish nation. Rather than play marginal and middleman economic roles as Jews did in the Diaspora, a new Jewish nation would be born working on the soil of *Eretz Israel* (the land of Israel). Such a revolt was also inevitably directed against religious orthodoxy, which was viewed as the embodiment of a ghettoized diaspora mentality—backward and stifling.[4] Nonetheless, despite the antireligious stance of many Labor Zionists, and despite the orthodoxy of the religious Zionists, both would eventually find themselves as coalition partners in Zionist politics before the Jewish state was declared and in almost all Israeli governments between 1949 and 1976.

A pattern of secular-religious cooperation emerged very early in Zionist political history in the form of a working alliance between Herzl, a "general" Zionist (in other words, a non-socialist, middle-class, secular nationalist), and what became the religious Zionist movement. The issues which prompted this exercise in expediency, and the questions which came out of it, remained central to Zionist and Israeli politics for the next eight decades. In its program, the World Zionist Organization, founded at a congress in Basle, Switzerland, in August 1897, declared its goal to be the creation of "a home in Palestine secured by public law" for the Jewish people.[5] Herzl's Zionism was of a secular, formal, political nature: he saw the Jewish problem as that of a stateless people, resolvable only politically, that is, through statehood. What exactly the "Jewishness" of this state would entail was undefined—the Basle program spoke solely of the need to foster national sentiment and consciousness among the Jews. However, by the time the Third and Fourth Zionist Congresses met (in Basle in 1898 and 1899) the content of this consciousness became the catalyst of a major dispute.

An internal opposition to Herzl emerged that became known as the "Democratic Fraction." Its spiritual guide was Asher Ginsburg, an intellectual from Odessa better known by his nom de plume, "Ahad Ha'am" (One of the People"). Already in the year of the First Zionist Congress this "agnostic rabbi" had chastized Herzl's strictly *political* approach and advocated a national-cultural renaissance, lest Herzlian Zionism result in a "State of Germans or Frenchmen of the Jewish race."[6] It was not that Ahad Ha'am and his followers opposed the political dimension of Zionism; rather, in their view, this dimension was inadequate by itself, especially since they recognized that the modern epoch had ushered in a profound *spiritual* crisis for Judaism. The Democratic Fraction, led by the young Chaim Weizmann and Leo Motzkin, endeavored to place cultural and educational work on the agenda of the Zionists Organization, and also fought Herzl's often autocratic methods of running the movement. Their efforts bore fruit when, after a fierce battle at the Fifth Zionist Congress in 1901, a resolution was passed which committed the movement to national-cultural educational work. This induced a reaction not only from Herzl, who opposed the fraction for his own political reasons and out of fear that the "culture" issue would fragment Zionism, but also from the orthodox Zionists as well. The latter believed that an adventure in national culture and education would lead to a secular and cultural definition of Jewish nationhood and hence would subvert Judaism which, in their eyes, could only be defined in religious terms. The religious Zionists were, in fact, fighting a war on two fronts. While some of the earliest nineteenth-century proto-Zionists like Yehudah Alkalai and Zvi Hirsch Kalischer were rabbis, large segments of orthodoxy vehemently opposed Zionism on the grounds that it was a profane movement seeking to push the hand of God by means of a Jewish return to the Holy Land. Those orthodox Jews who embraced Zionism as such had to confront not only the Ahad Ha'ams and later the socialists, but also rabbis throughout Europe who harshly condemned them for entering into an unholy alliance with secular nationalists.

The religious Zionists responded both organizationally and ideologically. Organized by Rabbi Itzhak Yosef Reines, delegates from some thirty European cities converged on Vilna in March 1902 to form the religious Zionist organization Mizrahi. (Literally "Easterner," Mizrahi is the Hebrew acronym for *merkaz ruhani* or "spiritual center.") Under Reines' leadership Mizrahi, later one of the founding components of Israel's National Religious party, mobilized its delegates to confront the Democratic Fraction at the Second Conference of Russian Zionists in Minsk the following summer. There, Ahad Ha'am gave the opening address and called on the delegates to "conquer" Jewish schools on behalf of Zionism. He articulated this as a specifically pluralistic endeavor, insisting that both modernists and traditionalists within the Zionist movement needed to "recognize the points of union and of difference between them" and that each ought to make "national revival" the heart of their educational efforts. However, "on this foundation each is at liberty to erect its own superstructure in its own way, without hindrance or interference from the outside."[7] After substantial debate with Reines and the Mizrahi delegates, a resolution passed creating two committees representing the two trends to deal with education, although a Mizrahi conference the following March declared this decision non-binding.[8]

Herzl encouraged the formation of Mizrahi, sent a personal contribution to its organizers, and helped them get financial aid.[9] Its slogan became: *"Eretz Israel le'am Israel al pi torat Israel"* (The land of Israel for the people of Israel according to the Torah of Israel).[10] In the ensuing decades Mizrahi developed its own distinct philosophy which represented a religious traditionalism in search of both a response to the modern, profane world, and a justification for practical activities in it. Simultaneously, it developed its own institutions and organizational and educational infrastructure in Palestine and elsewhere. While Reines and numerous Mizrahi leaders wrote extensively on the ideology of religious Zionism, its most articulate formulation was undoubtedly made by Avraham Itzhak Kook, a talmudic scholar and Kabbalist who became the first Ashkenazi Chief Rabbi of Palestine in the 1920s. Kook saw in the return of the Jews to the land of Israel an anticipation of the coming of the Messiah. He argued that just as the Torah and people of Israel were holy, so too was their land, which was never to be regarded "merely as a tool." He insisted that "Eretz Israel is not something apart from the soul of the Jewish people.... Eretz Israel is part of the very essence of our nationhood; it is bound organically to its very life and inner being. Human reason, even at its most sublime, cannot begin to understand the unique holiness of Eretz Israel."[11] Hence land, something this-worldly, had central *religious* significance and its rebuilding, even when done by sacrilegious Marxist and radical Zionists, was part of a divine plan leading to the End of Days. He insisted that while "Jewish secular nationalism is a form of self-delusion, the spirit of Israel is so linked to the spirit of God that a Jewish nationalist, no matter how secularist his intention may be, must, despite himself, affirm the divine."[12] Once, when attacked for this claim, Kook replied with an analogy from the Talmud: When the Temple stood in ancient Jerusalem, none but the High Priest, dressed in vested garments on the Day of Atonement (Yom Kippur) could enter the Holy of Holies, the most sacred place in the sanctuary. However, observed Kook, when the Temple was being constructed, any laborer could go where necessary at any time. Accordingly, the secular pioneers of twentieth-century Zionism should be viewed as engaged in the building process of a yet unfinished Temple.[13]

This ideology/theology was uniquely suited to the actual political life that religious Zionists came to pursue. By the 1930s the Labor Zionists, led by David Ben-Gurion, emerged as the leading force within the Jewish national movement. The social democratic Mapai party and its successors would retain this position for nearly half a century; Mapai was what Maurice Duverger in his classic study, *Political Parties*, called a "dominant party." It remained larger than all other parties for an extended period of time and its "doctrines, ideas, methods...style" came to be "identified with an epoch."[14] Formulations such as Kook's provided an ideal foundation for the role religious Zionism was to play as junior partner in coalitions with Mapai's secularists. One could characterize this as a system of semi-coerced and coercive pluralism. The willingness of religious Zionists to accept the existence of other, secular parties and to work with them was undoubtedly due, in part, to their deep sense of solidarity with their people; however, their options were limited, so within this framework they sought to use their political position to expand the influence of orthodox, religious precepts in the daily life of Palestinian, and then Israeli, Jewry.

An additional dimension was added in the 1920s that helped facilitate the ties between Labor and Religious Zionists. Mizrahi's "Young Guard," impressed by socialist ideas in the eastern Europe of its origins and by the Labor Zionist movement in Palestine, began developing a new vocabulary based on the idea of *"Torah ve'Avodah"* (Torah and Labor). The chief theorist of this trend, Shmuel Haim Landau, called on religious Zionism to emphasize the effort to transform Jews into a national, religious, *laboring* community, working on the soil of the Holy Land. Mizrahi, complained his followers, was dominated by middle-class elements and ideas. As the Labor Zionist movement argued that diaspora Jewry was trapped in marginal and middleman positions in their host societies and could only be recreated as a nation by entering all levels of production (especially agriculture) in their own land, so Landau presented his own religious version of these notions, also claiming that a society divided by classes was alien to the Jewish spirit. "Torah cannot be reborn without labor," he wrote, "and labor, as a creative and nation-building force, cannot be reborn without Torah."[15] Those who embraced *"Torah ve'Avodah"* formed their own organization in 1922 called Ha'Poel Ha'Mizrahi (the Mizrahi Worker), which emphasized religion, nationalism, and the value of manual labor. Ha'Poel Ha'Mizrahi created its own institutions and rapidly became the dominant force in the religious Zionist camp.[16]

If Ha'Poel Ha'Mizrahi and Mizrahi represented orthodox "parties of participation" within the Jewish national movement, other religious elements who were later to play important roles in Israeli politics emerged parallel to them as anti-Zionist "parties of separation."[17] Rejecting not only Zionism but also cooperation with secular forces within Jewry, the Agudat Israel (Union of Israel) was formed in 1912. Its founding convention at Kattowitz declared that

The Jewish people stand outside the framework of the political peoples of the world and differ essentially from them: the Sovereign of the Jewish people is the Almighty, the Torah is the law that governs them and the Holy Land has been at all times destined for the Jewish people. It is the Torah which governs all the actions of Agudat Israel.[18]

That the land was "destined" for the Jews did not, in the view of Agudat Israel, mean that an effort should be made with secularists to recreate a Jewish state there—an action reckoned to be equivalent to pushing the hand of God. The opposing religious Zionist perspective is perhaps best summarized in a statement by Reines shortly before Agudat Israel's birth: "I prefer to make common cause with secular Zionists who desire to maintain the unity of the Jewish people, rather than unite with religious Jews who seek division."[19] Agudat Israel's attitude toward Zionist settlement efforts ranged from ambivalent to hostile; in Palestine it became a dominant force in the "Old Yishuv," the orthodox community which pre-dated Zionist settlement and was both opposed to Zionism and shocked by the mores of the secular Zionist pioneers with their collective farms and freer relations between men and women. Finally, parallel to Ha'Poel Ha'Mizrahi came the formation of an Agudat Israel counterpart, Poalei Agudat Israel (or "PAI," Workers of Agudat Israel).

Both the Mizrahi and Agudat Israel movements, as well as their labor offshoots, were based on community subcultures within Jewry. In their opposing paths we can see two different responses by religious traditionalists to the modern world.[20] One embraced an ideology that assumed a partial accommodation to and interaction with the modern world through activities within, first, a broader national movement and then a nation-state.[21] The other countered this with an ideology of separatism and an assumption that was at once political and non-political: that the Jewish people is defined strictly as a religious body. Agudat Israel only reconciled itself to the Zionist project with the advent of Hitler and the birth of Israel. Its evolution may be cautiously characterized as a shift from anti-Zionism to non-Zionism.[22]

By the time Israel's independence was proclaimed, Palestinian Jewry had developed an extensive network of political, communal, religious and (underground) military institutions. For all practical purposes, a government within a government functioned, although lacking the final attributes of sovereignty. As early as 1920, a representative elected assembly (the Asefat ha'Nivharim) was created, and it, in turn, elected an executive arm known as the National Council (the Va'ad Leumi). Article 4 of the British Mandate allowed for the creation of "an appropriate Jewish agency" to work with the authorities on behalf of the Jewish community, and Article 15 guaranteed freedom of conscience, freedom of worship and the right of each community in Palestine to maintain its own schools.[23] The transformation of Palestinian Jewry from an autonomous community under British rule into a sovereign community in its own state was greatly facilitated by all these factors, and the religious Zionists fought their own political battles within these frameworks.

Crucial to this evolution was a principle of political-religious organization that had originated during the Ottoman rule of Palestine. In the Millet system, which was carried over into the mandate and later in some ways into the State of Israel, the governing authority allowed each religious community substantial autonomy to manage its own affairs. The Zionists were able to build on this for their own purposes, and it also strengthened the power of specifically religious Jewish institutions. The Asefat ha'Nivharim attained legal status in 1927 on the basis of the Religious Communities Ordinance of the previous year.

During the Ottoman period (which ended with the British occupation of Palestine in 1917), a chief rabbi (the Haham Bashi) served as religious and political leader of Palestinian Jewry by the graces of Istanbul.[24] Through the same means by which the Asefat ha'Nivharim was recognized by the mandate, the British authorities, urged on by Mizrahi, created a centralized religious authority for Palestine Jewry composed of a Rabbinical Council (elected by rabbis and communal leaders) and two chief rabbis, one Sephardi and one Ashkenazi. Since the founding of these institutions, Mizrahi (and later the National Religious party) maintained substantial influence over their composition, while the Agudat Israel and the Old Yishuv refused to recognize their authority and formed their own institutions.

The various communal bodies created by Palestinian Jewry provided many arenas for conflict between the religious and the secular. However, within these structures there existed a system of what Liebman and Don-Yehiya call "institutionalized pluralism." A diversity of parties, organizations and movements were funded, allowed to set their own financial priorities, and concurrently participated in various Yishuv-wide decision-making bodies.[25] The fact that these bodies were voluntary and lacked means of coercion led the various Zionist parties to form generally inclusive coalitions among themselves in order to run them. Circumstances also tended to force moderation on most parties. Between 1922 and 1948 (the years of the mandate) the Zionist movement was engaged in a bitter struggle for national independence, fighting the Arabs and the British against the backdrop of the Nazi catastrophe. After Israel's birth, ongoing war played a similar function. Still, the very fact of sovereignty after 1948 necessarily compelled the Zionist leaders to confront problems they hitherto had been able to avoid, since they were now governors and legislators of their own state.

II

Israel's first national elections took place in January 1949. Among the seventeen parties contesting them were four that were avowedly religious in character and aims: Mizrahi, Ha'Poel Ha'Mizrahi, Agudat Israel, and Poalei Agudat Israel. Running together as an electoral alliance known as the United Religious Front, they received a total of 16 out of the 120 seats in Israel's parliament, the Knesset. The leading party was Mapai with forty-six seats, and on March 8 David Ben-Gurion became Israel's first prime minister. His government relied on a parliamentary coalition including the religious parties and the small Progressive party.

This coalition inaugurated Ben-Gurion's political strategy of isolating the extreme right (in particular, Menachem Begin's Herut party) and avoiding dependence on the parties to his left in order to maintain his parliamentary majority. His dictum that any government coalition could be acceptable, save one that included Begin or the Israeli Communists, made the religious parties central to his plans. The United Religious Front of 1949 did not survive, but Mapai's coalitions with Mizrahi and Ha'Poel Ha'Mizrahi did. The latter two parties merged in 1956 to form the National Religious party (or "Mafdal," after its Hebrew acronym). The "historic alliance" between the dominant Mapai and the smaller Mafdal lasted throughout the entire period of Labor hegemony in Israeli politics with the exception of three very brief periods. In contrast, the Agudat Israel spent 1952–77 in opposition to Labor, and Poalei Agudat Israel did so between 1952–60 and 1969–77.

The structure of Israeli politics, in particular its electoral system of proportional representation, gave the religious parties power far beyond their seats in the Knesset and corresponding support in the population. Recent estimates of the proportions of religious and non-religious Jews in Israel vary. Safran estimates that about 30 percent of Israel's (Jewish) population prefer a fully secular state, 15 percent advocate a theocracy, and the remainder are divided in inverse proportion between those who would prefer some link between religion and state and those who would prefer a separation but would accede to some ties. Liebman and Don-Yehiya, on the basis of various surveys, state that *datim* (or Orthodox Jews) compose less than 20 percent of Israel's population, while the other 80 percent are "secular" or "traditional" (the latter referring to those who honor and maintain customs).[26] No Israeli party having ever won an electoral majority, the leading parties—Mapai and its Labor party successor until 1977, and the Likud from then until 1984—entered into agreements with Mafdal, among other parties, to guarantee the parliamentary majority necessary to sustain a government. Mapai regularly promised that the religious status quo would be maintained and rewarded its coalition partners with ministerial portfolios and other concessions. It is in the battles over these elements of political barter that state-religion relations have been largely shaped.

As in the dispute between Ahad Ha'am and Herzl about the nature of the Zionist enterprise, these struggles represent broader contentions over the very nature of the Jewish state and its society. The political problem may be seen in a statement by Shlomo Goren, former Ashkenazi chief rabbi:

The act of giving the Law on Mount Sinai was an act of imposition and an infringement, as it were, on one's freedom of choice. When it comes to shaping the image of our national life we are commanded by the Torah and by the ethics of the prophets to employ the coercive power of the state.[27]

In the eyes of the religious parties, Zionist and non-Zionist, a Jewish state can ultimately only be a theocracy; it must be governed by Halakhah (Jewish law), which comprises prescriptions for virtually all aspects of social, political and personal life. Since Israel lacks a written constitution and in its place the Knesset enacts what are known as Basic Laws (*Hukei yesod*), the religious parties seek to influence Israeli society through shaping legislation. In their view, the Jews have a constitution with which to regulate their national existence in the Halakhah. For example, Rabbi Yehuda Leib Hacohen Maimon, a moving force in the creation of the Chief Rabbinate in the 1920s and later a cabinet minister, argued,

Our Torah does not differentiate between the Jewish State and the Jewish religion. Israel's Torah includes not only commandments regulating man's conduct toward the Almighty but also man's obligations toward his fellow man and toward the State. The laws and commands of the Torah embrace not only the life of the individual and the community but also the life of the State in all its aspects, general and particular.[28]

Similarly, Moshe Haim Shapira, a Mafdal leader and holder of numerous cabinet posts for his party between 1949 and 1970, insisted that the ideal of religious Zionism was "a Torah-based state," since "there is but one Law that ought to govern all spheres of life in resurgent Israel. Moreover, this Law ought to extend to the non-Jewish as well as the Jewish citizens of the State, with the sole injunctions being of a purely religious character. This Law . . . is none other than Israel's Torah as interpreted by our sages throughout the generations."[29]

Such views are hardly congruous with modern notions of pluralist democracy and are certainly irreconcilable with the spirit of Israel's Declaration of Independence, which, incidentally, both Maimon and Shapira signed, and which avows that the Jewish state "will ensure complete equality of social and political rights to all its inhabitants irrespective of religion, race or sex" and "will guarantee freedom of religion, conscience, language, and culture."[30] In his classic defenses of liberty, John Stuart Mill argued that the silencing of an opinion contrary to our own implies an assumption of our own infallibility.[31] Although the leaders of the religious parties have not advocated abolishing freedom of speech in Israel, and while they do not assume their *own* infallibility, they do assume the infallibility of the source of their political beliefs. Nonetheless, the political system within which they function is that of Western democracy; hence my earlier use of the terms "semi-coerced and coercive pluralism." Despite the undemocratic tendencies and sources of its ideology, Mafdal is an active participant in the country's political life, accepting the rules of the game and seeking to use them to implement its own purposes, as do political parties in most Western democratic systems. The Agudat Israel, on the other hand, participates within the political system with much more reticence and with goals more limited than those of Mafdal. We could characterize the National Religious party as a self-conscious religio-political movement and party, in contrast to the Agudat Israel which is a religious movement involved, sometimes more, sometimes less reluctantly, in politics. This is reflected also in party organizational structure: that of the Mafdal is comparable to other parties while the ultimate authority in the Agudat Israel is its *Moetset Gedolei ha-Torah* (Council of Torah Sages), which is composed of leading rabbinical authorities on Halakhah.

While both Mafdal and Agudat Israel seek to enhance the role of religious orthodoxy in Israeli life, the Mafdal's role was, until the Begin years, the more politically salient because of its ongoing participation in Israeli governments. In reaching coalition agreements, it has, as we have noted, insisted on the maintenance of the status quo in religious affairs. This means in theory that the existing (and always tenuous) balance between religion and state should not change. In practice, however, the status quo has remained anything but static: In Israel's three and a half decades religious influences and controls have steadily increased under Labor and even more under Likud governments. In the 1977 elections, one small secular party went so far as to assert in its platform that "the mystique of the status quo" had become, through coalition agreements, "a means of extortion in the hands of the religious parties, at the expenses of human rights and civic rights, in a manner and a method conflicting with the principles in the Declaration of Independence and of the foundation of democracy."[32]

In the years of the Likud rule (1977–84), the Agudat Israel took part in the governmental coalitions, substantially expanding its influence over legislation, but without accepting ministerial responsibility. It is estimated that while Agudat Israel's four Knesset votes made up only 6 percent of the coalition composing Menahem Begin's government, some 36 percent of the coalition agreement was composed of items to curry its favor.[33]

Mafdal's "traditional" cabinet portfolios were those of the Ministries of Religions and the Interior. The first has jurisdiction over the affairs of all religions in Israel and, in particular, the state-supported religious institutions (partly excluding education). Control of the Ministry of the Interior allowed Mafdal to oversee both local government and funding going from the national government to local projects, authorities and institutions. This obviously entails enormous powers to aid financially the institutions and localities that the incumbent favors. For reasons we shall turn to shortly, the Interior Ministry was also crucial for Mafdal because of its role in determining who is classified as a Jew in Israel. A third ministry, that of Education and Culture, was a long-sought prize that eluded Mafdal until the advent of the first non-Labor government in 1977. In a sense, this brought Religious Zionism full circle; the original stimulus to form Mizrahi was, after all, a dispute over culture and education within the World Zionist Organization. With a new coalition partner in the Likud, Mafdal attained a role that it had long hungered for and believed rightly its own, that of national educator. During the Mandate three autonomous Jewish school systems existed in Palestine under the general direction of the Va'ad Leumi: a General Zionist educational system, a Religious Zionist educational system (run by Mizrahi), and a Socialist Zionist system (run by the Histadrut, the trade union confederation). With statehood, Ben-Gurion pursued a policy of *éta-tisme* (*mamlakhtiyut*) through which he sought to subordinate various national institutions to state, rather than party, control. He wanted to merge the three educational systems into one, but was compelled by his religious coalition partners to maintain a religious system and to merge only the other two. The Labor movement thus yielded one of its central instruments of socialization while Mizrahi maintained its own.[34] For secular, especially socialist parties in power, religious education and state funding for it is a perennial problem. For example, in the spring of 1984 educational reform served as a catalyst to unite opposition to the French socialist government, and in Salvador Allende's Chile what had been three years of basically decent relations between the Church and the Popular Unity government were disrupted by a national education reform which aimed to expand state control over schools and introduce a program of socialist humanist education in all schools, including those of the church.[35] Israeli Labor, however, never faced these problems, since the precedents of the Millet system and institutionalized pluralism, along with the need for coalitions with religious parties, led to an acceptance of a state-supported religious education system.

Israel maintains both secular and religious legal systems. The Jewish, Muslim and Christian religious courts are primarily concerned with questions of personal status such as marriage and divorce. The maintenance of these courts is in the jurisdiction of the Ministry of Religions, which is also responsible for local religious councils and the rabbinate. Since Mafdal control of the ministry has meant effective control of these institutions, it has therefore had important influence on who were chosen as chief rabbis or as members of the Chief Rabbinical Council. Mafdal has also used these powers virtually to bar official recognition of Conservative and Reform branches of Judaism within the Jewish state and to restrict their activities.

It is nonetheless impossible to classify Israel as a theocracy because, aside from matters of personal status, Israeli law is the product of a democratically elected national legislature, not religious stricture. The Supreme Court of Israel has ruled that without express parliamentary legislation, no governmental bodies can enforce or legislate religious behavior; hence the emphasis placed by the religious parties on parliamentary work and broadening the jurisdiction of religious courts.[36] In sum, Israel remains a secular state in which elements of theocracy have consistently gained ground.

Nowhere has the issue of religion and state been fought out with more vigor—and inconclusiveness—than in the debate over "Who is a Jew?" a matter which goes to the heart of Jewish statehood. In July 1950, the Knesset passed a Basic Law known as the Law of Return by which any Jew may become of right an *oleh* (immigrant to Israel). Two years later a Nationality Law gave citizenship to every *oleh* under the Law of Return. These laws established a principle of affirmative action: any member of a long-persecuted and homeless Jewish people could claim automatic citizenship in the Jewish state. However, these laws were the inevitable source of political dispute because the religious parties sought to have a Jew defined in strict accordance with Halakhah. A brief examination of one of the leading controversies over the Law of Return will illustrate the complexity of the problem.

Oswald Rufesien was a Jew who had been active in the Zionist movement in his native Poland. After the Nazi invasion, he posed as a German Christian and aided in the rescue of Jewish lives, served in the partisans and, while hiding from the Gestapo in a convent, converted to Catholicism. Adopting the name of Brother Daniel, he entered the Carmelite order as a monk, with the hope of joining its chapter in Palestine. He arrived in Israel in 1958 and applied, under the Law of Return, to be classified as an *oleh*, claiming that although now a Christian by religion, by nationality he remained a Jew. Plainly, this presented the most perplexing of problems for Israeli authorities. By a strictly secular definition of Jewish nationality, Brother Daniel ought to have been granted his request; religion is generally not determinant of nationalities. On strictly religious grounds he ought to have received citizenship, since according to Halakhah a Jew is a person who is born of a Jewish mother or is properly converted to Judaism. Apostasy is irrelevant. Nonetheless, Brother Daniel was refused. The Israeli Supreme Court ruled in 1962 that under strict interpretation of Halakhah Brother Daniel was indeed Jewish, *but not under the Law of Return*. In this law, wrote Justice Moshe Silberg for the majority, the word "Jew" had a secular definition and a meaning "as it is usually understood by the man in the street." As such, "A Jew who has become a Christian is not called a Jew."[37]While barred from *oleh* status, Brother Daniel was free, like any non-Jew, to become a naturalized citizen.

A major cabinet crisis occurred in 1958 specifically over how nationality was to be designated on Israeli identification cards. Under the Registration of Inhabitants Law, these cards list both an individual's nationality and religion. The Interior Minister, who is responsible for the law's administration and who was then a socialist, issued a directive to make population registration practices more uniform: a Jew was to be regarded as any individual who declared himself or herself so in good faith. If parents declared their child Jewish, he or she would be regarded as Jewish. This directive provoked fury from the religious camp because it clearly ignored Halakhah. In an effort to prevent a split in the governing coalition, the cabinent created a special subcommittee which added a stipulation to the directive stating that an individual who declared himself or herself Jewish could not profess another religion. Mafdal, still finding this compromise unacceptable, withdrew from the government. Prime Minister Ben-Gurion was eventually forced to yield, and a member of Mafdal became Interior Minister.

A decade later Benjamin Shalit, an Israeli Jew who had married a non-Jew abroad, sought to have the Interior Ministry register his children as Jews by nationality, leaving their religious classification unspecified, since both parents were atheists. The Minister of the Interior refused but was overruled by the Supreme Court. This, too, provoked the predictable storm, and the Chief Rabbinate went so far as to tell the Interior Minister (Mafdal's Moshe Haim Shapira) to disobey the court. After a vigorous struggle between Labor Prime Minister Golda Meir and the National Religious party, the premier yielded on most major points; an amended Law of Return was passed by the Knesset in 1970 stipulating that a Jew was someone born of a Jewish mother or converted to Judaism, providing the individual did not embrace another religion. The sole demand to which Meir refused to accede was that conversion had to be according to Halakhah, which would have effectively meant that Reform and Conservative conversions abroad would be invalid in Israel.[38] In the winter of 1984–85 a national unity government headed by Labor's Shimon Peres was jeopardized when the religious parties once again sought to amend the Law of Return.

Until 1967 the religious parties sought to use the levers of legislation first and foremost to make a non-traditional society, built in great measure by secular nationalism, into a more orthodox, religious entity. The working relation between Mapai/Labor and the National Religious party rested on a tacit understanding: Labor got its way in foreign and social policy and gave its partner sway on important religious affairs. Neither Agudat Israel nor the National Religious party were particularly concerned with foreign issues. The Six Day War, however, created an entirely new reality.

III

Following the 1948 war most Israelis accepted their armistice boundaries as permanent. Before Israel's birth the extreme right wing of the Zionist movement, the "Revisionists," were the most vocal advocates of an integral nationalism, insisting on Jewish rights to all of ancient Israel, although such claims did find (sometimes strong) echoes in the religious and socialist camps. However, between 1949 and 1967 only the tiniest of minorities took the notion of pressing territorial claims seriously. When Israel defeated the three Arab armies that had been mobilized on its borders in June 1967, the Israeli government made plain its intention to trade occupied land for peace. The response of the Arab world came in the form of the "three Nos" issued at the Arab League summit conference in Khartoum in the fall of 1967: no talks with Israel, no recognition of Israel, no peace with Israel. Confronted with such formulae, Israel prepared for a long stay in the occupied areas and made clear that while compromise was still possible, "defensible" borders would now be demanded and there could be no return to the status quo ante.

What was predominantly a question of self-defense for the mainstream of the ruling Labor movement, took on an entirely different dimension among elements of the religious Zionist community. Israel had captured the eastern half of Jerusalem, including Judaism's most sacred site, the Western Wall (the sole remaining structure from the Temple of the Second Commonwealth). In addition, the West Bank of the Jordan River had been seized. This area, designated by the 1947 United Nations (UN) partition plan as part of a Palestinian Arab state and annexed by Jordan after the 1948–49 war, was of enormous religious and historical significance to Judaism. Instead of "West Bank," the biblical designation of the areas, *"Yehudah ve'Shomron"* (Judea and Samaria) more and more became common parlance. The messianic element in Religious Zionism was restimulated.[39]

The pattern of religious Zionist politics in the ensuing period contrasts sharply with western European patterns. Berger notes that generally speaking—and with significant exceptions—in western Europe "the dominant pattern has been a tight association between religion and the Right" for some two centuries. That pattern has begun to break down, and significant support for left political attitudes has emerged among clerics in France and England, for example.[40] This has opened new possibilities for cooperation between socialist movements and religious elements in their societies. In Israeli politics, the reverse seems to have occurred. Religious Zionists imbibed radical ideas in the 1920s, later had a long-term alliance with social democrats, but then began to take on a new face in the 1970s. In the decade between the 1967 war and the defeat of Israel Labor party in 1977, the National Religious party was transformed from a coalition partner docile in foreign affairs, to a party containing a powerful element opposed to any territorial concessions in Judea and Samaria, and pressing avidly for settlements in all areas of the occupied territories. (Labor encouraged settlements in the West Bank as well, but generally tried to restrict them to security zones lacking significant Arab populations.) Slowly a Mafdal emerged that was closer to the Israeli right wing (which regrouped in 1973 as the Likud) than to its old Labor partner.

Concurrently, Mafdal's older generation found itself increasingly challenged by its "Young Guard," led by Zevulun Hammer and Yehudah Ben Meir. The Young Guard sought to broaden both the party's appeal and its agenda, and as Ben Meir put it in 1974, oppose an "a priori inclination towards coalition with Labor."[41] Most significantly, the Young Guard encouraged and identified with those who wanted to settle the West Bank and claim sovereignty over it. A vigorous integral religious nationalism had emerged. The land more and more became the chief concern of the Young Guard, and their strength and influence within Mafdal continually grew despite efforts of more dovish elements within the party to fight a rearguard action against them. The Young Guard's desire to expand Mafdal's horizons—there was talk of broadening the party along the lines of Western Christian Democrats so as to be in a position to assume power one day— was partly undermined by its own narrow nationalism and emphasis on territory.

The same winds propelling the Young Guard to the forefront of the political arena led to the creation of Gush Emunim (the "Bloc of the Faithful"), first within the National Religious ranks and then as an extra-parliamentary—and often extralegal—movement seeking to prevent any territorial compromise on the West Bank. Its spiritual guide was Rabbi Zvi Yehuda Kook, son of the late chief rabbi. Building on his father's messianism and emphasis on the holiness of the land of Israel, he asserted that the beginning of the redemption was being heralded by settlement in Judea and Samaria. In no uncertain terms he warned believers that "any concession or annulment of Israeli control over even the smallest part of our homeland, and its transfer to Gentile authority is absolutely prohibited by the Torah and is simply theft of our land."[42] The Gush organized demonstrations, built new settlements, and often defied the government on the assumption that it had a higher authority.

Events in 1981 and 1982 compelled serious rethinking within religious Zionist ranks. Unable to compete with the right-wing parties as the embodiment of unswerving, strident nationalism, and weakened when a Mafdal minister of Moroccan origins who was facing corruption charges formed his own party (Tami) aimed at Sephardi voters, Mafdal won only half (6) of its previous number of Knesset seats in the general elections of 1981. A debate began following Israel's invasion of Lebanon in the summer of 1982, the massacres at Sabra and Shatila, and a call from Gush Emunim for the annexation of southern Lebanon because ancient Israelite tribes had dwelled there. Some Mafdal leaders fretted in public that a form of extremist nationalism was eclipsing religious concepts and that the Religious Zionist effort to balance and synthesize the elements of land, people, and Torah was being lost; the land of Israel now seemed to dominate all. Hammer, renowned for his unremitting support of Gush Emunim, announced on Israeli television that he needed "to rethink many things" and suggested that "the Land of Israel is not the only factor in my view of the world. We must also think of the people who live on this land."[43] He also expressed concern that his party had shifted too much of its emphasis away from religion and toward nationalism.[44] Hammer's longtime colleague, then Deputy Foreign Minister Yehudah Ben Meir, openly stated that Gush's pronouncements on Lebanon would "lead us to eternal war and has nothing to do with Eretz Israel."[45] These comments, which amounted to a volteface, aroused the anger of Gush Emunim.

Religious Zionism seems to have entered a period of unprecedented turmoil, ironically in the aftermath of a period in which its influence expanded greatly. The extent of Mafdal's identification with the Likud governments of Begin and Shamir provoked a crisis in its own identity. Significantly, Ben Meir, once a leader in the struggle to undermine the "historic alliance" between Labor and Mafdal and to open the way to a coalition with Likud, stated in late 1983 that "Mafdal has a covenant (*brit*) only with the Holy One."[46] In the 1984 Israeli elelctions Mafdal dropped from six to four seats. The party fragmented, with some of its following going to new and old parties that were more vociferous nationalists, and also to Tami. The ire of Israel's non-Western Jewish communities was also aimed in 1984 both at Mafdal and Agudat Israel, who are dominated by Ashkenazi Jews, and the "Shas" (Sephardic Torah Guardians) party was formed as a split from Agudat Israel.

IV

The 1984 elections resulted in the formation of a national unity government based on the country's two largest parties. It was thus secure in its parliamentary majority, and in these circumstances Labor and Likud had the option of excluding or undermining the influence of the religious parties; both, however, chose to protect the latter, seeing them as possible junior coalition partners in the future. As such, for both practical political reasons, as well as the more fundamental ones we addressed earlier, the politics of religion and state will continue to be the source of ongoing political tension in Israel.

Since the country's birth, its theocratic elements have not been triumphant, but have continuously gained ground. As we pointed out, what is today defined as the religious status quo is much more to their liking than it was in 1949, and their success has been partly the function of the very structure of Israeli politics. In addition, the large influx of tradition-minded Jews from Arab countries in the 1950s reinforced those who favored a more religious flavor to Israeli public life. Particularly significant is another factor: the decline of Labor's dominance. The secular political force that ruled Israel and Zionism for half a century exhausted itself both intellectually and politically long before its defeat in 1977. Whether Labor's return to power as head of the national unity government will yield dramatic changes is an open question, especially since in defeat it did little to renew its own spiritual and ideological verve.

"A clear line ought to be drawn between freedom and anarchy," a Mafdal leader once argued, largely summarizing the mainstream orthodox approach, "If modern Israel's character were to be identified with the whims and fancies of the non-observant, nothing would remain of the historical link with classical Israel."[47] Yet, Israel today is a land of many vibrant Judaisms. Commentators and scholars perennially raise the specter of a *Kulturkampf*; this danger seems real, at least as long as orthodoxy monopolizes— or tries to monopolize—Jewish religion and culture. *Kulturkampf* may be postponed due to the pressing reality of Middle Eastern wars, but it probably cannot be avoided altogether unless orthodoxy accepts or genuinely resigns itself to pluralism, religious freedom and tolerance in ways it hitherto has not.

NOTES

1. I am indebted to Drs. Gary S. Schiff, Robert M. Seltzer and Steve J. Zipperstein for reading this essay in manuscript form and providing invaluable, insightful criticism. In addition, I wish to thank the following people with whom I talked while preparing this study: Rabbi Avraham Melamed, (then) member of Knesset for the National Religious party; Rabbi Richard Hirsch, executive director of the World Union for Progressive Judaism; and Rabbi Uri Regev, secretary and spokesman of the Council of Progressive Rabbis in Israel. Any conclusions drawn herein, however, are my own. Note: in the text and notes I have rendered transliterations consistent except where there is a spelling that is common usage or where a translation employing another spelling is used.

2. Theodor Herzl, *The Jewish State* (London: H. Pordes, 1967), p. 71.

3. Quoted in Arthur Hertzberg, *The French Enlightenment and the Jews* (New York: Schocken Books, 1970), p. 360.

4. The revolt against orthodoxy, and the conception of Zionism as a national, not religious, movement was not, however, restricted to the socialists and was shared by most of the middle-class and right-wing Zionists.

5. "Program of the World Zionist Organization (Basle)," in J. C. Hurewitz, ed., *The Middle East and North Africa in World Politics: A Documentary Record*, vol. 1, 2d ed., rev. (New Haven, Conn.: Yale University Press, 1975), p. 466.

6. Ahad Ha'am, "The Jewish State and the Jewish Problem," in *Ten Essays on Zionism and Judaism* (London: George Routledge and Sons, 1922), pp. 45–46.

7. Ahad Ha'am, "The Spiritual Revival," in *Selected Essays of Ahad Ha'am* (New York: Atheneum, 1970), p. 304.

8. See Moshe Rinott, "Religion and Education: The Cultural Question and the Zionist Movement 1897–1913," *Studies in Zionism* (Spring 1984).

9. S. Zalman Abramov, *Perpetual Dilemma: Jewish Religion in the Jewish State* (Jerusalem and New York: World Union for Progressive Judaism, 1976), p. 68.

10. The slogan was coined by Meir Bar-Ilan.

11. Abraham Isaac Kook, "The Land of Israel," in Arthur Hertzberg, ed., *The Zionist Idea* (New York: Atheneum, 1969), p. 419.

12. Abraham Isaac Kook, "Lights for Rebirth," in Hertzberg ed., *The Zionist Idea*, p. 430.

13. Similarly, Kook pointed out that it was Herod who built the Second Temple. See Zvi Yaron, *Mishnato shel Rav Kook* (Jerusalem: World Zionist Organization, 1974), p. 339.

14. Maurice Duverger, *Political Parties* (London: Methuen and Co., 1978), p. 308.

15. Shmuel Haim Landau, "Towards an Explanation of our Ideology," in Hertzberg, ed., *The Zionist Idea*, p. 439.

16. On Ha'Poel Ha'Mizrahi see Aryei Fishman, " 'Torah and Labor': The Radicalization of Religion within a National Framework," *Studies in Zionism* (Autumn 1982).

17. These are the terms of Gary S. Schiff, *Tradition and Politics: The Religious Parties of Israel* (Detroit, Mich.: Wayne State University Press, 1977).

18. Quoted in Abramov, *Perpetual Dilemma*, p. 74.

19. Quoted in Samuel Rosenblatt, *The History of the Mizrachi Movement* (New York: Mizrachi Organization of America, 1951), p. 25.

20. On the question of modernization and the Israeli religious parties see Schiff's *Tradition and Politics* and the critique of Schiff in Eliezer Don-Yehiya, "Origins and Development of the *Aguda* and *Mafdal* Parties," *Jerusalem Quarterly* 12 (Summer 1981).

21. It should not be forgotten, however, that Mizrahi saw in the re-creation of the Jewish nation the beginnings of messianic redemption and the rebirth of the *ancient* Jewish commonwealth.

22. The 1937 World Conference of Agudah endorsed the creation of a Jewish state despite a fierce internal struggle.

23. "The Mandate for Palestine," in J. C. Hurewitz, ed., *The Middle East and North Africa in World Politics: A Documentary Record*, vol. 2, 2d ed., rev. (New Haven and London: Yale University Press, 1979), pp. 306–8.

24. The Haham Bashi was Sephardi and not recognized by the Ashkenazi community in Palestine.

25. Charles S. Liebman and Eliezer Don-Yehiya, *Religion and Politics in Israel* (Bloomington: Indiana University Press, 1984), pp. 23–24.

26. Nadav Safran, *Israel, the Embattled Ally* (Cambridge, Mass.: Harvard University Press, 1981), p. 200; Liebman and Don-Yehiya, *Religion and Politics in Israel*, p. 3.

27. Abramov, *Perpetual Dilemma*, p. 215.

28. Yehuda Leib Hacohen Maimon, "Religion and the State," in Yosef Tirosh, ed., *Religious Zionism: An Anthology* (Jerusalem: World Zionist Organization, 1975), p. 164.

29. Moshe Haim Shapira, "The Mission of Religious Zionism," in Tirosh, ed., *Religious Zionism*, pp. 118–19.

30. "Declaration of the Establishment of the State of Israel," in *Laws of the State of Israel: Authorized Translation from the Hebrew*, vol. 1, Ordinances 5708–1948 (Jerusalem: Government Printer, 1948), p. 3.

31. John Stuart Mill, *On Liberty*, in *The Philosophy of John Stuart Mill*, Marshall Cohen, ed. (New York: Philosophical Library, 1961), p. 245.

32. Citizens Rights Movement (*Ratz*), *Platform for the 9th Knesset* (Tel Aviv, February 1977), p. 5.

33. Ira Sharkansky, "Religion and State in Begin's Israel," *Jerusalem Quarterly* 31 (Spring 1984): 40.

34. In the school year 1952–53 (the last in which the three systems existed), 43.4 percent of Israeli students attended Labor schools as opposed to 27.1 percent in the general trend and 19.1 percent in the Mizrahi schools. See Aharon F. Kleinberger, *Society, Schools and Progress in Israel* (Oxford: Pergamon Press, 1969), p. 121. As of 1980, some three quarters of Israeli school children attended the secular state schools with most of the remainder in the religious state schools. There are, in addition, a small number of state-recognized, but not supported, schools. See *State of Israel: The Ministry of Education and Culture, Report for the Years 1979–80/1980–81* (Jerusalem, June 1981), p. 5.

35. See Brian H. Smith, "Christians and Marxists in Allende's Chile: Lessons for Western Europe," in Suzanne Berger, ed., *Religion in West European Politics* (London: Frank Cass, 1982), p. 116.

36. Abramov, *Perpetual Dilemma*, p. 179.

37. Ibid., pp. 287–88. My presentation of the Brother Daniel case closely follows Abramov's superb discussion. Secular parties often have proposed their own definitions of Jewishness. A recent example is that of Shulamit Aloni and several Knesset members of like mind from the Citizen's Rights and Labor parties who proposed that a Jew is "one who ties his or her fate to that of the Jewish people," and one who was, in his or her native country, a member of the Jewish community or registered as a Jew there. See *Jerusalem Post International Edition*, December 1, 1984.

38. Especially see Abramov for detailed discussion of this and other issues concerning personal status or privacy as they pertain to questions of religion and state in Israel.

39. Parallel currents profoundly affected segments of the non-orthodox population, including Labor which had within its ranks its own advocates of "Greater Israel." In contrast, the Agudah, as a non-Zionist party, never became infatuated with the newly held territories.

40. Suzanne Berger, "Introduction," to Berger, ed., *Religion in West European Politics*, pp. 1–3. In the same volume also see in particular, Renaud Dulong, "Christian Militants in the French Left," and Kenneth Medhurst and George Moyser, "From Princes to Pastors: The Changing Position of the Anglican Episcopate in English Society and Politics."

41. Aryeh Rubinstein, "Religious-Party Politics in Israel," *Midstream* (January 1976): 41.

42. Michael Shashar, "The State of Israel and the Land of Israel," *Jerusalem Quarterly* 17 (Fall 1980): 62.

43. *Jerusalem Post*, October 11, 1982.

44. *Jerusalem Post*, October 1, 1982.

45. *Jerusalem Post*, October 5, 1982.

46. *Maariv*, December 30, 1983.

47. Zerach Warhaftig, "The State of Israel—a Jewish State," in Tirosh, ed., *Religious Zionism*, p. 203.

4

Jewish Approaches to Pluralism: Reflections of a Sympathetic Observer

JOHN T. PAWLIKOWSKI, O.S.M.

It is always perilous for an outsider to write about the perspectives of another religious tradition. The problem becomes even more fraught with difficulty when it is a matter of a Christian reflecting on Judaism, given the historic intolerance manifested by Christianity toward the Jewish people. Moreover, the devastating experience of the Holocaust, to which the Christian tradition contributed, has been the context for a significant amount of recent Jewish thinking on politics and nationhood. On the other hand, with appropriate caution, a Christian analysis can also make a distinct contribution because it is relatively free of the tensions commonly found among internal expositors. It can state strengths and weaknesses with a certain measure of objectivity not always possible for such commentators. That is why I chose to accept the task of offering some reflections on Jewish self-definition insofar as they touch upon the general theme of this volume. I do so with a background of years of study in Judaism and extensive contact with a wide spectrum of contemporary Jewish opinion. But I also do so with the full realization that it is not for me to define the most appropriate political expression of Judaism for Jews. After centuries of persecution and homelessness, after the searing trauma of the Shoah, I am ultimately bound to leave that decision to the Jewish people and its leadership. Overall reflections are appropriate; attempts to stamp this or that option as preferable when one is not directly affected by the life-and-death decisions that may be involved are not.

One more disclaimer needs to be made. In an essay as brief as this it is not possible to offer a comprehensive view of Jewish thinking on a particular topic. Hence I shall only discuss a few representative authors in order to illustrate what one Christian commentator believes are some of the principal questions with which Judaism must continue to struggle in relation to the theme of this volume. I would like to focus on four of them: (1) religious pluralism, (2) Zionism and the Jewish land tradition, (3) power, and (4) the rise of Oriental Jewry.

Over the years Judaism has had little need to worry about a theology of religious pluralism based on its tradition, since it lacked the sovereign state power to impose anything on anyone. Its principal preoccupation was staying alive in the face of frequent conversionist onslaughts. For some Jews, especially in eastern Europe, this often meant withdrawal into a closed world where life could be organized in an entirely Jewish manner. For many Jews in the West a high degree of accommodation to the prevailing culture became the more common answer. These Jews usually accompanied this assimilationist tendency with a strong commitment to the notion of church-state separation. Where Jews thought it hopeless to protect their religious ethos through legal means, retreat into a ghetto seemed the best solution. In countries with a strong sense of religious pluralism Jews were often in the forefront of legal challeges to any incursion of religious perspectives into state affairs. Their dominant attitude, at least at the leadership level, was that the more religiously neutral the public sphere, the better for Jews.

With the emergence of the State of Israel a new set of problems faced Judaism, one that had not been present for nearly two millennia. Now in possession of the power to shape a national state, Jews had to deal with the question of minority religions in that state. I do not wish at this point to enter an evaluation of the ways in which Israel has handled this issue by means of law since 1948. Let me focus rather on the attempts to wrestle with the issue on a theoretical plane. It is no accident that two of the most significant attempts in this regard have been made by Israeli scholars David Hartman and Shemaryahu Talmon. Their viewpoints, insofar as they influence public policy perspectives within the government, will have a direct impact on the question of faith and political pluralism.

For Hartman, an exaggerated stress on truth remains the primary reason for past and present instances of interreligious conflict. Truth, he insists, does not serve as the primary religious category for Judaism. He calls for a new pluralistic spirituality rooted in a radical and complete abandonment of historic claims to absolute truth on the part of Judaism, Christianity and Islam. He rejects any intermediate position which regards the commitment to pluralism as merely a temporary position to be assumed by a given religious group while it awaits the assured and final confirmation of its own faith-perspective with the advent of the eschatological age. These are his precise words:

We cannot in some way leap to some eschaton and live in two dimensions; to be pluralistic now but to be monistic in our eschatological vision is bad faith. We have to recognize that ultimately spiritual monism is a disease. It leaps to the type of spiritual arrogance that has brought bloodshed to history. Therefore we have to rethink our eschatology, and rethink the notion of multiple spiritual communities and their relationship to a monotheistic faith.[1]

It is Hartman's firm conviction that the heritages of Judaism and Christianity will survive only if Christians and Jews recapture a basic principle that is of divine origin—*through the way you live, I will be known*. Intimately involved in any serious commitment to this principle is the willingness of Jews, Christians and Muslims to acknowledge that their own peculiar faith-stances and religious visions are of equal stature. Abandonment of any and all claims for the superiority of any one religion stands at the heart of such a pluralistic perspective for Hartman. He is not naive, however, in recognizing the radicality of what he is proposes. It represents a definite break with the biblical tradition, which even in its more universal moments still remains far more absolutist. This biblical absolutism has been in large part responsible, he argues, for the massive injustice frequently perpetrated against outsiders by religious groups by the use of coercive state power.

A second proposal for a Jewish theology of religious pluralism is to be found in the writings of Shemaryahu Talmon. In a presentation originally delivered at a multilateral conference sponsored by the World Council of Churches' Commission of Dialogue with Peoples of Living Faiths and Ideologies, he sets out several principles that he believes must undergird such a theology.[2]

The first principle is that such a theology must draw upon the particularistic resources of each faith community. He has little regard for any approach to the question through the search for common bases among all religious traditions. He insists that each religion should contribute its own distinctiveness to the joint search for such a theology. Only the conclusions of each group, not the reasons for them or the method of arriving at them, should be considered in the dialogue. Though the positions of Hartman and Talmon seem quite far apart, they appear to agree that the only legitimate way of judging another group is by how it acts on what it thinks.

Talmon's second principle for a theology of religious pluralism stands in sharp contrast to Hartman's view. As Talmon sees it, we cannot pretend that most religious traditions do not harbor in varying degrees dreams of univeral acceptance whether by force or by less objectionable forms of persuasion. He writes:

The utopian views of Christianity and Islam have traditionally envisioned the ideal state of mankind as the embracing by all humans of their respective prophets of dogma. Judaism, at the very least, looks forward to the obliteration of idolatry, and the universal acceptance of the one God and His moral code.... If such ultimate aims are denied, we are false to these individual outlooks.[3]

Talmon then turns to what he believes to be the crucial question. How can the various faiths construct a theology of religious pluralism if each really yearns for universal adherence to its own particular spiritual truth? While the dilemma may at first appear hopeless, Talmon holds there is a way out. It hinges on the development of a shared mentality among the world's major religious groups. Having placed their respective eschatological goals on the table, each faith community will subsequently agree to consider the task of building world community as fundamentally non-eschatological or, at best, pre-eschatological. This will involve the emergence of a firm resolve on the part of all religions that the process of building interdependence must never become the occasion for activist eschatological realization and for the proselytization that it implies. Talmon thus clearly differs from Hartman in his rejection of the abandonment of eschatological truth claims as a pre-condition for the development of authentic religious pluralism on a worldwide scale.

The questions raised by Hartman and Talmon will prove crucial in my estimation of Jewish perspectives on religious pluralism in North America and Western Europe, but in a particular way of the policies of the State of Israel. I wish to make it quite clear that I am not speaking here simply of individual religious liberty, but of the very ethos of the nation situated in a region where religious identification remains fundamentally important. Further, what I say is not meant to be especially critical of Israeli policy to date; rather, its concern is with the future. We face here problems that have by no means been solved in the United States or in other Western nations. Especially pertinent to the discussion will be the future *character* (not merely status) of Jerusalem.

Both Talmon's and Hartman's perspectives seem to imply that any Israeli state must make greater room in its national ethos for minority religious viewpoints. It seems that the spirit of world community for which Talmon explicitly calls, and which is also implicit in Hartman's perspective, involves definite dialogue among the three religious traditions represented in the region. As the chief political force it appears that Judaism has the obligation to promote such dialogue. This is especially the case with regard to Jerusalem. Again, let me repeat that I am not addressing the question of political status[4] nor those of access to holy places or of the freedom to worship. Even under unified Israeli political rule in Jerusalem, which the overwhelming number of Israelis desire, the question of Jerusalem's spirit would remain an issue for discussion and negotiation. If Jews are to take Talmon's clear advocacy of building world community seriously, obviously Israel, and especially Jerusalem, is the place to begin.

It seems to me, however, that Hartman's position would move us even beyond Talmon's unquestioned commitment to community building. For Hartman's call for an end to any notion of religious superiority, eschatological or pre-eschatological, would profoundly affect how Jews might envision the ethos of both Israel and Jerusalem. His view seems to imply less dominance of the Jewish perspective and more sharing of the national ethos with Muslims and Christians; and this, he would argue, is necessary not just for the sake of a viable political community in Israel and throughout the world, but for the spiritual growth and development of Judaism (as well as for Christianity and Islam). As I interpret the implications of his thought, Islam and Christianity need to be seen as vital resources for the spiritual well-being of a Jewish nation, not simply as tolerated minority groups existing in greater or lesser detachment from the heart of the life of the state.

One further implication that emerges from the Talmon thesis has to do with the use of political power to combat proselytizing. This has traditionally been an extremely sensitive matter for Jews and for good reason; and legislation has been passed by the State of Israel to prohibit proselytizing. This issue raises some important and pertinent theoretical questions. Is it a violation of religious pluralism to use state power to prevent proselytizing if it is considered a religious duty, as it has been by both Christians and Muslims? If so, are there are distinctions to be drawn regarding the form that such missionary activity may take? Obviously, the ultimate answer to this problem is for all groups to adopt Talmon's non-proselytizing principle. But short of such consensus, is it not a violation of the spirit of religious pluralism to prevent such activity by political restraints?

My personal viewpoint is that, given the great danger of indiscriminate application of such legislation, it would be better to seek an end to such proselytizing through extralegal means that will lead to voluntary compliance. Let me add that this problem is even more acute in many Islamic states. This may be one area where the Christian experience—especially the kind of reflection that led up to the passage of the Second Vatican Council's Declaration on Religious Liberty and which is expressed in the writings of such Christian theologians as John Courtney Murray, S.J., who were directly involved in the authorship of this declaration—could provide a useful challenge for both Judaism and Islam.

Moving on to the second issue which I deem significant for our theme—that is, Zionism and the Jewish land tradition—we enter a complex world which few Christians understand with any degree of sophistication. Far too many Christians approach Zionism in very simplistic terms, when in fact there has always existed a wide variety of understandings of what Zionism should mean.[5] And this has been true not only on the level of political theory but also in terms of the actual shape of the national state to which Zionism has given birth.[6] In approaching this issue, it is imperative to comprehend the almost mystical Jewish attachment to Zion that is quite pervasive. Israel (and it is very difficult to separate the theological ideal from the concrete state) and more particularly the city of Jerusalem with which it is virtually synonymous are absolutely pivotal for Jewish self-definition. Abraham Heschel captured well how deeply Israel as a spiritual/physical entity and its heart, the city of Jerusalem, permeate Jewish consciousness in his volume *Israel: An Echo of Eternity*:

Jerusalem is more than a place in space...a memorial to the past. Jerusalem is a prelude, an anticipation of days to come....It is not our memory, our past that ties us to the land. It is our future....Spiritually, I am a native of Jerusalem. I have prayed here all my life. My hopes have their home in these hills....Jerusalem is never at the end of the road. She is the city where waiting for God was born.[7]

And the noted Israeli ecumenist, R. J. Zwi Werblowsky, underscores Heschel's point about the virtual interchangeability of Zion and Jerusalem:

The meaning of Jerusalem as it subsequently determined Jewish self-understanding and historic consciousness is spelled out in the prophets and in the book of Psalms. Jerusalem and Zion are synonymous, and they came too mean not only the city, but the land as a whole and the Jewish People (viz. its remnant) as a whole.[8]

As sympathetic as a Christian outsider might be to the profound attachment to Zion/Jerusalem that is at the center of Jewish tradition, certain questions inevitably arise when we place it in the context of the theme addressed in this volume. Will such a deep attachment to Zion ever allow for a distinction between land and state that can adequately provide for political and cultural expression by the Christian and Muslim minorities who share the land? And how and where ought limits to be placed on political activity that claims to have its roots in this Zionist ideal?

Many Jews, mostly Israelis, have struggled with this problem. Regrettably, far too few American Jews or Jewish organizations, despite the professed centrality of Israel for their self-identity, have ever confronted the issue in anything more than a minimal way. The election of Rabbi Meir Kahane to the Israeli parliament brought the issue to the attention of the world press. In this extreme case American Jews and Israelis have reacted in a highly commendable fashion. But the deeper question still remains virtually untouched—at least, so it appears to an outside spectator of the Jewish scene. Small steps have recently been taken to address the matter. One example has been the selection of an Arab citizen of Israel to kindle the official national lights for Independence Day, 1984. But the overall significance of such a step for the meaning of Zionism and its relation to the state has not been discussed very much. In fact, coupled with the growing nationalist identity of Palestinians living in Israel, the current situation seems to be deteriorating.

Several Israeli analysts have spoken of such deterioration. Moshe Gabai, director of the Institute for Arabic Studies at Givat Haviva, has spoken of the absence of integrated social frameworks in Israeli national life:

The cultural and social differentiation between Arabs and Jews has become institutionalized. To this very day there are no integrated or common frameworks. The
basis of Arab identity, from the point of view of ethnic origin, language, religion
and nationalism, guarantees a separate Arab existence—the concentration of Arab
populations in specific territorial enclaves and separate institutions such as schools,
media and voluntary organizations. All this hinders the creation of an overall Israeli
culture and identity, and common social frameworks.[9]

Further, Dr. Haim Gordon, who has developed a project in peace education based on the Buberian dialogue model at Ben Gurion University in
Beer Sheva, concludes, "the relations between Jews and Arabs in Israel have
gone from worse to terrible in the past five years, and few persons have
the courage to swim against the tide."[10]

Admittedly, the integration of the Arab minority into Israeli life is not a
one-way street. The Arab community has yet to decide to what extent it
wishes such integration and to make its wishes clear. Should it virtually
reject any integration, a new dilemma will result. Can a state remain healthy
with two totally separate political communities? One Israeli response to
this question is to argue for an end to Zionist ideology as the process of
the normalization of Jewish life in Israel continues. Writing in *Dissent*,
Menachem Brinker argues that the crucial problems facing the Israeli community today are primarily "Israeli-civic" and only secondarily "Zionist-
ideological." For him, Zionism, though important, was only a means to an
end—the safety of the Jewish people:

The Zionist movement had one simple goal: to bring a majority of the Jews to an
independent state. Once this is done, the Zionist idea and the Zionist movement
earn a place of honor—in history. The continued existence of a Zionist movement
is on the way to becoming not only superflous but harmful.... The pressing issues
of today are no longer issues for which Zionism has answers.[11]

For Brinker, it would seem, the religious perspectives of Heschel and
Werblowsky hinder the genuine resolution of Israel's current problems,
including the creation of a cultural and political ethos in which minorities
enjoy the fullest possible equality.

The debate in Israel will go on for some time to come. My suspicion is
that the kind of radical, non-Zionist solution proposed by Brinker will not
win the day among the vast majority of Jews, including both those who call
themselves Progressive Zionists and those who belong to such religiously
based Zionist peace groups as *Oz ve'Shalom*. Moreover, it is likely that
discussion will intensify in American Zionist circles where thus far it has
been minimal. David Polish, a longtime proponent of Zionism, has written
of the need for Jews to continue to wrestle with the full implications of
Israeli state sovereignty. The mere fact of such sovereignty has not answered
all the relevant questions, especially in the religious sphere.[12]

Although to a large extent this is an intra-Jewish debate, it affords appropriate moments for Christians to raise questions and engage in actual dialogue with Jews. The same holds true for Muslims. On the Christian side, I have argued that attitudes toward the sacredness of the land constitute one of the primary differences between Christianity and Judaism.[13] This is not to claim that Christianity ought not have regard for the land and fully implant itself in history. Rather, it is the assertion that though Christianity may consider the Holy Land of special significance, ultimately every place is as holy as the next because of the Incarnation. Therefore one cannot speak of a "diaspora Christianity" as of a "diaspora Judaism." Nevertheless, a useful, mutually enriching discussion can result from an interchange between the Christian viewpoint and that mystical attachment to Zion as a special place of salvation articulated by such Jewish theologians as Heschel.

An equally profitable discussion would ensue from a comparison of Jewish attempts to relate the spiritual vision of Zion to the problems of a multiethnic state with the way in which Western Christian churches have solved the problem under the strong influence of the spirit of the Enlightenment. The perspectives presented by the Second Vatican Council's Declaration on Religious Liberty, and especially by John Courtney Murray, S. J., in his own writings, need to be compared with Zionist perspectives, religious and secular. Many Christians in the West will probably feel uncomfortable with the seeming overidentification of state and religious vision in the writings of Heschel, Werblowsky and others like them, but the Brinker proposal should appeal to them. On the other hand, an encounter with Zionism will challenge many of the assumptions of those of us who basically identify the church-state separation model as the ideal for Catholic theology and not merely as pragmatic accommodation. Moreover, in light of events such as the Holocaust we in the West need to confront some serious questions about the role of religious symbols in our own general cultural ethos. There is danger that we may limit religion far too much to the sphere of the individual, allowing the public realm to be gradually stripped of any sense of transcendence. And if that happens, can personal religious commitment survive? I suspect that in many ways Muslims are in principle much more sympathetic to the vision of religious Zionism than are most Western Christians. I doubt that either Israel or many Islamic states will adopt in full the Enlightenment answer to this dilemma that has found favor in the West and is espoused by such Israelis as Brinker.[14] Besides, the perspectives of Brinker and of the civil libertarians in Israel are too simple. They raise many important questions about the rights of both non-observant Jews and Arabs in Israel; but their humanistic state model does not so easily resolve the problem of pluralism facing Israel as they contend.

Jacob Agus and Manfred Vogel have in somewhat different ways made an approach to the Zionist question that elicits the same sort of questions. For Agus the theological dimension of Israel can only be used to project a *vocation*. The re-emergence of the state has made it possible for the Jewish people to transmit more easily certain divine-human values internally and to the rest of humankind. But there is always the danger that "the state, reflecting the ethnic base of Jewish consciousness, may become a surrogate for the superstructure of the faith. The beginning may be viewed as an end, the opportunity as a fulfillment."[15] Agus goes on to assert the need for Jews to see Israel as a part of the universal messianic vision. But he also asserts that Christians have the obligation to acknowledge the indispensable role that the concept of Jewish homeland plays in the historic problem of Jewish survival and in the building of the Kingdom of God: "They have to accept the necessary *existence* of the state as a realm of opportunity for the realization of Jewish and universal values."[16]

Central to Vogel's perspective on the land question is the sense of peoplehood. Land, while important, is in fact secondary and derivative with regard to Judaism's basic faith stance. But the land remains vital for the realization of Israel's redemptive vocation. Minus a land in which meaningful sovereignty can be exercised, the very workings of the redemptive vocation are impossible. It cannot be denied that Jewish faith has survived the absence of land. Such preservation of faith would have been impossible if the Jewish sense of peoplehood had disappeared. But such survival constituted a mere shadow of authentic Jewish existence. In Vogel's words, "In diaspora existence Judaism could only mark time. It could only, so to speak, hold the fort. For the resumption of the active pursuit of its redemptive vocation it had to await and hope for the restoration of the land."[17] The common thrust in both Agus and Vogel is a functional approach to Jewish state sovereignty. A Jewish state and its consequent political power are not so much ends in themselves, as they appear to be in the writings of "spiritual Zionists," but only means to an end. One could, perhaps, classify Agus and Vogel as "moral Zionists." Neither has, however, spelled out the full implications of their viewpoint in terms of the problem of pluralism. Does their moral Zionism prevent, for theological reasons, even the consideration by Jews of any abrogation of state sovereignty (that is, some new federation of peoples in the Middle East)? I do not see this as being practicable in the foreseeable future because of the current lack of peace and trust in the region, and maybe it will never be. Still, the question as to whether state sovereignty is *de fide* for Jewish theology as the moral Zionists interpret it is an issue worth pursuing on the theoretical level.

This question might become especially critical with regard to Jerusalem. It would be interesting to learn of Agus' and Vogel's reaction to the spiritual Zionists' claim that Jerusalem and Zion are synonymous. Does this mean that Jewish faith at this moment could not countenance any concept of shared sovereignty in Jerusalem? I am not speaking of a redivision of the city along its former lines, but rather of the possibility of a new creative plan that would accord a measure of real sovereignty to the various groups in Jerusalem in the context of a comprehensive peace agreement. This may not be possible at the moment; but could it nonetheless be considered a political ideal proper to a Jewish believer?

There are other questions that may be put to Agus and Vogel, particularly in light of the reflections of Talmon and Hartman. To what extent do the Christian and Muslim understandings of the fulfillment of the kingdom become important for the achievement of Judaism's redemptive vocation? If to any degree, then does Christian and Muslim access to state sovereignty become a critical issue? Agus speaks of Israel becoming a means of fulfilling "universal values," while Vogel seems to focus only on the Jewish redemptive vision. But each still has to grapple with the question of whether Christian and Muslim particularity has anything to contribute to the fulfillment of Israel's redemptive vocation, which for both of them seems to be the primary theological justification for the exercise of Jewish state sovereignty.

In concluding this section, let me issue a warning to my Christian brothers and sisters. The questions that I have raised are in no way meant to be a general indictment of Israel's treatment of its minorities. While certain deficiencies do exist—and some of these I deem to be serious—Israel has still done a far better job in ensuring a measure of pluralism and minority rights that any other Middle Eastern state. Moreover, many of the problems that I have raised for consideration have not been resolved fully either by Christianity or by Western political thought. They have been raised in a spirit of dialogue and in invitation of my Jewish colleagues, both in Israel and in the West, to respond with questions of their own about Christian teaching on faith and political pluralism.

The third area selected for discussion is the use of power. I have raised it because a number of Jewish writers, especially those for whom the Holocaust experience has become a starting point for contemporary Jewish religious identity, have stressed its utter centrality to contemporary interpretations of Jewish existence. Richard Rubenstein is one of these, and in a somewhat more nuanced and indirect way so is Emil Fackenheim. But the "centrality of power" thesis has been most cogently pursued by Irving Greenberg. As Greenberg reflects on it, a crucial lesson to be gleaned from the trauma of Auschwitz is that all people need to acquire an adequate measure of power to survive. "Power inescapably corrupts," he writes, but "its assumption is inescapable" after the Holocaust. From the perspective of contemporary Judaism Greenberg claims that it would be immoral to abandon the quest for power. The only option in the post-Holocaust world, if we are to avoid repetitions of the human degradation and evil of the Nazi period, is to combine the assumption of power with what Greenberg calls the creation of "better mechanisms of self-criticism, correction and repentance." Only in this way can we use power "without being the unwitting slaves of bloodshed or an exploitative status quo."[18]

As an ethician in the tradition of Reinhold Niebuhr, I remain quite sympathetic to the call to struggle with the "humanized" use of power to achieve justice in our day. But the issue of power does raise problems for our theme of faith and political pluralism. To the degree that large numbers of Jews subscribe to Greenberg's prescription of their post-Auschwitz self-definition (and there are dissenters to this position), the general commitment to pluralism and outreach to minorities will be correspondingly lessened, particularly in Israel. This is because the power model tends to set up an *antagonistic* relationship toward the Other, rather that a cooperative one. Greenberg himself alludes to this implication of his thought:

Power must be widely distributed to insure that it will not be absurd. This sets up a dialectic of power which must be applied to Israel as well as to all power-wielding nations. The ideal would be maximum self-government for Palestinians and Arabs as a check on Jewish abuse. But such self-government can only be accepted if it does not threaten the existence and security of the Jewish People.[19]

The final sentence is critical for any Jewish approach to pluralism that would take its cue from Greenberg's power model. It makes clear that, for such an approach, pluralism must remain close to the end of any list of priorities in the exercise of Jewish state sovereignty. Greenberg's model also seems to discourage both Jewish and non-Jewish populations in Israel from the kind of commitment to enhanced integration of Jews and non-Jews within the Israeli state that was discussed earlier in this essay. Pluralism, according to the Greenberg perspective, would appear to be the result of the organized harnessing by each group of its power potential. Greenberg would also apply the same power model to Jews in the United States. He applauds the increased involvement of American Jews in political lobbying groups. He considers it unfortunate, however, that Jewish power groups still remain too vulnerable and marginal: what power is available should be used to the hilt. He quotes with approval the statement of Manes Sperber: "After the Holocaust, Jews have a moral obligation to anti-Semites to be powerful so as never to tempt them into such evil behavior again."[20] Such an approach, if it carries the day, will undoubtedly mean a significantly more modified stance with regard to pluralism in America than has been the case till now, at least for Reform and Conservative Judaism.

It needs to be added at this point that though Greenberg has brought to the fore the Jewish identity question in America in connection with his power model, the issue has been actively deliberated for some time. The rise of the "new ethnicity" in American life has occasioned this, and while no clear consensus has yet emerged, it appears that particularity is in the ascendency.[21] But let me caution that this conclusion does not necessarily mean a total abandonment of the classical American Jewish commitment to religious and political pluralism. William Cutter and Alan Henkin, for example, have argued that the rebuilding of strong particularistic bases in the lives of American Jews may allow for a serious fleshing out of a new understanding of, and commitment to, universalism within American Judaism, and one that will reach beyond the controversy surrounding the historic liberal Jewish conception of universalism.[22] It should be noted before concluding our consideration of Greenberg's view, that while his stress on the power model for Jewish self-identity today may alter the Jewish approach to external pluralism, he himself believes that it will give new impetus to pluralism internal to Judaism, for in light of the Holocaust previous internally Jewish debates seem not only petty but life-threatening. His model, he is convinced, will help create new forms of Jewish organization that will allow for a wider variety of Jewish belief and practice as they forge Jews into an effective political power base in America and bring about greater social cohesion within the Jewish population of Israel.

There is no doubt in my mind that a dialogue about the power model needs to take place between Christians and Jews, including Muslims as far as that is possible. Certainly, Christians must enter such a dialogue fully cognizant of their historical abuse of power, especially against the Jews. Nevertheless, I remain convinced that Jews, who have not had the experience of power for very long, can profit from the ongoing reflections on power and on its ever easy degeneration into brutal force that mark recent Christian theology and such church documents as the American Catholic Bishops' Peace Pastoral.[23]

The final point that seems important to me in any consideration of Judaism and political pluralism is the gradual emergence of Oriental Jewry in Israeli society. These are largely the people who have fled from Arab countries during the past several decades. Depending on which researcher you follow, Oriental Jews now constitute, or come close to constituting, the majority of Israel's cultural, political and social life and will undoubtedly alter its national ethos.[24] The effect of this demographic shift on diaspora Jews remains uncertain. The religious and political experience of Oriental Jews is quite different from that of Jews with Western roots. They are generally unfamiliar with Western political traditions, including its stress upon pluralism, and with Christianity; and the Nazi Holocaust is not in their lived experience.

At this point it is simply too early to predict how Oriental Jewry might permanently influence Israel's approach to political and religious pluralism. Some in the Jewish community have argued prematurely that, because Oriental Jewry has little familiarity with political models other than despotism and has suffered greatly on many occasions under Arab rule, it will pull Israeli society away from its present democratic tradition and take a hard line against any accommodation with the Arab community. This too-quick assessment of Oriental Jewry's potential influence on the ethos of Israel has been challenged, and rightly so. Former President Yitzhak Navon, himself an Oriental Jew, has consistently warned against automatically assuming that the Oriental Jewish community will bring about a decided turn to the right in all dimensions of Israeli politics, particularly the relationship with the Arabs. Likewise, Inge Lederer-Gibel of the American Jewish Committee, one of the most perceptive writers on this topic in American Judaism, has forcefully denounced the haughtiness of many Jews—including elements of the Israeli peace movement which she fundamentally supports—for simply dismissing the possibility of any contribution by Oriental Jews to Arab-Jewish rapprochement. She claims that, in so doing, they are pushing the Oriental Jews into league with the radical right.[25] Dr. Shlomo Elbaz, a lecturer in comparative literature at the Hebrew University in Jerusalem and a leader in the East for Peace movement, voices the same complaint. He says: "Even the Peace Now people whom we regard as our allies say that the *Edot Hamizrah* are a barrier to peace. Nothing could be further from the truth."[26] There is little doubt in my mind that the Oriental Jewish traditions bring with them a wealth of religious insights with political implications that will have to be digested by Jews, both in Israel and in the Diaspora, as well as by sympathetic observers of Judaism. Apart from what may be gained by exposure to a largely untapped source of religious wisdom, the incorporation of this segment of the Jewish people into the dialogue about religion and political pluralism may force us in the West to recognize that our understanding of such matters has been too exclusively Western. This is not to play down in any way the positive contributions of Western political thought and experience to the development of this theme, but simply to say that the whole answer may not lie in Western political wisdom. Dialogue not only with Oriental Judaism but with the entire Oriental religious/political tradition is increasingly necessary if this problem is not to remain an exclusively Western concern. We in the West have much to give to the East in this realm. But for us to be heard by the East in a constructive way requires that we stand ready to learn from it and not assume the automatic superiority of our own current resolutions of the faith/political pluralism issue. Additionally, encounter with the Oriental Jewish tradition will help Christians (and Western Jews as well) to break through certain stereotypes of Judaism as a Western religion and as particularistic in contrast to supposed Christian universalism. Though far smaller in numbers, Judaism has been as multicultural as Christianity, and in some instances has been far more receptive to the notion of adjusting its religious expression to the indigenous religious and political ethos than has been the case with the Christian churches. Moreover, Western Jews will have to modify some of their simple equations of Judaism with the Western tradition. In other words, the rise of Oriental Jewry may lead us to an enhanced awareness of internal Jewish pluralism.

Finally, Oriental Jewry may provide an important bridge, both for Western Jews and for Christians, to the world of Islam. Although the relationship between Oriental Jews and the Muslim world has often been marked by Muslim repression, it has also occasioned a history of constructive interchange that is ripe for re-examination by scholars. No one pretends that such a mediatory role for Oriental Jewry will be easily assumed, given recent history. But it is there to be pursued.

So much, then, for one outsider's view of how contemporary Judaism is handling the relationship between faith and political pluralism. The present is a confusing period but not necessarily an uncreative one. One thing is certain: Christian self-reflection will be enriched if the churches enter serious dialogue with the Jewish people on this topic so crucial for justice and social harmony in our age.

NOTES

1. David Hartman, "Jews and Christians in the World of Tomorrow," *Immanuel* 6 (Spring 1976): 79.

2. Shemaryahu Talmon, "Towards World Community: Resources for Living Together—A Jewish View," *The Ecumenical Review* 26 (October 1974): 617.

3. Ibid.

4. I have addressed this elsewhere: "Rethinking the Palestinian Question," *Worldview* 17, no. 10 (October 1974): 41–44; "The Evolution of Christian-Jewish Dialogue," *The Ecumenist* 22, no. 5 (July/August 1984): 65–70; and "Jews and Christians: The Contemporary Dialogue," *Quarterly Review* 4, no. 4 (Winter 1984): 23–36.

5. For a discussion of the UN Resolution on Zionism and Racism, see my essay, "Anti-Zionism = Anti-Semitism: Fact or Fable?" *Worldview* 19, nos. 1–2 (January/February 1976): 15–19.

6. For a succinct summary of various Zionist trends, see Manfred Vogel, "The Link between People, Land and Religion in Modern Jewish Thought," *Sidic* 8, no. 2 (1913): 15–32.

7. Abraham Heschel, *Israel: An Echo of Eternity* (New York: Farrar, Straus and Giroux, 1969), pp. 18 ff.

8. R. J. Zwi Werblowsky, "The Meaning of Jerusalem to Jews, Christians and Muslims," The Charles Strong Memorial Lecture (Australia), 1972, reprinted from *Jaarbericht Ex Orient Lux*, 23 (1973–74): 11.

9. Moshe Gabai, "Israeli Arabs: Problem of Identity and Integration," *New Outlook* (October/November 1984): 23.

10. Haim Gordon, "Buberian Learning Groups: Education for Peace in Israel," *Journal of Ecumenical Studies* 21, no. 3 (Summer 1984): 629.

11. Menachem Brinker, "The End of Zionism? Thoughts on the Wages of Success," *Dissent* (Winter 1985): 81–88.

12. David Polish, "Israel: Some Halachic Theological Perspectives," *Journal of Reform Judaism* 31, no. 1 (Winter 1984): 44–59.

13. See my volume *Christ in Light of the Christian-Jewish Dialogue* (New York: Paulist Press, 1982), pp. 127–33.

14. For more on this issue, see my essay, "The Holocaust: Its Implications for the Church and Society Problematic," in Richard W. Rousseau, S.J., ed., *Christianity and*

Judaism: The Deepening Dialogue (Scranton, Pa.: Ridge Row Press, 1983), pp. 97–102.

15. Jacob Agus, *The Jewish Quest: Essays on Basic Concepts of Jewish Theology* (New York: Ktav, 1983), p. 230.

16. Ibid., p. 234.

17. Vogel, "The Link between People, Land, and Religion in Modern Jewish Thought," p. 29.

18. Irving Greenberg, *The Third Great Cycle in Jewish History* (New York: National Jewish Resource Center, 1981), pp. 25 ff.

19. Ibid., p. 25.

20. Manes Sperber, *The Ethics of Jewish Power: I* (New York: National Jewish Resource Center, 1984), pp. 1–2.

21. For a wide-ranging discussion of the pluralism question in American Judaism, see the articles by David Ellenson, Irvin M. Blank and William Cutter/Alan Henkin in *Journal of Reform Judaism* 26, no. 2 (Spring 1979): 47–82.

22. William Cutter and Alan Henkin, "Universalism and Particularism: Where Ends and Means Collide," *Journal of Reform Judaism* 26, no. 2 (Spring 1979): 74–75.

23. For an amplification of my own views on power and peace, see "Power and Peace: A View from the Christian-Jewish Dialogue," *The Bible Today* 21, no. 3 (May 1983): 184–90; and "Power and the Pursuit of Peace: Some Reflections," in John T. Pawlikowski, O.S.M., and Donald Senior, C.P., eds., *Biblical and Theological Reflections on the "Challenge of Peace"* (Wilmington, Del.: Michael Glazier, 1984), pp. 73–89.

24. For more on the Oriental Jews and Middle East Peace, see my essay, "The Evolution of Christian-Jewish Dialogue," pp. 65–70.

25. See Inge Lederer-Gibel, "Radical Chic in Israel: Excluding the Sephardim," *Christianity and Crisis* 44, no. 16 (October 15, 1984): 367–73; *Three Israelis—Three Successful Sephardim Speak of Themselves, Their Land, Their Future* (New York: American Jewish Committee, 1983); "Moroccans in Israel: My Family's Anguish," *Response* 23 (Fall 1984): 91–103.

26. Shlomo Elbaz, *Jerusalem Post*, International Edition, July 8, 1983, p. 26.

PART II

CHRISTIANITY

5

Christianity Within the Political Dialectics of Community and Empire

MATTHEW L. LAMB

INTRODUCTION

As the twentieth century draws to a close, humankind on this planet faces challenges of unprecedented gravity. For the first time on this stage of world history, we humans can envisage the possibility (some would say the probability) of a self-inflicted abrupt and almost apocalyptic nuclear end of the human drama as we have known it till now. Since the curtain rose upon human history, the drama has been rent by wars and conflicts in which some emerged as victors and most were destroyed or enslaved as victims. The human drama has been marked by pell-mell successions of roles which could be designated as winners versus losers, victors versus victims, masters versus slaves, empires versus colonies, superpowers versus weakly underdeveloped countries. The titantic irony of the nuclear arms race is that it has the potential to end these scenarios of heroic victors and crushed victims. Physically dominative power is reaching its apotheosis. Should extensive nuclear warfare occur, there would be no victory parades. Any surviving victims would envy the dead. The pride or *hubris* which has fueled the massive war machines of history, which has scripted so much of the human drama in terms of power dominating and exploiting other humans, could quite literally *end* the planetary drama. The masks of "victory to the conquerors and woe to the conquered" have been stripped from the face of dominative power, revealing its awesome evil as death. The dialectic of master and slave, of victor and victim, ends in the universal victimhood of all human beings.[1]

The world religions cherish within their traditions important resources and memories which, if incarnated in the lives and practices of religious believers, could contribute to the radical change or conversion of the human drama away from death and toward life.[2] Among all life forms on this planet, humans are the only ones known to care for their dead. Burial provides the most primitive or primordial evidence of specifically human life. In diverse ways all religions grapple with the mysteries of victimhood and death as immanent in human life and yet transcending as well. Salvific transcendence might be expressed in terms of denial, as in Buddhism, in terms of trans-migration, as in Hinduism, or in terms of transformation, as in Judaism, Islam and Christianity.[3] The central stories or foundational narratives of the world religions reveal paths of right conduct toward fuller life for those gifted with the call to change from the narrowness of the ways of death to the expansion of minds and hearts through enlightenment and faith. But the gifted call can be refused; it is always more of an imperative than an indic-ative. Religious authenticity can shatter, twisting the symbols of life into tools of deadly animosity. The cries of the victims are drowned out by the clatter of crusades and holy wars as religion is pressed into the service of dominative power bent upon imposing its will, come what may. Religion can be—and too often has been—used to extol and legitimate the victors of history and to distract the victims from their longings for freedom and dignity.

I shall address the topic of religious, and specifically Christian, convictions and public action by first outlining the ambiguous legacies of both Chris-tianity and of modernity. The urgency of our contemporary situation has not a little to do with these ambiguous legacies. I shall then discuss the political dialectics of community and empire by first analyzing what I call the radical politics of pluralism and then showing how such pluralist political dialectics relate to community, empires or superpowers, and Christianity. In this study I contrast what I term an-archy and mon-archy on the one hand, and syn-archy on the other. The words are hyphenated and designate respectively no (*an*) principle (*arche*), one (*mon*) principle (*arche*) or pluralist cooperative (*syn*) principles (*arche*) for creating, sustaining and changing social orders. Mon-archy tends to create, sustain and change social orders "from the top down," excusing its impositions with the belief (or defense mechanism) that the "bottom" would otherwise be an-archy. Syn-archy tends to create, sustain and change social orders from the "bottom up" by nurturing and expanding the freedoms of "the bottom."

THE AMBIGUOUS LEGACIES OF CHRISTIANITY AND MODERNITY

Pluralism is both a fact and a value. Pluralism is a fact, as it always has been within nature, history and religion. Christianity is no exception. Almost all types of pluralism have and will be found within Christianity—economic, social, ethnic, political, cultural and religious pluralism. The fact of pluralism raises the question of the value of pluralism. Pluralism means differences. Some differences are complementary to one another. Other differences are contradictory to, or mutually exclusive of, one another. Still others may be genetically related to one another. Leaving aside a very old problem, that of the one and the many, I would argue that pluralism is a value to be cherished and fostered insofar as it is intrinsic to the humanization and personalization of life on this planet.[4] The whole of human history, as well as of Christianity, could be presented as an ongoing experiment, or vast series of sets of experiments, aimed at discerning the values and disvalues of pluralism. To what extent do the differences constitutive of pluralism promote the human good? One might argue that the question is unanswerable, since there are many contradictory notions of the human good, so that the pluralism is only another name for a fundamental an-archy, a fundamental lack of any universally valid principles for discerning between contradictory differences.[5]

Yet to argue for a *fundamental* an-archy is logically and ontologically an impossibility, for any argument has some principle of discerning order if it is not mere unintelligible babble. Ethical agnostics are wont to consider themselves intelligent: the better their arguments for a fundamental an-archy regarding the human good, the more their own cognitive performance subverts their intended position.[6] Pluralism as a value is not an-archy. The pluralism of values so evident in the human drama does not mean a fundamental relativism of values. The crucial issue is how to mediate such a pluralism of values, with its complementary and contradictory differences, in ways that promote responsibility and freedom. If an-archy as a fundamental relativism of values is unacceptable, the fear of such an-archy has often contributed to many historical forms of what I term mon-archy. Where an-archy asserts no possible principles of discerning freely between contradictory differences in values, mon-archy attempts to settle the issue by imposing the values of particular individuals or groups upon others through various forms of dominative power. Mon-archy in this sense is a fundamental inability to relate pluralism to responsible human freedom, deciding instead to impose sets of social and cultural meanings and values upon others. This would include many, probably most, of the political forms of monarchy, but it would also include many other forms of social organization where the particular interests of some are "universalized" through dominative power.[7] Power is dominative to the extent that it represses the interests and questions, and the actions expressing those interests and questions, of those seeking to expand effective human freedom.[8]

The legacies of Christianity and of modernity in the West are profoundly ambiguous in regard to free and responsible mediations of pluralistic differences. I shall sketch some of the main components of these ambiguous legacies under the metaphor of three major betrayals: the betrayal of Christian faith, the betrayal of empirical reason and the betrayal of dialectical

reason. The metaphor of "betrayal" connotes both how these three major
sets of traditions in the West *could* have promoted more effective human
freedom and good than they in fact have, and how their failures to do so
demand of us, not a total repudiation of their ambiguous achievements, but
a discerning recovery of those aspects in the sets of traditions which would,
if actualized, subvert their failures.[9]

From Judaism Christianity inherited a revelatory intensification of the
transcendent unity of the Divine immanent within the plurality of a people
called out of slavery. The struggles between monarchy and the prophets
were later intensified to the point of apocalyptic expectation: from the
Davidic kingship to the kingship of Yahweh. Jesus both inherited and transformed this apocalyptic expectation. The unity of God is *not* revealed in
power dominating and controlling historical chaos, but is revealed in nar-
rative invitations to a discipleship of faith, hope and love empowering the
lowly and poor to become the children of God, who is Love.[10] Jewish
theology both stressed how God is so transcendent in unity that there can
be no images of God and the Divine Name cannot be uttered, and emphasized the immanence of the Divine in the liberating identity of the Exodus
narratives. Christianity likewise emphasized how the transcendent God is
immanent in the preaching and life of Jesus, and also stressed how in him
God became one with the poor and the powerless, with those non-identified
with the "world" and called to the freedom of the Kingdom of God.[11]

In the first centuries both Jews and Christians suffered for their refusals
to capitulate to the sacralist prejudices of the Roman Empire. Both the
lordship of Yahweh and the lordship of Christ were recognized as prohibiting any acknowledgment, however cynical and pro forma, of the emperor
as divine.[12] Within Christianity, however, the temptations to sacralism were
strong. Sacralism is the identification of religious values with forms of secular
power: identifications of churches with the Kingdom of God, of Christ's
lordship with the mighty and powerful of this world. The Constantinian
dilemma was paradigmatic. Augustine and many monks would articulate in
thought and in communal practice the need for the apocalyptic reign of
God to transform radically the imperial sacralism of the Roman Empire.
Athanasius and other bishops would dogmatically break the mon-archical
aspirations of imperial ideology by affirming how the unity of the Godhead
is community of persons.[13] But Constantine had, as other mon-archs after
him, his court theologians. Eusebius of Caesarea would oblige, along with
others, in rewriting history from the perspective of the victors, the emperors
as divinely graced, if not divinely natured.[14] Christianity became Christendom. Although altar and throne were separated, more often than not one
would reinforce the authoritarian prejudices of the others.[15]

I shall not trace here the series of betrayals and recoveries in Christianity
down to our own day. The monastic missionaries preached and lived the
Gospel as freeing and educative empowerments of "the so-called barbari-

ans," whereas the tactics of a Charlemagne tried to press the monasteries into his imperial designs.[16] The efforts of the mendicants and their theologians transformed the classical Graeco-Roman heroic social virtues through evangelical faith, hope and love. Those efforts were thwarted by later scholastics who legitimated the imperial ambitions of popes and monarchs in the Holy Roman Empire.[17] Reforming prophets and theologians rejected the inquisitorial authoritarianism of Rome for the sake of the Gospel, only to find their spiritual renewal often co-opted by the powers of the emergent nation-states.[18] The Cross would be continually betrayed by the Sword as colonization brought new peoples and lands into the struggles for monarchical power. By the seventeenth century the West began to have its fill of the pogroms, crusades, inquisitions, wars of religion, and the other excesses and repressions of a decadent Christendom.[19]

The first phase of the Enlightenment began to draw together the constitutive elements of a critically empirical reason. The religious convictions of faith were too divisive of public actions in their conflicting sacralisms. The successes of the emerging intellectual convictions in empirical natural sciences broke the mon-archical cosmologies of decadent scholasticism. Nature did not operate in accord with mon-archical or hierarchical orderings of the spheres. As the empirical methods of observation, hypothesis formation, experiential verification, and incipient industrial applications began to spread, proponents of empirical reason turned to the study of man and society.[20] Freedom *of* religion was championed by those who, like the Deists, found a basis for belief in intelligible natural laws rather than in the contested revealed religions. Empirically oriented human and historical studies increasingly challenged the authoritarian hegemony of Christendom, as they called attention to the plurality of concrete particulars not identifiable with the cultural conceptualism and uniformity of the *ancien régime*.[21]

The liberally critical thrust of empirical rationality, however, was betrayed by new forms of old alliances. The old orders of hierarchical sacralism gave way to new forms of bureaucratic secularism.[22] As capitalist industrialization expanded, empirical reason became identified with methods of quantification and technical manipulation. Although the natural sciences would gradually uncover the wondrous unity-in-diversity of planet earth, technical industrialization would increasingly regard nature as an energy reservoir and dump site for its expanding megamachine.[23] A social Darwinism would legitimate the "survival of the strongest," while a Max Weber would, despite his sad disclaimers, legitimate the fiction of value-neutral facticity and the supposedly inevitable subsumption of democracy into bureaucracy.[24] Politics became the prerogative of a social engineering trying to play off competing pressure groups. Culture capitulated to the demands of mass industry as all aspects of modern secular life were invaded by a technical or instrumental rationality which had betrayed the critical potential of empirical reason.[25] If the first phase of the modern Western Enlightenment put its hopes for enlightened social policies not in the churches but in the new academies, educational and research institutes, these more often than not betrayed their trust by legitimating the dominative interests of the highest bidders. The intellectual conviction of progress through a "pure" empirical reason would gradually crumble as instrumental rationality would deliver undreamed of physical power to the expanding military machines. The titanic irony of such betrayals can be seen in the possibility of nuclear annihilation. A major rationalization for these betrayals of empirical reason consisted in the belief that reality is fundamentally only matter-in-motion.[26] A massive nuclear holocaust would indeed only leave our planet with matter-in-motion as it obliterates all higher forms of life.[27]

A second phase of the modern Western Enlightenment began in the last century with efforts to differentiate the methods of the human sciences from those of the natural sciences (Dilthey) as well as efforts to transform personal and social living through the emancipatory imperatives of psychoanalysis (Freud) and of the socioeconomic critique of ideologies (Marx). These efforts were the hesitant emergence of dialectical reason. In maintaining that the description and explanation of "facts" required only more or less mechanical conjunctions of observational techniques with techiques of theoretical measurement, empirical reason was betrayed by naive "realism." Such a naive realism was a betrayal since its empiricism and positivism were unverifiable beliefs or ideologies that did not articulate the actual praxis or performance of empirical reason.[28] Against such betrayals of empirical reason, with their naive realist sunderings of fact and value, dialectical reason would reintegrate the fact and value in Dilthey's project of a critique of historical reason, in Marx's critique of psychic pathologies. This hesitant emergence of dialectical reason repudiated neither the Enlightenment project nor the critical potential of empirical reason. Quite the contrary. Analogous to the reformers in Christianity, these efforts were an intensification of empirical reason. Just as reformers appealed to faith and the Gospels over against what they considered the incrustations of a distorted and betrayed institutionalization of Christianity in Roman Christendom, so Dilthey, Marx or Freud appealed to reason and enlightenment over against what they considered the distortions and betrayals of the meanings and values within human communication and emancipation, whether in empiricist scientism and historicism (Dilthey), or in capitalist societies (Marx), or in the repressive optimism of bourgeois consciousness (Freud).[29]

Such a dialectical reason contains, therefore, elements of what Jürgen Habermas refers to as the quasi-transcendental, as interests practical in the hermeneutical-historical sciences and as emancipatory in psychoanalysis and in the critique of ideologies. These elements of dialectical reason have by no means been integrated into complementary methods of reflection and action.[30] But their hesitant emergence did introduce divergent patterns of rational reflection on value convictions. They began offering suggestions on how to resolve hermeneutically, ideologically or therapeutically fundamental value conflicts. Whatever the differences between them, the writings of Dilthey, Marx or Freud began to establish the needs for (1) a serious intellectual and critical commitment to integrate values into reflection, (2) a reflective realization of how reason was not yet realized in history, society or psyche, (3) a growing suspicion that such a realization could not be through technical or instrumental rationality, and (4) a recognition that such projects of dialectical reason could only be achieved by attending to the *victims* of either cultural-historical amnesia (Dilthey) or socioeconomic exploitation (Marx) or psychopathological obsessions and illusions (Freud).[31]

But this second phase of the Enlightenment was only a *hesitant* emergence of dialectical reason. Its beginnings were ambiguous even in its originators. Little wonder, then, that their dialectically practical reason would be swallowed up and betrayed by the almost inexorable "progress" of scientism, technocracy and instrumental rationality.[32] Hermeneutics and history would betray any trace of dialectical reason as they became prerogatives of value-neutral techniques in an ivory-tower scholarship, legitimating the secularist bureaucratic and cultural prejudices in dominative nations. As Arendt, Gadamer, Habermas and others have shown, they often did this in the name of a Cartesian quest for the certitude of a *fundamentum inconcussum* (unshakeable foundation), while in fact such scholarship was usually based upon the more financially and academically remunerative "foundations" of expanding nation-states.[33] Similarly, the dialectically transformative potential of psychoanalysis, as well as other depth psychological therapies, was betrayed by both a scientistic reduction to techniques of "adjustment" to pathological social "realities," and a professionalization of analysis which, as Bettelheim, Laing and Szasz among others have argued, has contributed not a little to the commercialization and privatization of psychiatry.[34] Finally, the series of betrayals within Marxism have successively reduced its critical and dialectical power to the platitudes and propaganda of rigid state socialisms, tightly controlled by suffocating bureaucracies and rigid party class systems. As Marcuse sadly commented, such betrayals indicate how "the means for liberation and humanization operate for preserving domination and submission, and the theory that destroyed all ideology is used for the establishment of a new ideology."[35]

Today the innocent beliefs of the Enlightenment in progress through pure reason, whether empirical or dialectical, seem undermined by the devastations of global and local wars, by the Holocaust, by increasing militarism and nuclear arms races, by widening gaps between rich and poor, by a dwindling confidence in democracy on the part of both capitalist and communist "experts." The intellectual convictions of modernity are no longer modern. Like Christianity, modernity now has a history. And that history—our history—of supposedly pure reason has brought us even more victims than the old, impure religions. In response to the betrayals of Christianity with its competing mon-archical sacralisms, modernity either proclaimed a freedom *of* religion (as in the primarily middle-class revolutions) or a freedom *from* religion (as in Marxist revolutions). Instead of religious institutions, secular educational and research institutions would collaborate with governments in forming enlightened public policies. As states divorced themselves from churches, they wed themselves to academies. (No wonder, you might say, reason lost its purity!) But techniques of legal separations, whether of church and state or highly unlikely ones of state and academy, do not address the roots of the problems. Such strategies of institutional separation are heavily infected by what Gandhi perceived as an underlying temptation in modernity: we want to create institutional systems that are so good that we don't have to be good.[36] Academies in late capitalist and in state socialist countries have witnessed a more or less pervasive *Betriebsblindheit* (yours not to question why, yours but to get good grades and jobs) with an increasing professionalization or technical rationalization of inquiry.[37]

Pluralism has suffered an eclipse. Secularist mon-archical systems in late capitalism and state socialism now compete for global hegemony, forcing their dominative either/or options on Third World countries. Cultural pluralism seems faced with selling out to either a "tyranny of tolerance" (Marcuse) or totalitarianism. Genuine public discourse seems less and less effective in really establishing consensus policies. Politics seems stamped with either motivism or decisionism.[38] The wars and repressions amid such global rifts make the atrocities of past pogroms, crusades and wars of religion almost appear tame by comparison. Modern secular secret police (KGB, CIA, and all the others) have such extensive surveillance and sophisticated torture techniques that they dwarf the perversions of their predecessors who worked for the Spanish Inquisition or for other Catholic and Protestant political powers from the fifteenth century onwards.

Do the ambiguous legacies of Christianity and of modernity leave us only the options of either an enlightened cynicism or an enlightened conviction? Does the end of innocence for both religious faith and rational inquiry lead to a condition in which, to quote Yeats, "the best lack all conviction, while the worst are full of passionate intensity"?

POLITICAL DIALECTICS OF COMMUNITY AND EMPIRE

The metaphor of "betrayal" suggests two related observations. First and foremost the three betrayals suggest the seriousness of our contemporary situation. Karl Jaspers wrote: "For more than a hundred years it has been gradually realized that the history of scores of centuries is drawing to a close."[39] Something large and ominous seems to be emerging from the subterranean depths of the human drama on this planet. We might want to brush it off by means of our convenient categories of the past such as apocalyptic rhetoric, utopian protest or millenarian fervor. But such labels have a hard time sticking to something like the nuclear arms race. Who is *really* expecting an abrupt apocalyptic-utopian-millenarian change in the historical drama? Very quiet and rational arguments are being made that the real dreamers are those who, *despite* the overwhelming empirical evidence of history and statistics, maintain that in this *unique* instance weapons that are mass produced will not be used! By a paradoxical twist, the betrayals of Christianity and of modernity have led, in this momentous issue, to the implausible *coincidentia oppositorum* in which those who maintain the necessity of continuing the nuclear arms race because of the realities of dominative power in an immoral and imperfect world (shades of Niebuhr), must also express a quite fantastic faith in the rational infallibility of machines, military and political leaders (against all historical evidence) not to occasion or cause a nuclear holocaust. Such militaristic millenarianism as that evidenced in Jerry Falwell's *Listen America* finds its roots, I believe, in this paradoxical twist—not to mention Watt's musings on an environmental second coming.[40] Mon-archical "realists" are forced by the realities of power to make blind and irrational leaps into an-archical utopianism or apocalyticism.

A second observation suggests that, if we are to face creatively and courageously the seriousness of our situation, we must initiate a *politics of pluralism* which respects the conflicting religious, moral and intellectual convictions in ways that avoid the illusory opposites of an-archy and mon-archy. This is the *kairos*, in the Tillichian sense, with which the nuclear arms race confronts us. Such a politics of pluralism must be truly *radical*, must go to the roots of our endangered condition. Neither the rhetoric of co-existence nor the techiques of social engineering among competing pressure groups are adequate. Neither politics nor pluralism as they are usually understood and practiced, as Alasdair MacIntyre has so brilliantly argued, will see humankind through this dark night.[41] For politics in a pluralistic world have, until now, usually relied upon techniques of separation in order to achieve some measure of tranquil co-existence. Internationally this has meant the transition from colonies (old imperialism) to "spheres of influence" (new imperialism). Within nation-states such techniques of separation have led to the bureaucratization of managing "public opinion" and conflicting pressure groups which underlies, as Jürgen Habermas has shown, the increasing de-politicization of societies.[42] In such a context pluralism either succumbs to the dominative ethos of those groups mon-archically controlling and/or manipulating the nation-state, or retreats into so-called "sectarian" reservations of ritual and memory with, perhaps, a hope one day, in league with other groups, to become dominant itself. The Christian Right in our country is now making just such a move.[43]

A radical politics of pluralism, however, would require more genuine forms of participation in political life. I should like to outline, much too briefly, some of the constitutive elements for such a politics of pluralism.

First I shall discuss Christianity within a political dialectics of pluralism, and then Christianity within a major mode of such a dialectics, namely those of community and empire.

POLITICAL DIALECTICS OF PLURALISM AND CHRISTIANITY

The ambiguous legacies of Christianity and of modernity were presented under the metaphor of betrayal in order to indicate an analogous pattern or process in the distortions or alienations which "betrayed" the creative originations of the religious convictions of Christians and the intellectual convictions of modernity. That pattern or process is a dialectic, but the dialectic is not between an-archy and mon-archy. Indeed, we have seen that an-archy, which states that individual freedom ultimately means a relativism of all meanings and values and so equates pluralism with relativism, is only the other side of mon-archy, which enthrones one set of meanings and values as ultimate arbiter through a dominative power legitimated deterministically or voluntaristically. Historically, pluralism and truly responsible freedom always end up the loser when the dialectic is misunderstood in this fashion.[44] Instead I would argue that the real dialectic is between an-archy and mon-archy on the one side, and what I term syn-archy on the other.

An-archy claims there are no common or universal principles governing free choice. Mon-archy claims that common or universal principles must be extrinsically imposed either through a voluntaristic (or decisionistic) will to power or through elites imbued with deterministic knowledge. Syn-archy maintains that human freedom is constituted by intrinsic orientations toward principles of attentive intelligence in quest for truth and responsible love. Such principles or orientations as intrinsic to freedom can only be approximated through, or by means of, freedom.[45]

Both an-archy and mon-archy agree that pluralism and order ultimately exclude one another, while syn-archy affirms that pluralism and order ultimately include one another. For the order of syn-archy is not based upon any utopian ideal (an-archy) or millenarian ideal (mon-archy) but upon the concrete free and pluralistic efforts of countless human beings to expand their effective freedom through free and pluralistic means. Syn-archy accepts human beings where they are but does not leave them there, insofar as "where they are" represses or oppresses their own orientations toward intelligent truth and responsible freedom.[46] The transformation is not extrinsically imposed but invites change from within by appealing to self-correcting processes of learning and acting intrinsic to pluralist human freedom. An-archy excoriates universality as inimical to pluralism. Mon-archy imposes a particularistic universality and coerces all other particularities to be mediated through its dominative universality. Syn-archy affirms the manifold particularities of our pluralistic world and insists that any genuine universality will only be mediated through self-correcting processes of learning and doing immanent within those particularities.[47]

There is evidence of movements toward such syn-archical pluralism as self-corrective toward truth and freedom within the contemporary traditions of Christianity and of the Enlightenment's two phases.

In Christianity we are witnessing the beginnings of a true *ecumenical* orientation. The old *oecumene* of a Constantinian or Holy Roman Empire variety was motivated by mon-archical pretensions. The new ecumenism, while it occasions fears of an-archy in many, is really based upon syn-archical presuppositions. For this ecumenism—whether directed at other Christians, at other world religions or at secular or atheistic humanism—does not rest upon any of these diverse orientations to renounce their deeply held convictions. Rather it calls upon all human beings to respond to the dynamics of dialogue with others which arise out of those convictions. It beckons Christians to appropriate more deeply and genuinely their own traditions and the Gospel of Jesus Christ. It calls for reforms and renewals in Christianity where those traditions have either been distorted, or where the circumstances out of which the diverse and conflicting traditions have changed, or where those traditions are now in conflict with a genuine living of the Gospel, or are now in conflict with the deepest aspirations of human freedom.[48]

The ecumenical movement within Christianity calls for a unity through diversity, through the imperatives of a quest for freedom in responsibility to truth. It trusts, not in the dominative imposition of uniformity, but in the self-corrective processes of genuine dialogue. The ecumenical movements within the world religions are based upon the growing (if sometimes threatened) realization that all manifestations of the Divine within all the world religions are manifestations of compassion and solidarity with the victims of history. Ecumenism calls attention to the convictions of religious faith as convictions arising out of symbols, narratives and cognitive claims engendered by love, not by fear.[49] Indeed, I would suggest that the ecumenical movement within Christianity arose in great part out of the experiences and dialogues of so-called mixed marriages. The dialogue in and of freedom is not mere talk; it leads to reform and renewal inasmuch as it generates self-critical reflection and action within Christianity itself. This is evident in the Jewish-Christian dialogues which are leading to Christian self-criticism of Christianity's own large role in fomenting or legitimating anti-Semitism.[50] This process is also emphasizing the foundational importance of praxis in the dialogues between secular humanist scientists and Christians, and especially in dialogues between atheists and Christians. As Hans Küng observes:

The early rationalist criticism of religion in the eighteenth century, the classical criticism of religion in the nineteenth and early twentieth centuries, and more recent criticism have one thing in common: rejection of religion as a whole is connected with rejection of institutionalized religion, rejection of Christianity with rejection of Christendom, rejection of God with rejection of the Church. This was true already of La Mettrie and Holbach; it was true especially of Feuerbach, Marx and Freud. And this precisely is true also of present-day criticism of religion.[51]

The Christian churches bear a particular responsibility for the rise and spread of modern atheism. Feuerbach, Marx and Freud were not metaphysicians troubled merely by the "idea" of God; they were committed and intelligent human beings disgusted with how the authoritarian and bourgeois practices of Christian churches were both causing and legitimating oppressive and repressive projections, alienations and pathological illusions.[52]

The self-criticism within both Christianity and secular or atheistic humanism resulting from the ongoing dialogues are already beginning to bear fruit. Depth psychologies and theologies are beginning to engage in much-needed cross-fertilization and collaboration. Political and liberation theologies are integrating much-needed insights from economic and sociological critiques of alienation and ideologies, with dramatic political and publicly transformative effects in Eastern Europe (Poland) and Latin America. Eurocommunism has abandoned, for more than just tactical reasons, its atheistic pre-judgments.[53] Syn-archical orientations are also evidenced in the dialogues and debates between empirical science and religion as is clear practically in the collaborations between theologians and scientists regarding the ethical ramifications and implications of science and technologies, and is clear theoretically in the development of Christian theologies which integrate scientific categories, methods and conclusions.[54] We should not underestimate the advance in political and public awareness these dialogues have made. Fundamentalist mon-archists have had to dress up, for example, their objections to evolution in pseudo-scientific garb both in Russia (Lysenko) and now in the United States (creation-science.)[55]

The successors of the first phase of the Enlightenment, the advocates and practitioners of empirical reason, have also in the course of ongoing dialogues and discoveries undergone extensive self-corrective transformations. The mon-archical illusions of a monolithic empirical science with their reductionist projects of deducing all verifiable knowledge from one set of physical laws, like the other project of reducing all languages to a unified scientific language, have been progressively criticized and abandoned.[56] The pluralisms of methods and of matrices in which the empirical sciences are done have not resulted, despite the brilliant efforts of a Feyerabend, in anarchy.[57] Rather the philosophical reflections on empirical science in, for example, Kuhn, Lakatos, Radnitzky or Toulmin indicate an attention to the historical and social matrices of the sciences, and how the ongoing developments of methods are self-corrective even to the point of radical paradigmatic shifts.[58] Lakatos has shown, for instance, how neither an-archy nor mon-archy—what he calls the "tolerant skeptical enlightenment" and the "intolerant dogmatist enlightenment"—was able to do justice to Newtonian mechanics, let alone the Einsteinian or quantum mechanics paradigm-shifts of our century.[59] The ongoing natural sciences are discovering a universe of emergent probability which syn-archically collaborates in a series of complex interdependencies within the irreducible unity-in-diversity of nature.[60] Similarly, the empirical social sciences have begun to discover that bureaucratic rationality is somewhat illusory. What was thought to be a model of efficiency is increasingly seen as very inefficient. In fact, when bureaucracies work, it is not so much thanks to their mon-archical flow charts of authority and decision making, but thanks to informal and communal interpersonal relations among the so-called bureaucrats.[61] Philosophically the crumbling faith in instrumental rationality is leading to self-corrective reappropriations of the critical potential of pragmatism in Pierce, James and Dewey, indicating how they did not espouse the utilitarianism of much vulgar pragmatism.[62] Politically and publicly, empirical scientists are increasingly taking responsibility for value issues and forming unions of concern to promote dialogue and public debate on issues of vital importance regarding the impacts of sciences and technologies on nature and history.[63] Bio-medical science and research are explicitly calling for dialogues and collaboration with bio-ethics, and a syn-archic "holism" in medicine is slowly gaining ground, often despite the opposition of pharmaceutical multinationals.[64]

The successors of the second phase of the Enlightenment, the advocates and practitioners of dialectical reason, have also in the course of ongoing dialogues and debates undergone extensive self-corrective transformations. The ambiguities within the works of the originators of hermeneutics, depth psychology and the critique of ideologies—especially any tendencies to reduce their methods to those of the natural sciences—have been analyzed and many alternative corrections and radical paradigm-shifts suggested and argued. Depth psychologies have complemented and corrected Freudian therapies with a series of new approaches associated with Adler, Rank, Jung or Frankl. The therapeutic appropriation of the unconscious has uncovered not only what was expected by the architects of depth psychology, but also the ongoing praxis of therapy has itself uncovered many constitutive processes and occasioned major paradigm-shifts, as not only the archaeology but also the teleology of psyche became known (Ricoeur).[65] Indeed, dialectical reflection on, and appropriation of, values has led to a meta-level convergence of hermeneutics, depth psychology and the critique of ideologies. An illustration of this would be how hermeneutics has moved from the object-oriented, empirical and structural concerns of Dilthey and Betti, through the subject-oriented, normative and existential concerns of Heidegger, Bultmann and Gadamer, to the efforts of both the critical hermeneutics of Apel and Habermas, as well as the phenomenological hermeneutics of Ricoeur, to mediate object and subject, empirical and normative, structural and existential, elements through communication or language theories, through quasi-transcendental interests or phenomenology of texts and symbols, through praxis or poesis.[66]

The differences are important and deep, the convictions are divergent among these works, but the result is not an-archy. Similarly, the convergence is impressive but it hardly resembles an orientation to mon-archy. Instead these thinkers, as well as many others (such as Arendt, Becker, Horkheimer, MacIntyre, Peukert, Tracy, Berstein), warn against the pervasive lack of public discourse resulting from the mon-archical reductions of all issues and forms of living to techniques. Genuine pluralism and political publicness demand explicit reflection upon the dialectical praxis of communication and dialogue itself. The reduction of praxis to mere "practice"-as-technique has had the disastrous consequences mentioned above when discussing the betrayals of empirical and dialectical reason through instrumental or technical rationality.[67]

Recovering and transforming the classic distinction between praxis and technique, these authors in various and diverse ways indicate how technique, as the production or making of products or external objects, has become mon-archical in industrialized societies. The resulting privitization of individuals, and mechanization of discourse and policy formation, have seriously curtailed public consensus, reduced conflict to crisis management techniques, and politics to various techniques of social engineering. Praxis is human doing, performance or conduct in which the goals are *intrinsic to the performance itself* as free, ongoing self-corrective processes of learning. In other words, praxis is syn-archical, originating in and leading to intelligent discourse and responsible freedom.

As MacIntyre has demonstrated, only in this context of praxis—and not in the utilitarianism of techniques of rewards and punishments—does virtue as the expansion of freedom make any sense.[68] Gouldner and others have shown how this distinction provides for a Marxist analysis and critique of the ongoing developments within Marxism itself. Scientistic Marxism trusts in techniques of infrastructural manipulation, while Critical Marxism seeks to re-establish praxis as the infrastructural dynamics of self-correcting relations of production interacting mutually with suprastructural developments.[69] Marx's own rather an-archical hope in dissolving government, combined with his ambiguities on praxis and technique, left the door open to scientistic and bureaucratic mon-archical political and economic regimentation.

The crisis in both state socialism and late capitalisms, especially the economic crises, are demanding new and critical macroeconomic theories and praxes which would relate production processes and monetary circulation to the self-corrective heuristics of human praxis as an expansion of freedom in syn-archy. Late capitalism is a mon-archical materialization of idealism, and state socialism is a mon-archical idealization of materialism. Neither attends to the foundations of economic activity in human performance or conduct as immanently generated activity. Instead they seek to control or manipulate that activity through techniques of regimentation or advertising. Neither, therefore, is cognizant of how sooner rather than later immoral or unethical economic practices destroy economies. Neither understand how macroeconomic processes which intensify poverty and oppression are both evil and stupid even in economic terms.[70] Attention to the dynamics of genuinely public dialogue and debate on the part of the advocates of dialectical reason focuses reflection on the long-term significance of those movements of communal dialogue and action which are challenging the hegemony of late capitalist and state socialist "spheres of influence": movements such as Solidarity in Poland and the grass-roots religious communities in Africa, Latin America and Asia, or the grass-roots community organizing in Europe and North America, as well as in Russia and China.[71]

CHRISTIANITY, COMMUNITY AND EMPIRE

There is emerging a radical political dialectics of pluralism which transcends the illusory opposites of an-archy and mon-archy. Such political dialectics, with their self-corrective processes of inquiry and action, do *not* guarantee perfection. They do not offer new and better techniques with which to organize and control societies. They simply call attention to the value judgment that all institutions generated by humans are for the sake of humans and not the other way around. Hence, they regard as foundational what I have described as syn-archy, in order theoretically and practically to conduct themselves toward the expansion of effective human freedom. Syn-archy seems frail and of little account over against the dominative superpowers of yesterday and today. While the latter go about trying, in Gandhi's terms, to make and sustain systems that are so good that humans don't have to be good, syn-archy claims that all their efforts are doomed to eventual failure, since they ignore the human and pluralists *infrastructure* of any and all social organizations. They construct gigantic, dominative bureaucracies and war machines and transnational economics, but syn-archy points out that the massive idols have clay feet.

The political dialectics between an-archy and mon-archy, on the one hand, and syn-archy on the other are rapidly reaching crisis proportions. As Jaspers pointed out, scores of centuries are drawing to a close. The nuclear arms race is the apotheosis of the alienating and alienated tendencies of humans to ignore their own value and project all value outwards into the mon-archical systems they produce, which they then serve as values higher and greater than themselves. Nuclear weapons at the disposal of superpowers, and those who aspire to superpower status, enable them to intimidate both their own citizens and others with fears of an-archical annihilation. "Either submit to our mon-archical system or be blasted back into an-archy and possible extinction" is the option offered by competing superpowers. Security through dominative power has always been an illusion. Now the nuclear arms race has exposed this illusion. We have to return to basics. Superpower rhetoric and diplomacy will not get us out of this one! The centuries of empires and superpowers with their dominative power and wars to end all wars, with their pell-mell successions of a few victors and millions of victims, are drawing to a close. The illusory option between mon-archy and an-archy is rapidly becoming a dead end.

Syn-archy offers a way out of this with its radical political dialectics of pluralism. For those dialectics call attention to the infrastructural dialectics of communities. Community, like freedom, originates and ends in human praxis. When community promotes human questing for truth and responsible love, community, like freedom, flourishes. When community gives way to individual or group egoism with their desires and fears, community, like freedom, constricts, atrophies and may die. Community, like freedom and praxis, is as radically pluralist as all the spheres of human doing or performance. It is truly the infrastructure of all economic, social, political, cultural and religious living. But this universality of community immanently transcends (that is, mediates the universal through the particular). Community is destroyed or betrayed when it compromises with mon-archy in order to impose its particular meaning and values uniformly upon others. When this occurs, it either instigates or legitimates empire building. *No empire or superpower in history was ever the result of free choice on the part of all communities over which it extended its dominative power.* The universality of community is mediated through the pluralist particularities of human communities in dialogue and debate respective of the self-corrective processes of human learning and action.[72] When those processes are not respected, when the "easy" way out, mon-archy, is implemented, community, like freedom, is imperiled.

The tragedy of wars and violent conflicts is that their slaughter and maiming of human beings is the expression of the disintegration and destruction of communities and freedom within the warring groups. Wars of liberation, of insurrection against dominative mon-archical powers, are ethically justified only to the extent that they are a last resort, and only through them could genuine dialogue and debate once again become actual. Militarization, like technique, focuses upon either gaining or defending external control. Like technique, the danger is that militarization would become an end in itself and succumb to mon-archy. Such an ethical justification of wars of liberation does not apply to nuclear warfare among the superpowers. Indeed, it would not apply to many—if not most—of the wars in history insofar as these were military conflicts between mon-archical empires or superpowers, or those aspiring to empire building.[73] So-called "defense" can, I believe, only be ethically justified in terms of protecting genuine communities and freedom. It loses that justification when the very techniques of defense destroy genuine community and free dialogue and action. An added tragedy of modern militarism is that the basic needs of all human communities on this planet can be fulfilled if those communities were allowed to do so.[74] But the global rift caused by the superpowers, with the consequent displacement of capital, centralization of planning and militarism, are not allowing the local communities to provide adequately for their basic needs. Moreover, the very forces of production themselves, with advances in contemporary technologies, are beginning to provide the technical means for vast decentralization, debureaucratization and for extensive communitarian dialogue, debate and policy formation. But those forces of production are being hampered by mon-archical relations of production bent upon control and domination.[75]

A syn-archical understanding of community acknowledges it as the permanent infrastructure of any and all social organizations in the micro-domain (family, marriage, neighborhood), the meso-domain (cities, regions, nations) or the macro-domain (humankind). But this infrastructure does not function automatically. It is constituted by and in and for human freedom. Hence community can become restrictive or constrictive, it can decay and become the prey of desires and fears which alienate the self-corrective processes of learning and action. Community, when it flourishes, empowers its members toward the intelligent quest for truth, the responsibly free quest for good, the unrestrained play of symbol, ritual and art as beautiful. But these orientations are all too easily diminished or extinguished by the tendencies to an-archy and mon-archy.[76] Yet the infrastructure seems powerfully resilient. The quest for community and freedom keeps returning with every new birth; the dynamics of instinct and psyche try time and again to enter into collaboration with consciousness in order to realize freedom and community. The challenge of our time is to overcome the mon-archical alienations which try to press whatever is left of community into the service of its alienating ambitions.

A mon-archically biased psychology, sociology or political theory would claim that community as *Gemeinschaft* can only be instinctual whereas society as *Gesellschaft* is voluntary and contractual.[77] This is mon-archical because it fails to take into account the teleology of human instinct toward responsibility and freedom. Freedom is then mistaken for extrinsically oriented "contracts" which can be bureaucratically controlled and manipulated. Monadic individualism and mass collectivities go hand in hand under the aegis of technique.[78]

Nuclear arms have now exposed the dead end of such separations of community and society. As Jonathan Schell indicated recently: "By threatening life in its totality, the nuclear peril creates new connections between the elements of human existence—a new mingling of the public and the private, the political and the emotional, the spiritual and the biological."

He then recalls Hannah Arendt's notion of a "common world of word and deed" into which we are born, as it were, for a second time, and by which we are challenged to take responsibility for our physical birth. He then continues:

Now the whole species is called on literally to take on itself the naked fact of its original physical appearance—to protect our being through an act of will. Formerly, the future was simply given to us; now it must be achieved. . . .

This effort would constitute a counterpart in our conscious life of reason and will of our instinctual urge to procreate. And in so doing it would round out and complete the half-finished common world of pre-nuclear times, which, by the time nuclear weapons were invented, had enabled mankind to learn and to suffer but not to act as one.[79]

What Schell overlooks is that this effort to promote intelligent and responsibly free collaboration between public and private, between the spiritual and the biological, has been more and less successfully going on in the syn-archical praxis of trying to create and sustain communities. Admittedly, it has by and large been unsuccessful—else we would not now be in the predicament we are. But community, however fragile, is the only hope we have. Otherwise, "to act as one" would be to submit to what might be called a "Meta-Superpower" which would dominate and control the entire globe. It would be a mon-archical actualization of a Hegelian *Weltgeist* and, as Schell indicated himself, could not really guarantee the survival of the species, since it would feed on the very fears which generated nuclear arms in the first place.[80]

The authority of community is not dominative authority. The authority of community does not rest on external rewards or punishments to assert itself. Authority of community rests instead upon the power of free and conscious cooperation and consensus, which is the only genuinely human form of power (power as empowering free and responsible subjects). Communal authority, then, is a praxis which originates and issues in the expansion of genuine human freedom. To the extent that authority denigrates cooperation and consensus, to that extent its power becomes increasingly dominative and dehumanizing, as it seeks to maintain and extend itself through external enticements of fear of punishment. Cooperation and consensus are not only possible among contemporaries, they also extend down the ages, and so the authority of community can continue and transform, through its own contemporary dialogues and debates, the traditions of its own or another's past.[81]

Such a syn-archical understanding of authority uncovers, I believe, a dialectic of authority and power in opposition to the usual distinctions between "rational bureaucratic" authority and "personal charismatic" authority. As Weber developed these "pure types" of authority, he tended to base the distinctions between them on the differences between *Zweckrationalität* and *Wertrationalität*.[82] Thus the charismatic leader or prophet tends to *demand* acceptance of the values he (the examples given are all male) espouses or represents by the "miracles" or wonders with which he seems endowed. Little room is left for dialogue and consensus, for when this begins, Weber maintains, the rational or bureaucratic "routinization" of the charisma has begun. Rational and bureaucratic authority tends to the *Zweckrationalität* where actions are primarily concerned with various external goals or ends, and the authority and value of the latter are by and large not questioned. Thus Weber, and many after him, reduce authority to either instrumentally rational or bureaucratic techniques, on the one hand, or to highly subjective and "privatized" value-charisma on the other. Indeed, it can happen, according to Weber, that the routinization of charisma leads to anti-authoritarianism. The mon-archical presuppositions are obvious. Institutions of whatever kind roll on with their rational and bureaucratic authority and power, served by officials and members. Every once in a while a charismatic personality will come along and excite us, but if he starts a movement it too will eventually become an "iron cage."[83]

The trouble is that some of the iron cages have developed nuclear weapons and, if business as usual prevails, the probabilities of annihilation or anarchy are getting higher. As I mentioned before, the authorities who want business to go on as usual are forced by these circumstances to "rationalize" the arms race with what could only be described as a "miracle" from the viewpoint of history and statistics, namely, that such mass-produced weapons in this unique instance will not be used. As Einstein observed, since the discovery of nuclear power, everything has changed but our thinking. The only way out of these iron cages is through a growing conscious and reflective appropriation of the infrastructural communities, and a concerted concern to promote those heuristics of community which nurture the quests for truth, responsible freedom and beauty. Only then will we "recover" the authority of community as genuine cooperation and consensus. Only then shall we realize how illusory mon-archical dominative power is, and how real is the human empowerment of cooperation which fosters and expands effective freedom.[84] Each generation must enter this process if we are to avoid the temptation against which Gandhi warned.

Community is our only hope. Authority and power are within self-correcting processes of learning and doing. A student once remarked: "You mean all we humans have is ourselves!" Yes and no. Yes in the sense that all the mon-archical systems in which we project our trust are just so many expressions of our own human activity. They are our creations, and for us to allow them to turn around and control, manipulate and destroy *us* is the height of foolishness and stupidity. Indeed, it would take too long to show how all creative breakthroughs in human history have always come from persons within human communities.[85] But that is the case. Unfortunately, in the past the *expressions* of those creative breakthroughs have often been expropriated by mon-archical systems in order extrinsically to legitimate their power. Read Einstein's reflections on what happened to his theories.[86] Community is not just a tragic ideal, or a regulative ideal, it is the infra-structural reality which for too long has allowed its power and its authority to be pressed into servitude and alienation by competing mon-archical systems.[87]

No, we humans are not alone. If our present grave historical crisis of possible nuclear annihilation is without precedent, if it calls us to engage as never before in a radical politics of pluralism and syn-archy for the sake of our very survival as a species, the dialectic itself is almost as old as humankind itself. The world religions, with their calls to conversion (in freedom and truth) away from the idols of our own making and toward the living Divine Mystery, have echoed the dialectic in many ways. If before religious convictions were expropriated for mon-archical dominative power, the ecumenical movement is indicating how to recover the communitarian and pluralist authority and empowerment of religious convictions arising from a faith as knowledge born of love. If we humans can cooperate and seek consensus on issues of eternal life and death, then why in God's name and our own must we destroy ourselves over such trifles as capitalism and communism?[88]

Christianity began in Jesus' preaching of the coming reign of God. The *basileia tou Theou*, the reign, the kingdom, or empire of God reversed our all-too-human tendencies to identify God's empire with the dominative mon-archical systems or idols which have captured so much of the historical drama on this planet. The empire of God as proclaimed by Christ is a free gift and call to enter into communities of expectation, faith and love with the poor, the hungry, the sorrowful, the untold victims of sinful histories of domination and oppression.[89] The empire of God would "cast down the mighty from their thrones and exalt the lowly" (Luke 1:52). The parables of God's empire are parables of apocalyptic or revelatory empowerment, whereby the Divine Mystery beckons us to communities of faith, hope and love. As such, the parables were, as Perrin remarks, "bearers of the reality with which they were concerned."[90]

Through his own life-(praxis), death and resurrection, transformative re-ligious discipleship in community was constituted and the Parabler became the Parable. These communities of expectation, of incarnate hope in God's reign as Love, stand over against the mon-archical empires of world history. Toward the beginning of this essay I traced some of the many betrayals and recoveries of this political dialectic between community and empire. Chris-tian churches are complex combinations of both communities expecting the Kingdom and cultural or ritual "borrowings" from imperial and/or other mon-archical symbols and organizations. Betrayals occur whenever the for-mer are pressed into the service of, or identified with, the latter. This resulted in forms of theocratic Christendom. Whenever this occurs, however, there arise movements of renewal or reform in which the redemptive reversal proclaimed by Christ's *Basileia tou Theou* finds new expression in Christian praxis.[91]

This dialectic is misunderstood, I believe, when it is cast in the categories of church versus sect. Like Weber's supposedly "pure types" of authority, the distinction of church and sect tends to allow church authorities to repress within the churches the challenges for reform through redemptive reversals. In most cases it takes two to make a sect. Too often "sects" resulted from the rejection of their calls for reform on the part of church authorities.[92] For example, medieval sects were largely reactions to the mon-archical efforts of the so-called "Gregorian Reform" which tried to impose uniformity from the top down.[93] Such "top-down" strategies always seem to employ techniques of separation, as was evident in the Roman authorities' reactions to the Protestant reformers.[94]

The time has now passed for such strategies and techniques to be meaningful. The tensive dialectics of transformative dialogue and debate—such as those going on in the ecumenical movement—must challenge the churches to witness more vitally to the realities of redemptive community. Already this process is underway among the poorer churches of the Third World, in genuine efforts at reform and renewal "from below" in thousands of liberating grass-roots communities. The times demand, as Metz indicates, a Second Reformation from below, wherein the churches would reform those mon-archical residues of paternalistic conservatism and bourgeois liberalism, in order to practice church as empowering and freeing basic communities of expectation, faith and love. Within my own church, the Roman Catholic, which has perhaps suffered most from mon-archical betrayals, such a renewal (even there!) is underway.[95] We have nothing to lose in this process but our illusions and alienations.

Yet, as history teaches, humans, including Christians, seem to cling to their illusions and alienations more doggedly than they do to one another and their freedom. The *kairos* of our time is that our illusions and alienations have backed us into a nuclear corner. Either we shall begin to accept ourselves and one another, in cooperation and dialogue, or our illusions and alienations will blast our species into a darkness where no nation, no society, no culture, no religion will grace this earth again.[96] It is time Christians and other religious communities begin in earnest to cooperate and trust the freedom with which the Divine Mystery has graced them. It is time we begin really to live together (syn) in the pluralistic dynamics of freedom (archy). The life of faith will flourish in such a genuinely pluralistic world. For then we shall be knowingly and willingly appropriating in our own lives the mystery of creation out of which we were all born. For Christians such a redemption of creation is incarnated in the life, death and resurrection of Christ Jesus.

NOTES

1. On the dialectic of master and slave, cf. G.W.F. Hegel, *The Phenomenology of Mind*, trans. J. B. Baille (New York: Harper & Row, 1967), pp. 228–40. There is a relationship between this dialectic and the universal victimhood implicit in the nuclear arms race, cf. E. P. Thompson and D. Smith, eds., *Protest and Survive* (New York: Monthly Review Press, 1981); also Jonathan Schell, *The Fate of the Earth* (New York: Alfred A. Knopf, 1982). One of the few condemnations leveled by the Second Vatican Council was directed at any and all manifestations of total war, cf. *Gaudium et Spes*, par. 80.

2. Cf. Wilfred C. Smith, *Towards a World Theology* (Philadelphia: Westminster Press, 1981), pp. 3–44; Langdon Gilkey, *Society and the Sacred* (New York: Crossroad, 1981), pp. 15–25; Raimundo Panikkar, "The Contemplative Mood: A Challenge to Modernity," *Cross Currents* 31, no. 3 (Fall 1981): 26–72.

3. Cf. M. Eliade and J. M. Kitagawa, eds., *The History of Religions* (Chicago: University of Chicago Press, 1970); also F. Heiler, ed., *Die Religionen der Menschheit* (Stuttgard: Philipp Reclam, 1962), pp. 13–53.

4. Cf. David Tracy, *The Analogical Imagination: Christian Theology and the Culture of Pluralism* (New York: Crossroad, 1981), pp. 154–229. On personalization and humanization, cf. Matthew Lamb, "Christian Spirituality and Social Justice," (Toronto: St. Michael's College, 1982 Kelly Lecture), forthcoming.

5. Cf. Bernard Lonergan, *Method in Theology* (New York: Herder & Herder, 1972), pp. 235–49; Alasdair MacIntyre, *After Virtue: A Study in Moral Theory* (Notre Dame, Ind.: University of Notre Dame Press, 1981), pp. 1–59.

6. MacIntyre, *After Virtue*, pp. 103–13, 238 ff.; also Lonergan, *Method in Theology*, pp. 247–66.

7. Cf. Wolfgang J. Mommsen, *Theories of Imperialism*, trans. P. S. Falla (New York: Random House, 1980); William A. Williams, *Empire as a Way of Life* (New York: Oxford University Press, 1980); Harry Magdoff, *Imperialism: From the Colonial Age to the Present* (New York: Monthly Review Press, 1978); Irving L. Horowitz, *Beyond Empire and Revolution: Militarization and Consolidation in the Third World* (New York: Oxford University Press, 1981); A. Brewer, *Marxist Theories of Imperialism* (London: Routledge & Kegan Paul, 1980).

8. Thus dominative power is extrinsic force. On effective freedom, cf. B. Lonergan, *Insight: A Study in Human Understanding* (New York: Harper & Row, 1978), pp. 619–33.

9. This is the function of dialectics according to Lonergan, cf. his *Method in Theology*, pp. 128–30, 235–66. It also corresponds to Johann B. Metz's notion of subversive memory, cf. his *Faith in History and Society* (New York: Seabury-Crossroad, 1980), pp. 184–204.

10. Cf. Lee Cormie, "The Hermeneutical Privilege of the Oppressed," *Catholic Theological Society of America Proceedings* 33 (1978): 155–81 and references given there.

11. Cf. Ben F. Meyer, *The Aims of Jesus* (London: SCM Press, 1979); Matthew L. Lamb, *Solidarity with Victims* (New York: Crossroad, 1982), pp. 7–12 and references given there.

12. Cf. Hubert Jedin, ed., *Handbuch der Kirchengeschichte*, 3rd ed. (Freiburg:

Herder, 1973), 1: 147–62, 187–92, 249–60, 433–41. Also cf. the biased account in Edward Gibbon, *The Decline and Fall of the Roman Empire* (New York: Modern Library, 1937), 1: 382–504.

13. Cf. E. Peterson, "Monotheismus als politisches Problem" and "Christus als Imperator," in his *Theologische Traktate* (Munich: Kösel, 1951), pp. 45–147, 150–64. Also, Alfred Schindler, ed., *Monotheismus als politisches Problem? E. Peterson und die Kritik der politischen Theologie* (Gütersloher: Gerd Mohn, 1978).

14. Timothy D. Barnes, *Constantine and Eusebius* (Cambridge, Mass.: Harvard University Press, 1981), pp. 224–44.

15. Ibid., pp. 245–75. Also Jedin, *Handbuch*, II/1: 3–93.

16. Cf. Jedin, *Handbuch*, II/2: 265–82, III: 16 ff.; Peter Brown, *Society and the Holy in Late Antiquity* (Berkeley: University of California Press, 1982), pp. 103–95.

17. Cf. MacIntyre, *After Virtue*, pp. 154–68; M. Clagett et al., eds., *Twelfth-Century Europe and the Foundations of Modern Society* (Madison: University of Wisconsin Press, 1966); Eric Christiansen, *The Northern Crusades: The Baltic and the Catholic Frontier 1100–1525* (Minneapolis: University of Minnesota Press, 1980); J. Gilchrist, *The Church and Economic Activity in the Middle Ages* (London: Macmillan, 1969); Gordon Leff, *The Dissolution of the Medieval Outlook* (New York: Harper & Row, 1976).

18. Cf. Edward P. Cheyney, *The Dawn of a New Era*, 2d ed. (New York: Harper & Row, 1962), pp. 142–246; Lewis Mumford, *The Condition of Man* (New York: Harcourt Brace Jovanovich, 1973), pp. 152–200; F. L. Nussbaum, *The Triumph of Science and Reason* (New York: Harper & Row, 1953), pp. 61–197.

19. Cf. Peter Gay, *The Rise of Modern Paganism* (New York: Random House, 1967); Claude Manceron, *Twilight of the Old Order*, trans. P. Wolf (New York: Alfred A. Knopf, 1977).

20. Cf. Herbert Butterfield, *The Origins of Modern Science* (London: G. Bell and Sons, Ltd., 1965); Hiram Caton, *The Origin of Subjectivity* (New Haven, Conn.: Yale University Press, 1973).

21. William L. Langer, *Political and Social Upheaval, 1832–1852* (New York: Harper & Row, 1969), pp. 1–53, 181–237; Arno J. Mayer, *The Persistence of the Old Regime* (New York: Pantheon Books, 1981).

22. Cf. Jacques Ellul, *The Technological System* (New York: Continuum, 1980); Max Weber, *Economy and Society*, ed. Guenther Roth and Claus Wittich (Berkeley and Los Angeles: University of California Press, 1978), pp. 48–55, 212–98. On bureaucracy cf. vol. 2, pp. 956–1002. Cf. also Anthony Gliddens, *Capitalism and Modern Social Theory: An Analysis of the Writings of Marx, Durkheim and Max Weber* (Cambridge: Cambridge University Press, 1977), pp. 133–84.

23. Cf. Fritjof Capra, *The Turning Point: Science, Society and the Rising Culture* (New York: Simon and Schuster, 1982); Carolyn Merchant, *The Death of Nature* (San Francisco: Harper & Row, 1980); Andre Gorz, *Ecology as Politics* (Boston: South End Press, 1980).

24. Giddens, *Capitalism and Modern Social Theory*, pp. 178–82.

25. Max Horkheimer, *Critique of Instrumental Reason* (New York: Seabury Press, 1974); idem, *Eclipse of Reason* (New York: Seabury Press, 1974); Matthew Lamb, *Solidarity with Victims*, pp. 28–60.

26. Capra, *The Turning Point*, pp. 53–74, 101–63.

27. Jonathan Schell, *The Fate of the Earth* (New York: Alfred A. Knopf, 1982).

28. MacIntyre, *After Virtue*, pp. 60–102.

29. Matthew L. Lamb, *History, Method and Theology* (Missoula, Mont.: Scholar's Press, 1978), pp. 55–210; Michael Schneider, *Neurosis and Civilization: A Marxist/ Freudian Synthesis* (New York: Seabury Press, 1975); Martin Jay, *The Dialectical Imagination* (Boston: Little, Brown and Co., 1973).

30. Max Horkheimer, *Critical Theory* (New York: Herder and Herder, 1972), pp. 3–46, 188–252.

31. Rudolf A. Makkreel, *Dilthey: Philosopher of the Human Studies* (Princeton, N.J.: Princeton University Press, 1975), pp. 305–39, 413–21; Leszek Kolakowski, *Main Currents of Marxism*, trans. P. S. Falla (Oxford: Clarendon Press, 1978), pp. 335– 420; Judith Van Herik, *Freud: On Femininity and Faith* (Berkeley: University of California Press, 1982), pp. 9–106.

32. Thomas McCarthy, *The Critical Theory of Jürgen Habermas* (Cambridge, Mass.: MIT Press, 1979), pp. 40–52, 60–98.

33. Hans-Georg Gadamer, *Truth and Method* (New York: Seabury Press, 1975), pp. 192–234; Hannah Arendt, *Between Past and Future* (New York: Viking Press, 1961), pp. 41–90, 197–264; Fritz Stern, ed., *The Varieties of History* (Cleveland, Ohio: World Publishing Co., 1956), pp. 46–144.

34. Robert Boyers and Robert Orrill, eds., *R. D. Laing and Anti-Psychiatry* (New York: Harper & Row, 1971); Thomas Szasz, *The Myth of Psychotherapy* (Garden City, N.Y.: Anchor Books, 1979); David Ingleby, ed., *Critical Psychiatry: The Politics of Mental Health* (New York: Pantheon Books, 1980); Bruno Bettelheim, "Freud and the Soul," *The New Yorker*, March 1, 1982, pp. 52–93.

35. Herbert Marcuse, *Soviet Marxism: A Critical Analysis* (New York: Random House, 1981), p. xiv; M. Albert and R. Hahnel, *Marxism and Socialist Theory* (Boston: South End Press, 1981); Donald C. Hodges, *The Bureaucratization of Socialism* (Amherst: University of Massachusetts Press, 1981).

36. Raghavan N. Iyer, *The Moral and Political Thought of Mahatma Gandhi* (Oxford: Oxford University Press, 1973), pp. 113–292.

37. Samuel Bowles and Herbert Gintis, *Schooling in Capitalist America* (New York: Basic Books, 1976), pp. 18–51, 53–149.

38. MacIntyre, *After Virtue*, pp. 6–34; McCarthy, *The Critical Theory of Jürgen Habermas*, pp. 213–31, 358–85; David Smith, *Who Rules the Universities?* (New York: Monthly Review Press, 1974); Richard Bernstein, *The Restructuring of Social and Political Theory* (New York: Harcourt Brace Jovanovich, 1976).

39. K. Jaspers, *Philosophy and the World: Selected Essays and Lectures* (Chicago: Henry Regnery Co., 1963), p. 22.

40. Daniel C. Maguire, *The New Subversives: Anti-Americanism of the Religious Right* (New York: Continuum, 1982), pp. 1–56.

41. MacIntyre, *After Virtue*, pp. 103–13, 238–45.

42. Jürgen Habermas, *Communication and the Evolution of Society*, trans. Thomas McCarthy (Boston: Beacon Press, 1976), pp. 178–205.

43. Maguire, *The New Subversives*, pp. 87–140.

44. I believe that Alasdair MacIntyre's argument in *After Virtue* supports this observation. Both an-archy and mon-archy rest ultimately upon technique as controlling meaning and value, whereas syn-archy rests ultimately upon praxis and hence is constituted by the will to dialogue and to communicative competence in reaching

truly public policy. In this regard syn-archy as I develop it here is closely related to the works of the Frankfurt School.

45. The understanding of freedom I am referring to here is dependent upon the work of Bernard Lonergan. Cf. his *Insight*, pp. 595–633. For a complementary understanding of freedom as expanded effectively through virtuous practice, cf. MacIntyre, *After Virtue*, pp. 169–209.

46. Cf. Lamb, *Solidarity with Victims*, pp. 7–23, 28–55 and the references given there.

47. This aspect of syn-archy is equivalent to Lonergan's understanding of the self-correcting process of learning. Cf. his *Insight*, pp. 174–75, 286–303, 713–18.

48. For a contrast between contemporary ecumenism and the mon-archical pretensions of the classical *oecumene*, cf. Eric Voegelin, *The Ecumenic Age* (Baton Rouge: Louisiana State University Press, 1974), pp. 115–33, 300–307, and how this contrasts with the position of Karl Rahner, cf. his *Concern for the Church* (New York: Crossroad, 1981), pp. 77–186.

49. Cf. Lonergan, *Method in Theology*, pp. 101–24.

50. Rosemary Reuther, *Faith and Fratricide* (New York: Seabury Press, 1974).

51. Hans Küng, *Does God Exist?* (New York: Doubleday, 1980), pp. 324 ff.

52. Ibid., pp. 189–339.

53. Wolfgang Leonhard, *Eurocommunism: Challenge for East and West*, trans. Mark Vecchio (New York: Holt, Rinehart and Winston, 1978); G. R. Urban, ed., *Euro-Communism: Its Roots and Future in Italy and Elsewhere* (New York: Universe Books, 1978).

54. Cf. Gilkey, *Society and the Sacred*, pp. 75–119. Process theology is a prominent exemplification of this concern to relate theology and modern science, as well as the methodological orientation of these theologies influenced by Bernard Lonergan.

55. Cf. Maguire, *The New Subversives*, pp. 57–86 and references given there to the work as yet unpublished of Dr. Dean Fowler.

56. Gerard Radnitzky, *Contemporary Schools of Metascience* (Göteborg: Akademiförlaget, 1968), pp. 18–187.

57. Cf. Paul Feyerabend, *Against Method* (London: Verso, 1975).

58. Gary Gutting, ed., *Paradigms and Revolutions* (Notre Dame, Ind.: University of Notre Dame Press, 1980), pp. 27–74.

59. Imre Lakatos and Alan Musgrave, eds., *Criticism and the Growth of Knowledge* (London: Cambridge University Press, 1970), pp. 39–48, 91–196; Imre Lakatos, *The Methodology of Scientific Research Programmes*, ed. John Worrall and Gregory Currie (London: Cambridge University Press, 1978), pp. 193–222.

60. Cf. Lonergan, *Insight*, pp. 103–39.

61. Donald P. Warwick, *A Theory of Public Bureaucracy* (Cambridge, Mass.: Harvard University Press, 1975), esp. pp. 3–36, 183–218 and the references given there.

62. Richard J. Bernstein, *Praxis and Action* (Philadelphia: University of Pennsylvania Press, 1971), pp. 165–229; Karl-Otto Apel, *Charles S. Peirce: From Pragmatism to Pragmaticism*, trans. John Michael Krois (Amherst: University of Massachusetts Press, 1981).

63. Cf. Robert Goodman, *After the Planners* (New York: Simon and Schuster, 1972); Ruth Adams and Susan Cullen, *The Final Epidemic: Physicians and Scientists on Nuclear War* (Chicago: Educational Foundation for Nuclear Science, 1981); David

F. Nobel, *America by Design: Science, Technology and the Rise of Corporate Capitalism* (New York: Alfred A. Knopf, 1977).

64. E. Richard Brown, *Rockefeller Medicine Men: Medicine and Capitalism in America* (Berkeley: University of California Press, 1979); Arthur Koestler and J. R. Smythies, *Beyond Reductionism: New Perspectives in the Life Sciences* (Boston: Beacon Press, 1969); Karl R. Popper and John C. Eccles, *The Self and Its Brain* (New York: Springer International, 1981).

65. Paul Ricoeur, *Freud and Philosophy*, trans. Denis Savage (New Haven, Conn.: Yale University Press, 1970), pp. 419–551; Robert M. Doran, *Subject and Psyche: Ricoeur, Jung, and the Search for Foundations* (Washington, D.C.: University Press of America, 1977); Ernest Becker, *The Denial of Death* (New York: Free Press, 1973).

66. Josef Bleicher, *Contemporary Hermeneutics* (London: Routledge & Kegan Paul, 1980).

67. Paul Ricoeur, *Hermeneutics and the Human Sciences*, ed. and trans. John B. Thompson (London: Cambridge University Press, 1981), pp. 43–130, 222–73; Tracy, *The Analogical Imagination*, pp. 339–404; Helmut Peukert, *Wissenschaftstheorie-Handlungstheorie- Fundamentale Theologie* (Frankfurt: Suhrkamp, 1978), pp. 47–54; 252–310; Hannah Arendt, *The Human Condition* (Chicago: University of Chicago Press, 1958), pp. 175–325. For the references relative to Becker, Horkheimer, MacIntyre and Bernstein, refer to the above notes.

68. MacIntyre, *After Virtue*, pp. 169–89.

69. Alvin W. Gouldner, *The Two Marxisms* (New York: Seabury Press, 1980).

70. Cf. Michael Albert and Robin Hahnel, *Socialism Today and Tomorrow* (Boston: South End Press, 1981); M. Lamb, *Solidarity with Victims*, pp. 2–5 and references given there, 132–33 and references given there. Cf. also Michael Gibbons, "Insight and Emergence," in M. Lamb, ed., *Creativity and Method: Essays in Honor of Bernard Lonergan* (Milwaukee, Wisc.: Marquette University Press, 1981), pp. 529–42; Philip McShane, "Generalized Empirical Method and the Actual Context of Economics," ibid., pp. 543–72.

71. Michael Albert and Robin Hahnel, *Unorthodox Marxism* (Boston: South End Press, 1978); John McMurtry, *The Structure of Marx's World-View* (Princeton, N.J.: Princeton University Press, 1978); Stanislaw Starski, *Class Struggle in Classless Poland* (Boston: South End Press, 1982); Lawrence Weschler, *Solidarity: Poland in the Season of its Passion* (New York: Simon and Schuster, 1982); Rudolf Bahro, *The Alternative in Eastern Europe*, trans. David Fernbach (London: NLB, 1978); Kofi Appiah-Kubi and Sergio Torrese, eds., *African Theology en Route* (Maryknoll, N.Y.: Orbis Books, 1979); Basil Moore, ed., *The Challenge of Black Theology in South Africa* (Atlanta, Ga.: John Knox Press, 1973); Walbert Bühlmann, *The Coming of the Third Church* (Maryknoll, N.Y.: Orbis Books, 1976); Simon Leys, *Chinese Shadows* (New York: Penguin Books, 1974); Daniel H. Levine, ed., *Churches and Politics in Latin America* (Beverly Hills, Calif.: Sage Publications, 1979); Sergio Torres and John Eagleson, eds., *The Challenge of Basic Christian Communities* (Maryknoll, N.Y.: Orbis Books, 1981).

72. Roberto Mangabeira Unger, *Knowledge and Politics* (New York: Free Press, 1975) pp. 236–95; Glenn Tinder, *Community: Reflections on a Tragic Ideal* (Baton Rouge: Louisiana State University Press, 1980), pp. 148–99; Parker J. Palmer, *The Company of Strangers* (New York: Crossroad, 1981).

73. James Fallows, *National Defense* (New York: Vintage Books, 1981); David Holloway, "War, Militarism and the Soviet State," in E. P. Thompson and Dan Smith, eds., *Protest and Survive* (New York: Monthly Review Press, 1981), pp. 70–107; Thomas A. Shannon, ed., *War or Peace? The Search for New Answers* (Maryknoll, N.Y.: Orbis Books, 1980).

74. Francis Moore Lappe and Joseph Collins, *Food First: Beyond the Myth of Scarcity* (New York: Ballantine Books, 1977); Francis Moore Lappe, Joseph Collins and David Kinley, *Aid as Obstacle: Twenty Questions about our Foreign Aid and the Hungry* (San Francisco: Institute for Food and Development Policy, 1975); Susan George, *How the Other Half Dies* (Montclair, N.J.: Allanheld, Osmun and Co., 1977); Gerald and Patricia Mische, *Toward a Human World Order* (New York: Paulist Press, 1977); Joseph Gremillion, *Food/Energy and the Major Faiths* (Maryknoll, N.Y.: Orbis Books, 1978).

75. Dennis Gabor, *Innovations: Scientific, Technological and Social* (New York: Oxford University Press, 1970); Capra, *Turning Point*, pp. 263–420.

76. L. S. Stavrianos, *Global Rift: The Third World Comes of Age* (New York: William Morrow and Co., 1981); Loretta Schwartz-Nobel, *Starving in the Shadow of Plenty* (New York: G. P. Putnam's Sons, 1981).

77. Ferdinand Tönnies, *Gemeinschaft und Gesellschaft* (Berlin, 1887); Tom Bottomore and Robert Nisbet, eds., *A History of Sociological Analysis* (New York: Basic Books, Inc., 1978), pp. 151, 197–99, 440–42, 118–236.

78. David Riesman, with Nathan Glazer and Reuel Denney, *The Lonely Crowd* (New Haven, Conn.: Yale University Press, 1950); Howard S. Becker, *Outsiders: Studies in the Sociology of Deviance* (New York: Free Press, 1963); Frank J. Donner, *The Age of Surveillance* (New York: Alfred A. Knopf, 1980).

79. Schell, *The Fate of the Earth*, pp. 173–74.

80. Ibid., pp. 181–231.

81. MacIntyre, *After Virtue*, pp. 190–209.

82. Max Weber, *Economy and Society*, I: 24–26, 339, 212–65, II: 956–97; Max Weber, *On Charisma and Institution Building* (Chicago: University of Chicago Press, 1968), pp. 46–80.

83. Ibid., pp. 48–65.

84. Nancy Ring, "Alienation and Reconciliation," in M. Lamb, ed., *Creativity and Method*, pp. 249–64; Mark Morelli, "Horizonal Diplomacy," ibid., pp. 459–76 and references given in note 8 above.

85. Brewster Ghiselin, ed., *The Creative Process* (New York: New American Library, 1955); Arthur Koestler, *The Act of Creation* (New York: Dell Publishing Co., 1964); William Matthews, "Method and the Social Appropriation of Reality," in M. Lamb, ed., *Creativity and Method*, pp. 425–42. By community here I mean, of course, intentional and not only instinctual community.

86. Otto Nathan and Heinz Norden, ed., *Einstein on Peace* (New York: Avenel Books, 1981), pp. 509–640.

87. Lonergan, *Method in Theology*, pp. 356–68.

88. We have yet to appreciate the epochal significance of the ecumenical movement among the world religions. Cf. Wilfred Cantwell Smith, *Towards a World Theology* (Philadelphia: Westminster Press, 1981).

89. Refer to references given in notes 10 and 11 above.

90. Norman Perrin, *Jesus and the Language of the Kingdom* (Philadelphia: For-

tress Press, 1976); Ernst Käsemann, *Jesus Means Freedom* (Philadelphia: Fortress Press, 1969).

91. Gustavo Gutierrez, "Freedom and Salvation: A Political Problem," in *Liberation and Change* (Atlanta, Ga.: John Knox Press, 1977), pp. 3–94; Martin Hengel, *Christ and Power* (Philadelphia: Fortress Press, 1977); Gerd Theissen, *A Critical Faith: A Case for Religion* (Philadelphia: Fortress Press, 1979); Alfred Braunthal, *Salvation and the Perfect Society* (Amherst: University of Massachusetts Press, 1979).

92. Ernst Troeltsch, *The Social Teaching of the Christian Churches*, trans. Olive Wyon (Chicago: University of Chicago Press, 1981), I: 8–37.

93. Ibid., pp. 328–82.

94. Ibid., II: 461–514, 579–651, 691–805. Cf. also Timothy MacDonald, "The Ecclesiology of Yves Congar" (Ph.D. dissertation, Marquette University, 1982).

95. Johann Baptist Metz, *The Emergent Church* (New York: Crossroad, 1981). The renewed emphasis being given to local churches is reflected theologically in *The Catholic Theological Society of America Proceedings* 36 (1981). See also Sergio Torres and John Eagleson, eds., *The Challenge of Basic Christian Communities* (Maryknoll, N.Y.: Orbis Books, 1981).

96. Schell, *The Fate of the Earth*.

6

The Protestant Principle: Between Theocracy and Propheticism

MARTIN E. MARTY

Henri Desroche depicts three basic relations of faith-groups to their societies. Religion may *attest* when it integrates and is satisfied with a self-affirming society. When a society examines its own premises and reorganizes its constituencies and antagonistic elements, religion keeps its differentiating function but remains within the status quo. In this case the differentiating function appears as contending; I prefer to say now it *contests*. Third, in a society that is denying, challenging and refusing its right to exist, religion appears as a function of *protest*, revolting and subverting.[1]

The three forms are not chemically pure or always distinct. Especially when we bring in the issue of historical tenses, matters grow confused. Nostalgic religious groups, for example, may contest the present state of society in an appeal for return to the presumed earlier status quo, which they could have attested, and which, indeed, they do attest. Protest more often occurs when a religious group takes the side of a revolting or subverting group when the larger society is *not* "denying, challenging and refusing its own right to exist." This is the case with large elements of the Roman Catholic church in Latin American societies today. Still, Desroche's threefold typology can aid in sorting the parties and contentions in practical American life today.

My purpose is to be practical, not theoretical; to deal with power alignments as they affect public action today. Of course, these are all grounded in theory; and theory, in America at least, usually bonds with praxis. To be practical, however, I thought it well to begin in one dimension of public action: political, and especially legislative life. Attesting, contesting or protesting religious groups have a "practical" effect when they can inconvenience people who have political power. What, then, is the view from the state house window?

Most of the time, if I were a legislator in the flow that leads to support of the status quo, I would not be inconvenienced; for most of the time religion integrates and attests. *Religio societatis vinculum.* To Joachim Wach this was "the paramount force of social integration."[2] Emile Durkheim taught us to anticipate this sacral aspect of society, and the Gallup poll reinforces it. There is an American consensus and the religious rank and file cannot be sorted from it. The believer is much like W. H. Auden's "unknown citizen": he held the proper opinions for the time of the year. When there was peace, he was for peace. When there was war, he went. In Desroche's formula: *"a social experience of the sacred is identified with a sacral experience of society."*[3]

Practically, then, as a person in Congress I can read that about 80 percent of the American people are opposed to the affirmations of pluralism embodied in the U.S. Supreme Court "school prayer" decisions of 1962 and 1963, *Engel* v. *Vitale* and *Abington School District* v. *Schempp*. I can read on that about 80 percent favor a constitutional amendment that would legitimate some form of school prayer. Four out of five Americans "attest" the society that they presume once existed, and they will attest and confirm my efforts to reintegrate it on those terms. Similarly 80 percent tell the poll takers that they are ready for "equal time" to be given creationism and evolution in science classrooms of public schools. A legislator starts with a strong attesting base.

He or she must reckon, however, with well-poised contestors of these positions, most of them from religious groups. When school prayer amendments and legislative or judicial support for creationism become controverted, the main contesters come from a leadership minority in Judaism, Catholicism and Protestantism. Educators, scientists and humanists take a back seat to the contesters who can "prophetically" wield common symbols from religious lore against the attestations. Their arguments are sufficiently compelling; they are articulate and well placed enough that practically they can inconvenience me, so I have to pay attention to them.

Second, as a practical person in politics, I would become more alert, then, to the contending or *contesting* functions of religious groups. They do not usually proceed on the basis of anything like a consensus confirmed by poll takers at around 80 percent of the population. Joachim Wach speaks of the contesters as representing "protest within."[4] They appear at times when there is a redistribution of religious loyalties, but more often they represent "intramural contention" (*"la contestation interne"*). Bonhoeffer spoke of it as "resistance-submission." Here individual prophets rise, or there can be collective action by effective minority groups who have some leverage in the larger groups and the whole society.

Practically, as a person in Congress, I would have to notice such contesting on both what the media and I would call "the left" and "the right." The left today would be represented visibly and dumbfoundingly by a significant minority of the Roman Catholic bishops and an increasing coalition of Catholic, Protestant and Jewish leaders—and followers—who contest churchly support of the status quo in armament policies. In turn, they advocate nuclear disarmament in terms that inconvenience me. They seem to threaten national security in the face of Soviet threat, and they do threaten jobs in my constituency.

Practically, I do not have to pay much attention when the dissent comes from people named Berrigan or Coffin, for the media and I have long ago dismissed them as reflexive reactors, "generals without armies." Yes, they have vestigial power because they also draw on the common pool of symbols, and prophetic power because they invoke some of these symbols to depict benign futures that may have some attraction. I do pay more attention to the bishops, however, because their posture represents an apparent reversal, one that causes constituents in the church and the electorate to take notice.

"Throughout American history the Catholic Church and its bishops were probably the biggest hawks in our skies," observes Mary Hanna in *Catholics and American Politics*.[5] For them to question nuclear armament, to oppose administration policies in Central America, and to legitimate conscientious objection to the draft is surprising and therefore powerful, given the history of Catholic attesting in America. Hanna reminds us, so far as peace policies are concerned, that "World War I produced only one American Catholic conscientious objector; in World War II, there were only 200, nearly all of them followers of Dorothy Day's Catholic Worker movement."[6] Practically, I also had to pay attention to the bishops' support of workers in the Stevens textile strike a couple of years before. Who said that "mainline Christianity" is quiescent in the political sphere?

Practically, I would also be inconvenienced, if I sought the status quo, by coalitions between Catholic leadership, Catholic social action movements and various Protestant fronts. The media and I have been taught to neutralize and "reflexive bureaucracy" the boards and task forces of denominations and councils of churches. Yet when they contest national policies—for example, the current administration's policies as these affect the poor or matters of justice—they demand attention, especially when they appear in union with voluntaristic fronts, like Bread for the World. Here again, their power comes not from the mystification that goes with presumed numbers ("The N.C.C. which represents a constituency of x million," spooks out no one) but from the fact that they evoke response to common symbols. This was the source of power of Martin Luther King. He was not a charismatic leader (in the Weberian sense) who said, "It is written, but I say unto you."

He was a virtuoso leader who, turning to the prophets and the Declaration of Independence, spoke to a community that attested both and said, "It is written and I insist." As a legislator, momentarily I had to pay attention.

There is also contesting on "the right," which inconveniences me even if its members and I share many viewpoints and aspects of consensus. The same bishops who seem leftish on defense, foreign policy and social programs, are typed by the media and in the public mind in coalition with rightists on the issue of a constitutional amendment proscribing abortion. (The fact that this is the "single issue" that finds the Catholic leadership in alliance with the Right might very well suggest the need for re-examination of either the typologies or the deeper meanings of the abortion issue! But that is a topic for another day.)

In the other part of this coalition, then, I find myself in the company of people who had previously been attesters, supporters of consensus and status quo. Now, suddenly, they are discontented, shifting, contesting, "protesting within." They do so in the name of a presumed pre-pluralist past, the ethos of Protestantism's "Righteous Empire." Once there was a kind of monopoly or at least homogeneity in American life. The public schools were the main propagators of this vision in the era of liberal theist Horace Mann and the more conservative McGuffey readers. Back then, there could be school prayer and Bible reading and a crèche on the courthouse lawn. Back then, before pluralists made so much noise, there could be Ten Commandments on the public classroom wall, and the teaching of absolutes, *our* absolutes. All that is changed.

So there has risen a largely Protestant New Christian Right, which allies itself with Catholicism on anti-abortion, with some Catholics of the Phyllis Schlafly sort in opposing the Equal Rights Amendment, and with some Jews— of the neo-Conservative *Commentary* sort—who are ready to give privileged status to the ethos and ethics of earlier Protestantism because of its support for capitalism. These contesters, impatient with pluralism, represent problems similar to those that come with the Catholic bishops' stands. Speaking for the majority, they represent minorities, if polls are accurate, when it comes to issues like anti-abortion. Yet if the bishops or the Martin Luther Kings gain power by drawing on symbols shared with their larger believing communities, the New Christian Right draws power not only from its appeal to pre-pluralist nostalgia and simplicity. It also has mastered the techniques of propaganda, persuasion and organization of a late industrial society. Taking cues from another minority, the 2-million-member National Rifle Association, it has learned to keep legislators like me off balance. They can disenthrone or diselect me by mobilizing a few thousand impassioned, formerly quiet, voters.

There are three windows in my legislative office. I look out on a third, much smaller group, those who in Desroche's terms protest. They represent what Wach called "protest without." Desroche saw them standing in the prophetic tradition of Thomas Münzer—the "orgiastic chiliasm of the Anabaptists," to use Mannheim's phrase.[7] They no longer or never did share the terms of the larger society. They never were at heart theologically a part of the republic, or they have given up on it. Among these are groups as diverse and remote as the Hutterites, the Dukhobors, or the Jehovah's Witnesses. They tend to be politically passive; in the case of the Old Order Mennonites or Amish, often an "outside" lawyer from the American Civil Liberties Union has to represent their civil cases, so passive are they.

On the other hand, from time to time protest appears from the active left. In the late 1960s some militant blacks and feminists were ready to tear up the covenants of the "approved social contract," to use Ernst Gellner's phrase.[8] They may have been atavistic or recidivist in their desires to go to pre-political, anarchic and hence presumably free states. More often they spoke in the name of either utopianism, which by the nature of the case was untested, or of polities, which were believed to be alien in American society but which, they felt, had begun to be tested elsewhere—most of these being revolutionary socialist. The polls found at best minuscule and, in churches, even microscopic support for these Maoist, Che Gueveran, Frantz Fanonian, Regis Debrayan, or even Malcolm Xian proposals. Yet they inconvenienced me as a legislator who represents the existing public order and seeks the fulfillment of the promise of American life as it is prefigured in the Declaration—what I call a "working hypothesis for a humane society."

I am not particularly inconvenienced, however, by an academic wing of the protesting group, the advocates of liberation theology. From my window in Washington or Baton Rouge or Olympia it is a confusing phenomenon, powerful to the extent that it evokes some biblical symbols and ties in to some policies of the actually powerful—like the bishops. On the other hand, in most cases what is called liberation theology derives its protest ("protest without") argument from Marxist sources. These sources represent part of what Americans through the past century have evaded or suppressed or rejected. The symbolization is too alien to inconvenience me at present. The blacks who knock at my door are contesters, who "protest within" in order to become part of the existing and subtly transforming society. They do not draw on African or Marxist resources. I have not heard of the Gustavo Gutierrez or the Juan Luis Segundo cited by the restless Hispanics in my district. This does not mean that there is no potential in these arguments and resources, especially if there is a breakdown in the existing order. But if I know my history, I can expect that consequent upon such a breakdown, a socialist reconstruction in America would likely draw on existing symbols. It would no doubt result in a kind of "civil religious" theocracy called Christian Republicanism. I am a practical politician, with short-term outlooks, and the radical, alienated argument is not inconveniencing.[9]

So much for the practical lineup, or realignment. What is going on? From this point on, let us drop the "attesting" aspect of public action, simply assuming its prevalence. It is important to remember that attestation and integration belong to the promise of most contesting groups. After the present troubles, it is assumed that restoration would produce a society worth attesting again. In passing, take but one obvious example. The New Christian Right speaks in the name of symbols that regard America as *the* elect people, the chosen people, the people with a divine mission for the end time. First there must be a purging of internal alien forces, currently code named secular humanism. So long as the secular humanists' conspiracy retains power, one must contest the status quo in the name of the status quo ante. For the rest of this essay let us bracket that aspect and concentrate on the current elements: contesting, and its two kinds of intention and protesting with its more ambiguous intentions.

The code name for the combination of these "chemically impure" two is "the protestant principle." Despite the tendency of my title, this paper is not about the churchly Protestant response to pluralism in the public order. Instead it refers to Paul Tillich's familiar "protestant principle," which relies on no specifically Protestant ecclesial base. In its ontological or theological heart, this principle "is the guardian against the attempts of the finite and conditioned to usurp the place of the unconditional in thinking and acting."[10] While ecclesial Protestantism has ordinarily had theocratic tendencies, and still does (whether voiced by right or left)—which means that, given the chance, it would "run the show," or have a major part in a show it would enjoy helping run—Protestants join with Catholics, Jews and other believers in at least nominal support of the protestant principle.

For Tillich this principle ordinarily begins negatively, in protest against theocracy or ecclesial dominance, or in civil and public religious prophecy against absolutist claims made for any finite constructs, be they churches, political orders, movements and even one's own cause! On the positive side the principle asserts that God who grounds Being, issues justice and grace in ways that no finite expression can bound.

The protestant principle looks, on the one hand, to the necessity for "-cracy," for constructs of power, order, government and rule if there is to be justice. It recognizes that the Protestant churches and orders have often carried the logic of this impulse into theocracy and made it difficult for the principle to be effectively voiced or heard. On the other hand, it looks beyond prophecy to "propheticism." I picked up the term from some irretrievable citation in the 250-volume New Catholic Encyclopedia, and have no impulse or motive to search for this needle in that haystack. I took it to mean—and propose it—as the utterance of the protestant principle apart from its place in a polarity or dialectic, as a kind of end in itself. Sometimes this is done in millennial terms, as in the case of Roger Williams in colonial America: between the apostolic age and the return of Christ there can be no real church and no hint of theocratic order. Sometimes it is done in pathological psychological terms: the prophet is simply and egomaniacally a crabby sort. Most frequently it is a carrying out in isolation of the logic of the protestant principle without noticing the positive purposes of public order.

For working out this protestant "contesting" polarity in practical terms, I should like to embark on a case study. These terms prevent me from elaborating on biblical theory, on the majesties of Augustine or Aquinas, or on the roots of the modern protestant principle—either theocratic or propheticistic—in Calvin, Luther, Münzer or the Quakers. Nor do I take it that this should be an explication of the most recent mentors, from Jacques Maritain to Tillich and the Niebuhrs. I must disappoint those who expect my focus to be on the elevations of the World or National Councils of Churches.

Instead, the issue is most clear if we examine the most recent eruptions on the Protestant front, since the tendencies of movements are often most clear *in statu nascendi* and not *in statu mutandi*. For the past decade, it is the agglomeration of evangelical, pentecostal, conservative and fundamentalist Protestant movements that best bear examination. To deal with this faction or segment may be distasteful to those of elite or mandarin tastes, but my purpose is to be practical and not theoretical. But let me at least keep my elitist and mandarin credentials by quoting Alfred North Whitehead: "No religion can be considered in abstraction from its followers, or even from its various types of followers."[11] And, if some find the current Protestant polarities rendered most visible on the Right to their discomfort, let me assuage their discontents with another Whiteheadian line: "Great ideas enter into reality with evil associates and with disgusting alliances."[12] Let me also say that some of the advocates for new adjustments to pluralism, particularly on conservative Reformed soil, do not strike me as "evil associates" or "disgusting allies." They present arguments that deserve to be responded to, not ignored.

We have discontent with pluralism. The only way to express this discontent effectively is to enter the pluralist order, even if only to try to terminate it or to reduce its impact. As a result, the practical politician and the theoretician who grounds his or her work in concrete situations, not "in abstractions from a religion's followers," has had to readjust the vision of power alignments. A fundamental, seismic shift seems to be apparent in the American religious public order, one that may alter a resolution which took shape, some believe, between the lay revival of 1857–58 and the formation of the Federal Council of Churches and the issuance of the Methodist social creed in 1908.

After surveying that period, it seemed proper to me to tell the subsequent story of American Protestant political lineups in a two-party system, "public" and "private." New evidence suggests realignments. In the first issue of *This World*, the neo-conservative think-tank journal, Paul J. Weber writes on "Examining the Religious Lobbies."[13] He was able to isolate seventy-four "currently active groups" (plus one association, which we shall not include in this report). Of these, twelve were Roman Catholic, seven Jewish, seventeen liberal Protestant/ecumenical, and thirty-three conservative Protestant/ecumenical.

A Rip van Winkle awakened from dogmatic and political slumbers after a generation would rub his eyes: conservative Protestants only a decade ago protested liberal Protestant "meddling" in politics and declared it, according to their inerrant Bible, to be sinful and unbiblical. By the end of the 1970s, using the same inerrant Bible, they had declared such intrusion to be not only legitimate but biblically necessary. A discontent with pluralism impelled them to organize and speak up.

Weber documents the rise of these conservative groups. In the 1960s, the period of liberal social activism, "there were no new conservative groups" at all. As for the decades and the dates of founding:

	Liberal	Conservative
1800s	—	4
1900–40	6	1
1941–60	6	3
1961–70	7	—
1971–80	11	26
Total	30	34

The founding of twenty-six agencies or lobbies in the 1970s is only evidence of a wider discontent and stirring. Most of these were of the "single-issue" sort: nineteen of the conservative Protestant are single-issue, while only four of the liberal ones are. Politically, twenty-one single-issue causes are conservative while only four are liberal. Ecclesially, twenty-one conservative and nine liberal are "individual" as supposed to denominational, coalition, or mixed—and hence they represent that voluntaristic power that inconveniences legislators.

This new phenomenon may be so startling as to have to cause some of us to revise our typologies—a horrible thought. Sociologists like Dean Hoge have employed them and found them empirically verifiable into the 1970s, and David Moberg in conservative Protestant social scientific circles also tested and confirmed them in his book *The Great Reversal*. "The difference" between them, wrote Moberg, "is at root theological."[14]

Richard G. Hutcheson, Jr., has recently written:

For years we have characterized North American Christianity in terms of liberal social activism and conservative pietism, liberal involvement and conservative separatism, liberal this-worldliness and conservative otherworldliness. Martin Marty (in *Righteous Empire*) analyzed a century of historical trends in terms of two continuing parties, the public Protestants and the private Protestants, and we adopted this delineation. Reams of research as reported in such books as Dean Hoge's *Division in the Protestant House* and elsewhere, found socio-political involvement to be the surest litmus test for categorizing conservative and liberal Christians.

Now, all of a sudden, this neatly ordered typology has collapsed. The private Protestants have gone public.[15]

First, Hutcheson observed that the "young evangelicals" of the 1970s pressed for peace, an end to world hunger, economic justice and the like: "We welcomed them to the fold." Then came the election of 1980 and the New Christian Right: "And suddenly nobody was playing by the old rules." Adds Hutcheson: "The effect of all this will be more than a mere challenge to our public Protestant/private Protestant typology; it will be devastating to the entire religious status quo in the United States."[16]

In response, let me say three things. First, as a practical story-telling historian and not a theoretical typologizing sociologist or theologian, I find a change in circumstances that jostle typologies not a threat but a delight. Story-telling historians have nothing to talk about if there is no change. I shall delight some day to write chapters retrospective to the 1970s and dealing with "the great reversal of the great reversal," the reintrusion of once-active conservative Protestants, after a passive period, into reactivity.

Second, I am not yet ready to designate the reintrusive parties as "public," but at this time to see them as chiefly political, which is somewhat narrower. A public theology, it seems to me, must move beyond an ecclesially confined viewpoint in politics to one that legitimates or positively rationalizes those who share the republic but not the faith. "Better be ruled by a smart Turk than a dumb Christian," Luther is said to have said somewhere or other. The Persian Cyrus is theologically designated a leader of Yahweh's people without even knowing the name of the Lord. Amos cries out against confining the activity of the Lord of history to the chosen people. The new Protestant conservative theologians and activists until now have had too negative views of non-theists and too sectarian views of what is religiously licit to qualify as truly "public," though they are very overtly political.

Now, third, and perhaps most disconcerting—but redeemable in the eyes of some by recalling Whitehead's words about "evil associates and disgusting alliances," it strikes me that *formally* (though of course not always *substantively*) the New Christian Right, both in its high academic wings and in its street-fighting flanks, are structural correlates of the more familiar liberal activist expressions of decades past.

Let me momentarily forget Catholic and Orthodox Christians and turn ecclesially Protestant for a moment, because of the Protestant predominance in the American religious past when the parties formed. The most convenient term here—if not always the most clarifying—is "post-millennial," one which does not appear in the consciousness, to say nothing of the vocabulary, of most non-Protestants. It is not, I am happy to say, in the vocabulary of most Protestants, either, but it does not take much explaining to locate what the term intends or portends.

This post-millennial vision has been essentially theocratic. It contends that the end of history, whether conceived in mythic and symbolic terms associated with the Second Coming or whether demythologized, has operated with what Paul Tillich called a "metaphysics of progressivism" or a liberal-immanental view of revelation in which the always-coming Kingdom progressively keeps breaking in with more truth and light and greater potential for love and divine power and justice.[17] This theocratic tendency was present at root in Jonathan Edwards' vision of the Christian republic to come and in the consistent post-millennialism of the positive-thinking reformers and agents of benevolent societies during the first half of the nineteenth century, the Protestant empire's glory years. It returned, remythologized in Anglican (Maurice in England, Bliss and others in America) Christian Socialism and the Protestant Social Gospel. Walter Rauschenbusch's concept of "Christianizing" the social order was a liberal version of theocracy.[18] So, in the 1960s, were the resymbolized visions of Harvey Cox's *The Secular City* or Gibson Winter's *The New Creation as Metropolis*.[19] Rauschenbusch and George Herron could use mildly and non-violently Marxian tools of analysis, and Cox and Winter could find Marxian approaches more congenial. Theologically, however, theirs was a pluralistic theocracy whose pluralism was always being overcome by biblical and theological symbols and tendencies associated with "the kingdom" or "the city" or "the new creation." Being supple and sometimes subtle thinkers, they qualified their theocratic tendencies; but, if followed to the final consequences of their logic, they were at the theocratic pole.

On the opposite end there has been a long Protestant millennial tradition of prophecy that verges toward propheticism. It has necessarily been more rare, for here "contest" verges on "protest"; the assumptions move from "protest within" to "protest without." This was part of the Continental Anabaptist tradition, some of the English Puritan sectarian, and colonial American Antinomian, Quaker, and Baptist dissenting outlook. In the broadly extra-ecclesial sense, someone like Henry David Thoreau has been legitimately seen as the extender of Protestant logic to its propheticistic extreme. That is, he brings the transcendental or unconditional word and ethos to bear even at the expense of civil ordering. Here is H. Richard Niebuhr's "Christ Against Culture" motif, which has often been present on the Protestant soil made respectable by the passing of time and the appearance, in retrospect, of the heroic and the saintly from this dissenting camp.[20]

The propheticistic impulses belonged, curiously, to the pre-millennial tradition. Practically this was not usually apparent. The pre-millennialists devised, in the name of a "literalistic" reading of the prophetic books of the Bible, what James Barr conceives of as a "mythopoetic fantasy" worthy of a Blake or a C. S. Lewis.[21] The dispensationalists among them disvalued the present age and placed all positive meaning in events after the Second Coming and during and after the millennium. Coming to America soon after its invention in Scotland and England through small sects—Irvingite, Darbyite, Plymouth Brethren—it became virtually normative in Dwight L. Moody's evangelism and that which followed in its wake.

I said the propheticistic impulse was "curious" because, theology aside, these evangelists whose mission it was to rescue people from an evil world were, when they were political at all, attesters of the status quo. From Dwight L. Moody to the Billy Graham of the 1950s (though not of the 1980s) they were mere attesters of the approved American social contract, believers in the elect and chosen nation motif, celebrators of America's mission against atheistic socialist and communist challengers of capitalism, God's order and the like. Yet theologically they had no legitimation of churchly intervention in politics and chose expertise in the "private" realms. And, while being essentially attesters, they were practically critics, prophets—against a fallen America given to pornography, obscenity, worldliness, materialism and other vices.

What is new in this camp in the early 1980s is that the pre-millennial propheticism is disappearing. Somehow "cognitive dissonance" or the enjoyment of power has led pre-millennialists to turn worldly. Theirs is now the world that celebrates "born again" Miss Americas, the National Football League, Washington Prayer Breakfasts, television surrogates for nightclubs decorated with Jesus imagery, positive thinking for success in material affairs, "Graceful Losers" weight clinics and Christian charm schools. These are harmless and diverting. But theirs is now also the world of overt political attempts to alter the social contract or ethos by putative return to the earlier Protestant homogeneity to overcome pluralism.

Why, and why now the shift? First, they realized a loss of power to provide the symbols for the whole society. Commercial interests in mass media, the diversity of populations in public schools, the conflict of ethnic and religious constituencies in politics made these the three most vulnerable orders. *Ressentiment* was the next stage, a resentment directed against an outside foe, this time congealed not as "the infidel" but as "the secular humanist" in conspiracy against the faithful. Third came a spirit of revenge. In the 1920s they would displace and proscribe evolution. In *Segraves* v. *California* resentful and avenging declassé scientists found class not by having creationism legitimated but by finding evolution circumscribed and qualified.

Add to these a fourth motif, a revolution of rising expectations. One can speak of, sequentially as they have done during the period of base-broadening and compromise, a Protestant America, then a Christian, a Judeo-Christian, and now a "traditionally theist" nation (which even encompasses deistic Founding Fathers). And they have instruments for effecting restitution of this presumed lost order at the expenses of liberalism and nontheism or humanism, thanks to skillful uses of rapid mailing techniques and mastery of television and other media.

Let us briefly examine some options from the conservative camps. In an improbable source, the *Texas Tech Law Review*, John W. Whitehead and John Conlan provide a script or a scripture with their argument against "the establishment of the religion of secular humanism" and for the re-establishment of "traditional theism."[22] In this camp there is a competition of theocracies. Cleverly exploiting Justice Hugo Black's characterization of secular humanism as a possible religion (in *Torcaso* v. *Watkins*), they have stolen a page from sophisticated anthropology and judicial lore. Now they suggest that *all* value systems, ethoses, world views, outlooks or philosophies (including secular humanism and the teaching of evolution) *have* to be religions, complete with rites and theologies. They argue further that "the religion of secular humanism" is being paid for by the taxpayers who are traditionally theist and who are therefore a disenfranchised majority. These people of theocratic tendency are explicit about their desire to legislate privilege for the traditional theist view.

Now, this strategy includes ideology repugnant to the liberal theocrats of American Protestant history and it excludes the voices of those whom Reinhold Niebuhr called "the children of darkness" come to judge the ecclesial "children of light."[23] Yet structurally this does not differ that much from the theocratic post-millennial liberalism, which was always in the process of overcoming pluralism—sometimes, in the past, through overt anti-Catholicism and nervousness about Judaism—in the name of the coming Kingdom, as interpreted and dominated by Protestants.

On the opposite extreme, and far more sophisticated and academically respectable is the propheticist camp. Here are the middle-aged "young evangelicals" of the 1970s, the Post-Americans, *Sojourners, The Other Siders*, the Ronald Siders, who come from a variety of biblical viewpoints to a variety of political viewpoints. Some of them are frankly socialists, some advocates of non-systematic and mildly anarchic "simple living." Many are rooted in the Anabaptist tradition and concern themselves more with "Christ's victim people" than the assertion of positive power for the cause of peace. Others use biblical motifs to "protest without" in the most radical terms. Their theological heroes are people like Jacques Ellul, who asserts the Protestant principle against one's own cause most of all; William Stringfellow, whose unsmiling "biblical discernments" *always* find America wanting; John Howard Yoder who scrutinizes the Bible for peace and justice motifs to be applied in today's world.[24]

In all these cases, there is not much of a theocratic impulse, unless couched in such remote utopian terms that they have little practical appeal or consequence. Relying on "the principalities and powers" to assure the presence of an order in which the demonic will always prevail, they isolate the

Protestant principle and the prophetic impulse—and do so on the basis of "conservative" readings of the Bible and ecclesiastical ties as did their fore-parents. There may be no twists to the argument, new fronts for the causes and some different substance, but structurally they embody one aspect of the Protestant polarity.

Let me mention a third not really dialectical approach to pluralism. It is perhaps the most sophisticated of all. An excellent example of their argument issues from the Fellows of the Calvin Center for Christian Scholarship at Calvin College and reflects Netherlandish reform. Donald Oppewal and Gordon Spykman have proper names for their lineage, while Walfred Peterson seems to compromise it somewhat and Rockne McCarthy seems the outsider. (But he teaches at Dordt College, so the credentials are in order.) They have joined the theocratic militants in arguing that secular humanism has established itself as the privileged faith in the civil and public order. But instead of trying to overthrow it and re-establish Protestantism in the schools and through the legislatures, they take a different tack, one which to me reflects the Dutch resolution of *Verzuiling*, the rendering of civil life in columns—Protestant, Catholic, Jew and the like.

These Fellows have published *Society, State and Schools*, a celebration of pluralism and a critique of dominance by one element in the pluralism. The practical effect is to support notions or policies something like "tuition tax credits," which will allow positive-minded citizens (in respect to the republic) to find relief and support for nurture of meaning and value among their young in priviate schools.[25] They also propose minimum and maximum amendments to the constitution to legitimate their approach. I cannot here elaborate on the subtleties of their argument, which I commend to you. Typologically, they stand between the theocratic militants and the propheticistic critics, addressing without resolving the issue of pluralism, theologically and practically.

I believe that all these three positions, particularly the first and the third, are superimposed on centuries-old Protestant and millennia-old Christian proposals; however much their substance is directed to "single issues," their structure expresses different poles as these relate to the Protestant impulse, principle or establishment. Master them and you have a sort of road map for the more liberal Protestant and both liberal and conservative Catholic Christian advocacies and arguments of the day.

All these approaches occur in the face of a pluralist order that demands other and more from the theorists. The American who saw this best, even if he did not present fully satisfying proposals for our time, was John Courtney Murray, S. J. He was not a metaphysical pluralist and thus was not of a camp that should have a ready address to polity in practically pluralist America. As a Jesuit Thomist Natural Law Catholic monotheist he was not capable of affirming such an ontological pluralism as, say, William James was wont to do. He bracketed that issue to present his practical message most urgently: "Religious pluralism is against the will of God. But it is the human condition; it is written into the script of history. It will not somehow marvelously cease to trouble the City."[26] One need not agree with the first sentence in order to affirm the effect of the next two. Short of totalitarian efficiency in propagating, wielding and enforcing assent to one set of symbols, there will be religious and other pluralisms.

The theocrats would overcome, or always be in the process of overcoming, pluralism by seeking to persuade or coerce the public into assent to a single set of symbols and practical structures. Whitehead and Conlan and most of the New Christian Right work to that end. So, I have argued, did liberal Kingdom of God and utopian Protestants and, of course, before them the Catholics of Christendom and the Orthodox of Orthodoxdom.

At the opposite pole, caring little for "-cracy" but speaking much of "theo-," are those who evoke the protestant principle in the name of the Unconditioned against all finite resolutions, especially those of the powerful state. The Anabaptists of old and the radical conservatives of evangelicalism today join some liberation theologians in these apparently anarchic visions—not always in the name of a supplanting new order, but with a call to immediate ad hoc responses to divine mandates for justice.

Between them are some who "sit out" the argument over how to resolve the issue of the *communitas*, the larger community in the *communitas communitatum* that is a republic. They address pluralism by asking for freedom to be themselves in one of the subcommunities and from thence, as good citizens, to make some contribution to the larger whole while being released from the pressure to conform ideologically to the doctrines that, willy-nilly, fill the vacuum of values in pluralism.

The dialectical tradition associated in Protestantism with names like Paul Tillich and Reinhold Niebuhr could not take that third alternative, however much respect they may have for "sectarians." They leaned toward the theocratic element in support of civil order and public responsibility, and drew on the propheticistic extreme to call all resolutions and addresses to order into judgment under transcendent norms.

What David Tracy would call the analogical tradition was voiced in Protestantism by lesser figures like Emil Brunner and in Catholicism majestically by John Courtney Murray.[27] He smoked out the ideologies that had been privileged in American life. When he spoke out in the 1950s he still had to make explicit the Protestant interpretations of the American civil religion that paraded as universal interpretations. But he also issued Distant Early Warning signals that the "secular" conspiracy—"breathing together," in the positive sense—was also privileged, or sought privilege. I could argue, on his side, that the attempts to find a "universal" republican ethos—a position tended toward by significant figures from Thomas Jefferson and Benjamin Franklin to John Dewey and Sidney Mead and other "republicans"—also lead to particular, perhaps sectarian and certainly minority theologies. Why

give *them* privilege, ask other citizens inside pluralism? Why let *their* interpretations of natural law or reason displace our own or be sanctioned while
ours are disdained?

Let me be impractical and theoretical for a moment as I verge toward a
constructive closing statement in the spirit of John Courtney Murray. He
seemed to think that there has to be a minimal consensus if there is to be
argument. Argument is based on disagreement, not confusion. Disagreement
is as hard to reach as confusion is easy—and full agreement impossible. I
do not think it will be easy for enough Americans to concur on John Courtney Murray's sophisticated revision of natural law to find much consensus,
or on the new Protestants' revealed law to find any.

Yet Americans do have a common story, a common memory. We have
not been *mere* pluralists. When we have treated our biblical memory, cherished by the vast majority through the years, as a call to seriousness about
justice and freedom without imposing it as a creed on minorities, there has
been the beginning of argument and creative disagreement. Murray was
correct that "as we discourse on public affairs, on the affairs of the commonwealth, and particularly on the problem of consensus, we inevitably
have to move upward, as it were, into realms of some theoretical generality—into metaphysics, ethics, theology."[28]

Upward to *whose* theoretical generality? It is precisely this that theocrats
of left, right and center, Protestant militancy, liberal Judeo-Christianism or
"republican religion" would resolve by legislative fiat, perhaps at the expense of minorities. On the one hand, it might be good to "de-religiocify"
issues where possible. Not all meanings, values and ethical arguments have
to be upgraded into "ultimate concern" and formalized as religions by their
proponents or opponents. When everything is religious, nothing is religious.
On the other, when religious meanings are at issue, it is not necessary at
all times to exaggerate distinctives and turn into tribal solipsists. There are
shared meanings, intersecting and overlapping elements of consensus shared
across the subcommunities that make up the larger community. I have
sometimes played with Clyde Kluckhohn's almost playful sounding, paradoxical, but still helpful notion of "conditional absolutes."[29] A pluralist society cannot hope for much more than that. America was not born of more
than that.

When Abraham Lincoln—a theocrat who, as Edmund Wilson said, viewed
the Union as "religious mysticism" and yet was the supreme articulator of
the protestant principle—faced the issue, he kept the "theoretical generality" conditional and relative.[30] He asked citizens not to claim that they
were the expressors of the perfect will of God. They were to seek to discern
that will, so far as they could, remembering that "the Almighty has his own
purposes." That was a practical address to the pluralist issue, enough to get
the argument going. He spoke during the most uncivil moment of our
history, the Civil War. He was looking ahead to the restoration of a republic

of the sort Murray defined, following Thomas Gilby, O.P., as a "civilization
... formed by men locked in argument. From this dialogue the community
becomes a political community."[31] To say more than this at this point would
be impractical and thus beyond my scope.

NOTES

1. Henri Desroche, *Jacob and the Angel: An Essay in Sociologies of Religion*
(Amherst: University of Massachusetts Press, 1973), p. 37.

2. Quoted in ibid., p. 38; see also Joachim Wach, *Sociology of Religion* (Chicago:
University of Chicago Press, 1944), p. 381.

3. Desroche, *Jacob and the Angel*, p. 40.

4. Cited in ibid., p. 40.

5. Mary T. Hanna, *Catholics and American Politics* (Cambridge, Mass.: Harvard
University Press, 1979), p. 40.

6. Ibid., pp. 41–42.

7. Karl Mannheim, *Ideology and Utopia* (New York: Harcourt Brace Jovanovich,
1955), pp. 190 ff.

8. Gellner refers to it as the "true social contract" in Ernst Gellner, *Thought
and Change* (Chicago: University of Chicago Press, 1964), p. 123.

9. Desroche, *Jacob and the Angel*, pp. 36–47.

10. Paul Tillich, *The Protestant Era* (abridged), trans. James Luther Adams (Chicago: Phoenix Books, 1957), p. 163.

11. Alfred North Whitehead, as quoted in Sidney E. Mead, *The Lively Experiment:
The Shaping of Christianity in America* (New York: Harper & Row, 1963), p. 66.

12. Ibid., pp. 65–66.

13. Paul J. Weber, "Examining the Religious Lobbies," *This World* 1 (Winter/
Spring 1982): 97–107.

14. David O. Moberg, *The Great Reversal: Evangelism and Social Concern*, rev.
ed. (Philadelphia: Lippincott, 1977), p. 204.

15. Richard G. Hutcheson, Jr., *Christian Century*, October 7, 1981, p. 994.

16. Ibid. See also his *Mainline Churches and the Evangelicals: A Challenging
Crisis* (Atlanta, Ga.: John Knox Press, 1981).

17. Paul Tillich, *On the Boundary* (New York: Charles Scribner's Sons, 1966),
p. 75.

18. Walter Rauschenbusch, *Christianizing the Social Order* (New York: Macmillan, 1912).

19. Harvey Cox, *The Secular City* (New York: Macmillan, 1965); and Gibson
Winter, *The New Creation as Metropolis* (New York: Macmillan, 1962).

20. H. Richard Niebuhr, *Christ and Culture* (New York: Harper Brothers, 1951),
pp. 45–82.

21. James Barr, *Fundamentalism* (Philadelphia: Westminster, 1978), p. 195.

22. John W. Whitehead and John Conlan, "The Establishment of the Religion of
Secular Humanism and Its First Amendment Implications," *Texas Tech Law Review*
10, no. 1 (Winter 1978): 1–66.

23. Reinhold Niebuhr, *The Children of Light and the Children of Darkness* (New
York: Charles Scribner's Sons, 1944).

24. For a discussion of Ellul see Clifford G. Christians and Jay M. Van Hook, *Jacques Ellul: Interpretive Essays* (Urbana: University of Illinois, 1981); William Stringfellow commented on Ellul in "Kindred Mind and Brother," *Sojourners* 6 (June 1977): 13. For a pacifist-minded approach to politics in prophetic terms, see John Howard Yoder, *The Politics of Jesus* (Grand Rapids, Mich.: Wm. B. Eerdmans, 1972).

25. Rockne McCarthy et al., *Society, State and Schools: A Case for Structural and Confessional Pluralism* (Grand Rapids, Mich.: Wm. B. Eerdmans, 1981).

26. John Courtney Murray, *We Hold These Truths: Catholic Reflections on the American Proposition* (New York: Sheed and Ward, 1981), p. 23.

27. David Tracy, *The Analogical Imagination: Christian Theology and the Culture of Pluralism* (New York: Crossroad, 1981).

28. Murray, *We Hold These Truths*, p. 15.

29. Clyde Kluckhohn, *Culture and Behavior* (Glencoe, Ill.: Free Press, 1962), p. 277.

30. Edmund Wilson, "The Union as Religious Mysticism," in *Eight Essays* (New York: Vintage, 1954).

31. Murray, *We Hold These Truths*, p. 6.

7

Human Rights Theory: A Basis for Pluralism Open to Christian Ethics

JOHN P. LANGAN, S.J.

I

The notion of human rights has come to play an increasing part in political argument and practice as well as in recent moral and political philosophy and in the pronouncements of various church groups. The demand for the protection of human rights achieves a painful intensity in many parts of our world, while in other areas it can be put forward only intermittently and with grave difficulty and risk. In some societies it is an ordinary item in political discourse and reflection, while in others it is an alien and even threatening notion. While it is often linked with individualism and Western values by both its critics and defenders, the notion of human rights can be seen both as a source of community for non-governmental organizations and movements around the world, and as the object of a moral consensus formulated in the United Nations Universal Declaration of Human Rights (1948) and subscribed to by most nations of the world. Despite disagreements as to precisely what claims are to be included in human rights, it is presupposed by all that rights claims have a special urgency and importance. Political disagreements about the effectiveness and the costs of the Carter administration's human rights policy and about the worth of guarantees for human rights in Europe contained in the Helsinki Agreement of 1975 may make us raise doubts about the power of governmental actions to protect human rights abroad. But the widespread concern and hope that these and other initiatives have stirred show that large numbers of people feel that the issue of human rights is not a temporary political ploy but comes close to the heart of the common human enterprise even in an ideologically divided world.

The relationship between human rights theories and Christian ethics is a topic that involves complex systematic and historical considerations, and it is also a matter of pressing interest in our current world situation. So the scope of this paper will have to be limited to laying out some of the sources of tension and harmony between Christian ethics and human rights theories. The result will be a scheme of possibilities for systematic argument rather than a historical account of the relationship, though historical instances and themes will be referred to.

Two preliminary observations should be made. The first is that consideration of the relationship between Christian ethics and human rights theories is not intended to exhaust the possibilities for religious use and religious criticism of human rights theories. Obviously, similar though importantly different, accounts could be offered of the relationships between other traditions of religious ethics and human rights theories. The Christian tradition is, however, the one that is most familiar to me. Of more general importance, it is also the tradition within which and in criticism of which the most influential affirmations of human rights, both practical and theoretical, have been made.

The second observation is that in discussing human rights theories, I shall have in mind theories of the liberal tradition. Again, the primary reason for this restriction is historical. It was within the liberal tradition of political thought and more particularly in the great rebellions and revolutions which both used and were shaped by its categories and values, that the notion of natural or human rights came to serve as the moral category for the formulation of political and legal demands. When proponents of non-liberal values or critics of the various forms of liberalism demand their rights, they are working with a conceptual instrument that has been largely fashioned by the liberal tradition.

It is of particular importance for our enterprise that in the case of the liberal tradition we are not dealing with a moribund set of doctrines that have clearly lost all power to inspire both reflection and allegiance. For we have in the last decade witnessed a vigorous restatement of liberal principles and values in American political philosophy.[1] In that restatement, the notion of rights has been given an important and, in some respects, fundamental place. Thus Robert Nozick begins his influential *Anarchy, State, and Utopia* with the bald affirmation: "Individuals have rights, and there are things no person or group may do to them without violating their rights."[2] The notion of rights does not figure prominently in the major works of John Rawls, *A Theory of Justice*, but most of the human rights of traditional theory are included in what Rawls speaks of as a system of liberties.[3] Also, Ronald Dworkin has offered an important interpretation of Rawls' work. According to him, the deep theory behind Rawls' use of the social contract and his account of the original position for the choice of principles of justice must be based on a theory of natural rights.[4] On the other hand, the notion of rights plays an explicit and important part in the closely argued neo-Kantian work of Alan Gewirth on ethical theory, *Reason and Morality*.[5] Important presentations of the theory of rights have been offered by A. I. Melden[6] and Joel Feinberg.[7] Liberalism, then, like Christian ethics, has to be regarded as a complex and living tradition, capable of change, yet exhibiting certain persistent traits or tendencies.

I do not wish, however, to restrict my reflections on human rights theories to those theories which stand clearly within the liberal tradition. For one thing the United Nations Universal Declaration of Human Rights, by reason of its heavy emphasis on social and economic rights, is broader in its scope than the liberal tradition in most of its forms. Rather, I propose to regard human rights theories in the liberal tradition as the central cases which most clearly reveal characteristic features of human rights theories in general. Foremost among these features is the standing of human rights as universal moral claims. As I argue elsewhere, human rights (in contrast to rights that belong to human persons) are rights that every human person has simply by virtue of being a human person.[8] They are then universal and "natural," that is, they are possessed by all human persons prior to and independently of their acknowledgment by particular societies. They have moral urgency, but they are not simply absolute rights in the sense of being exceptionless (though there may be some absolute rights in this sense such as the right not to be tortured). I am in agreement with the position, though not with the terminology, of Joel Feinberg, who has written:

A human right must be held to be absolute in the sense that rights to life, liberty, and the pursuit of happiness are most plausibly interpreted as absolute, namely, as "ideal directives" to relevant parties to "do their best" for the values involved. . . . If a human right is absolute only in the sense in which an ideal directive is absolute, then it is satisfied whenever it is given the serious and respectful consideration it deserves, even when that consideration is followed by a reluctant invasion of its corresponding interest.[9]

I would also be in agreement with the two tests that Maurice Cranston proposes for determining whether certain universal claims are human rights: paramount importance and practicability.[10] I take issue, however, with the use of these tests to exclude the social and economic claims put forward in the second half of the Universal Declaration of Human Rights from the range of human rights. I should add that I believe that serious arguments in favor of recognizing social and economic rights can be advanced from within the liberal tradition of political philosophy and that I do not wish the central place given in the present paper to the liberal conception of human rights to be taken as excluding claims to certain social and economic goods from the range of human rights. One of the crucial difficulties that Feinberg and Cranston have with social and economic rights is that there does not seem to be an assignable person with the duty to satisfy these rights. This difficulty can, I would argue, be met by two moves: first, by insisting on the duty of mutual aid,[11] and second, by interpreting the duties corresponding to various social and economic rights as capable of being fulfilled, not directly by the provision of goods and services by individuals but by the establishment of just institutions in the society.[12]

In what follows, I shall speak of human rights theory. By this I mean a statement of the principal human rights together with those reasons that serve to provide immediate justification for a particular listing of human rights, indications of what principles are to have priority in the adjudication of conflicts of rights, and indications of the general outlines of the kind of social institutions that are required in order to satisfy human rights. This admittedly imprecise account is intended to divide human rights theories from more comprehensive theories of morality, politics and law on the one hand and from specific policy conclusions and recommendations on the other.

II

It is worth reminding ourselves at the outset that the Christian churches were far from enthusiastic when human rights demands first shook the political order of the *ancien régime*. The French Revolution, while it enjoyed some clerical support in its early stages, came to be seen as involving the rejection of religion as well as the affirmation of human rights. In many religious circles throughout the duration of the nineteenth century in France, in England, in Germany, and in Italy, revolution, secularization of church properties, atheism and the cult of reason, and the affirmation of human rights were all thought to be linked together and were all thought to be worthy of rejection and condemnation. Aversion to the "red fool fury of the Seine" and to the principles of 1789 in both their political and religious aspects continued to be a defining characteristic of the European Right until the Second World War and was strongly felt by both Protestants and Catholics. But it was the privileged position of Roman Catholicism in France that came most directly under attack. The French religious historian Bernard Plongeron has argued that the positive or negative response of national churches within Catholicism varied with their status as privileged majority (France) or oppressed minority (Holland).[13] We may also note the sympathy with which the Church of England regarded the French émigré clergy, a sympathy which, as E. R. Norman has pointed out, manifested "the need to give public support to religion, even if it was Catholic and foreign."[14]

Retrospectively, we are likely to feel that the churches and their leaders failed to distinguish between the defense of their privileges and their witness to religious values. But we should remember that some of their critics and opponents also failed to make this distinction and were clearly intent on the destruction of traditional Christianity in all its forms. But the French Revolution raised a challenge to the entire traditional order of Christendom, a challenge that was both secularizing and violent and that provided general reasons beyond the attack on the church itself for Christians to regard the doctrine of the Rights of Men with suspicion and even hatred. The new society of free thought and free trade, whether it was inaugurated by political violence or by technological innovation, was regarded by conservative Christians and by the leaders of established churches well into the twentieth century as destructive of traditional values of community and order. The point that I would like to make here is that those theories and those churches that rejected the principles of 1789, among which the demand for human rights was central, were interested not merely in protecting the position of the churches but also in preserving a certain form of pre-industrial society and its values, values which they took to be a social expression of Christian principles, an expression that was not merely legitimate but that was uniquely normative.[15]

In response to this negative reaction, those who promoted the principles of 1789 as well as those who wished to move beyond them (notably, but not exclusively, the Marxists) came to regard the continued affirmation of Christian faith as simply incompatible with the acceptance of a doctrine of human rights. This view is not so much a matter of showing logical connections as it is of suspecting links between certain social influences and traditional patterns of thought and evaluation. Accordingly, as the churches and many of their prominent and devoted members have taken up a variety of political and ideological stances, the grounds for this alleged incompatibility have become weaker and less persuasive. The mutual suspicion that marked relations between traditional Christians and advocates of the Rights of Man has either yielded to a mutual acknowledgment of rights (which is, in effect, a victory for human rights) or been transformed into a conflict between religion and secularism which, as in the Soviet Union and Eastern Europe, involved an effective restriction of human rights by the enemies of religion. The original Christian opposition to human rights theories on the ground of their secularizing and revolutionary character and their threat to traditional society has become outmoded as even established churches have accommodated to pluralism and secularization, as new agendas have been set for political struggle and as traditional society has been replaced by industrial and post-industrial society.[16] A contribution not to be overlooked in the resolution of this normative conflict within Western culture came from an unlikely quarter: the ultimately unsuccessful assault on both traditional Christian values and human rights by the National Socialists in Germany and their allies in Europe and elsewhere.

Interwoven with the Christian rejection of human rights theories on the ground of their disruptive and secularizing character was ecclesiastical opposition to freedom of religion and the removal of various forms of religious discrimination, such as religious tests for office holders. The assertion of religious freedom in the context of European Christendom can be seen both as a claim to a specific right and as a proposal to alter the character of the entire society. Accordingly, the opposition to religious freedom can be looked at in specific terms or as part of a general repudiation of a society whose legal and political structure is to be built on the recognition of human rights. Thus, the comprehensive intransigence of Pius IX in the face of human rights demands, as this was summed up in the Syllabus of Errors (1864), illustrates both the rejection of religious liberty as a specific right and the condemnation of the entire liberal picture of society. Among the condemned propositions of the syllabus was the denial that "civil liberty for any religious sect and the granting to all of full right to express any kind of opinion and thought whatever, openly and publicly, conduces to the easer corruption of the morals and minds of people and the spread of the disease of indifferentism."[17] What can be seen at work here is a concern for the public effects of freedom of religion and freedom of expression. But it is worth bearing in mind that Christians can be opposed to specific items in lists of human rights as well as to the concept of human rights in general. They can also, as the history of the American South evidences, be opposed to the extension of human rights to specific groups, even while they themselves take satisfaction in constitutional guarantees of their own human rights. Thus in both these ways there can be and have been more specific reasons for either Christian objections to human rights theories or at least for Christian discomfort with such theories.

A current example of this point is the difficulty that Roman Catholicism experiences in dealing with the demands of women for equal treatment and equal opportunity. It is relatively easy to show that the denial of ordination to women is not a violation of their human rights, since it can be argued both that a claim to ordination cannot be a human right because it is not a claim to something to which every human person is entitled by virtue of being a human person and because the good claimed is not an appropriate object of rights claims by either men or women. Thus it can be maintained, as Pope John Paul II holds, that the denial of ordination to women does not violate their human rights.[18] But the argument would be more difficult if we were to consider the matter in terms of the right of women and others to non-discriminatory treatment or to equality of opportunity. In reply, it can be argued that the church itself is not subject to the requirements of human rights doctrine, which is intended to apply to the actions and responsibilities of states or of civil societies and that fundamentally different considerations should be governing either for the church itself (such as divine law) or for religious groups generally (such as respect for tradition and cultural pluralism) or for voluntary associations.

The point of this example, regardless of how it may be resolved, is that it is possible for Christians to have religiously based objections to specific human rights. Difficulties of this sort can be addressed either by offering arguments to show that there is not a right of the type under criticism or that there are overriding considerations which stand in the way of acknowledging the right. Alternatively, one can argue that the particular elements in the religious tradition which are incompatible with acceptance of the specific right should be modified or reinterpreted, perhaps in the light of deeper or more comprehensive values in the religious tradition itself. These are, of course, moves that aim to bring about a harmony between human rights theory and the normative demands of a specific form of Christian tradition.

The effort to achieve a harmony between human rights theory and the norms of a particular Christian community with respect to such a specific issue as equal access to church office for women is one example of the difficult task of dealing with the normative dissonances that arise when people live simultaneously within different communities (domestic, religious, political, economic, social), each of which brings with it its own set of practices and institutions with their implicit and explicit norms. Recognizing the diversity and accepting the possibility of normative dissonances is a crucial step for individuals in acquiring the ability to function with effectiveness and equanimity in a complex and differentiated society. We learn to expect that private corporations will not operate by the same rules as government agencies, that banks will have different norms for decisions than parents, that churches can be both more participatory and more authoritarian than governments. The possibility of normative dissonance is, I would argue, inescapable whenever there are distinct social institutions or communities; the further possibility that this normative dissonance can produce significant political conflict is present whenever there is no consensus on the effective subordination of one institution or community to another.

Now, whenever the Christian community has argued for "the liberty of the church," whether this argument is made by Thomas à Becket or Martin Niemoller, by Mennonites or Huguenots, and whenever argument is made without arguing for a theoretic approach to political questions, it is in effect an argument for institutional pluralism and for the possibilities of normative dissonance and conflict which that implies.

This position does not always fit well with the aversion to internal political conflict which the Church took over from classical political philosophy and with the conception of a unitary political regime directing its subordinates to a common good that can be found in the political theory of Thomas Aquinas. But it was this position which Lord Acton pointed to as the main contribution of the church to the cause of human freedom. The insistence on the liberty of the church had a special potential for generating political conflict in the case of Roman Catholicism, precisely because of the visible authority structure of that church and its international connections. This became manifest as early as the investiture controversy in the eleventh century and continued through a long series of struggles with governments aiming at consolidating their hold on power and with revolutionary movements striving to alter the basic institutional framework of society. This struggle to protect its liberties and often enough its privileges as well impelled Catholicism to enter political conflict in the defense of institutional pluralism long before the Church was ready to accept or legitimate either political or religious pluralism. Something similar holds for the Calvinist or Reformed tradition as well, for in that tradition also the religious community was willing to function as a political actor in opposition to the government if necessary.

The acceptance of political pluralism came gradually with the increasing secularization of political society which implied, among other things, that political struggles were less likely to involve explicitly religious issues and with increasing acceptance in the Western world of such human rights norms as freedom of speech and freedom of association which provided that protection for the development of political pluralism as a continuing feature of the policy. The transition phase, however, often involved direct attacks on religious influence on social life and on traditional religious sources of power. Frequently, as in revolutionary France or revolutionary Russia or revolutionary Mexico, it saw the virtual elimination of the church and of lay politicians closely linked to the church from the political arena. The church reacted by aligning itself with extremely conservative movements and even with external adversaries of the new regime. Sometimes, as in the early years of the Third Republic in France, the church could be both an adversary of a political system which accepted pluralism and at the same time be a political actor practicing political pluralism itself. Many countries have had political parties organized on a confessional or quasi-confessional basis (such as clerical versus anti-clerical). This usually implies an acceptance of pluralism at least for those outside the church or religious community that supports the party. But it may also be accompanied by an expectation that members of the religious groups will support the chosen party, and political pluralism within the religious community may be frowned upon. There can also be situations in which one party and its allies are perceived to be consistently inimical to or even doctrinally incompatible with the views and interests of the church. So active membership in the Communist party in a country such as Italy is commonly regarded as incompatible with active membership in the Catholic church and at one time brought excommunication with it. Such a response puts a definite limit to political pluralism, but on the ground of the incompatibility of a given political party or doctrine with a particular religious tradition. Where there is no ground for such a judgment of incompatibility, both Catholicism and mainline Protestant denominations have come to accept and to respect the political pluralism of their members and even to appeal to this condition as setting a normative limit to the politically sensitive positions that may be adopted by the churches.

No major Christian church today is likely to be comfortable with the thought that it is the religious epiphenomenon or parasite upon some political movement or party, the thought given classic expression in the gibe that the Church of England was simply the Tory party at prayer. Discomfort can arise from a sense that the church is failing to reach out to or to remain in contact with significant parts of the population which it is its mission to serve, that in this regard the church is failing to be catholic or universal. Discomfort also arises from the suspicion that in such a situation the church is being made the instrument of some non-religious cause or project. This, of course, is a consideration that would weigh heavily even with those religious groups that never set out to include all elements in the larger society that were sectarian rather than catholic.

Against these lines of reflection which suggest the religious defects in a failure to accept pluralism, we should set the very strong tendency in contemporary liberation theology, both Catholic and Protestant, to argue that it is imperative for Christians to interpret the Gospel in terms of a political hermeneutic and that this interpretation will overcome the ideological distortions which protect the interests of oppressors and which blind people to the political content of the Gospel. The political program which faith requires is one that anticipates the Kingdom of God in which there is a community sharing the fruits of its labors on a non-discriminatory basis and enabling all of its members harmoniously to achieve the fullness of life. This, of course, is an objective which can allow for considerable disagreement about the means to its attainment and which can allow for political conflict and pluralism. The general assumption is that an authentic proclamation of the Gospel will direct its bearers to a political position that is universalist and egalitarian in its aspirations but that is resolute in the face of conflict. In this perspective, genuine political opposition to a socialist reordering of society is not a normal feature of political life which may be expected to continue indefinitely, but it is regarded as a temporary blindness that requires explanation. Liberation theology, traditional Christian theology and Marxism all have elements in their belief systems which stand in the way of accepting political pluralism. I would suggest that the crucial factor in whether a given form of liberation theology accepts or rejects political pluralism is whether its understanding of the nature of politics in the post-revolutionary situation allows for the possibility of significant political disagreement within the revolutionary party itself. The latter condition may, of course, fall far short of constitutional protection for the rights and liberties of dissidents, counter-revolutionaries, opposing political parties; but it seems to be an indispensable minimum for developing an acceptance of political pluralism as a legitimate phenomenon in a post-revolutionary world. We should also remember that no society finds all conceivable forms of political pluralism to be worth protecting or respecting. Normally, a willingness to accept the broad outlines of the current settlement (whether this be the settlement of 1558 or 1688 or 1832, or 1911 in the case of England, or the outcome of the Revolutionary War and the Civil War in America) is a necessary condition before a political group can function as a legitimate player in a pluralistic system.

III

But in addition to both general and specific Christian objections to the content of human rights theories, we also have to reckon with three lines of argument that have to do with the form of such theories, that is, with their use of the notion of rights and the practice of claiming one's rights as a primary guide to understanding the moral problems and demands of our life in society. The first two of these involve the choice of other notions and other experiences as paradigmatic for the reading of the moral demands of social life, at least for Christians. These two lines of argument can be put forward in various ways so that the effects on the theory and practice of human rights are quite different. Thus, it can be maintained that consideration of human rights is to be seen as epistematically dependent on conclusions about some more fundamental notion. Or it can be argued that there are pragmatic and utilitarian grounds for insisting on the priority of some other notion, which it would be more socially desirable or more religiously authentic to take as fundamental. The argument for the alternative notion can be taken to establish the view that human rights claims and the practices in which they function are secondary or are unnecessary or even harmful.

The two main notions that can be proposed as prior to the concept of human rights are obligation and grace. With the first of these, we come up against what Leo Strauss has argued is the distinguishing characteristic of liberalism, which he defines as "that political doctrine which regards as the fundamental political fact the rights, as distinguished from the duties, of man and which identifies the function of the state with the protection or the safeguarding of those rights."[19] Strauss presents Thomas Hobbes as the founder of liberalism because of his proposal to derive all our duties from "the fundamental and inalienable right of self-preservation."[20] Strauss also points to the contrast between Hobbes and pre-modern theorists of natural law with their emphasis on natural duties rather than natural rights. The priority of rights to duties can be attacked on various grounds. In its Hobbesian form it seems to involve treating the moral and political realms as instruments for the individual's self-preservation and the pursuit of his or her interests. From a political standpoint, insistence on the priority of rights increases both demands and constraints on the political institutions of society and is likely to be unacceptable both to Burkean conservatives and to contemporary neo-conservatives. From a theological standpoint it seems to involve an understanding of the human situation as one in which, rather than standing under God's commands and an obligation to do what is right, we are first of all subjects of legitimate demands. (There can also be theological objections to even the supposition of a state of nature in which human beings are not subject to basic moral restraints on their action; but this, I would suggest, is properly an objection to Hobbes' account of the state of nature rather than strictly to the priority of rights to duties.)

The thesis that the priority of rights to duties involves a misconception of our human situation under divine law can lead us to overlook the point that human rights theories are primarily designed to regulate the things that we do to each other rather than to define our relationship to ultimate reality. Thus, for instance, Nozick presents human rights as side constraints on what we may do to each other.[21] A properly constructed human rights theory should leave open both the question of the nature of ultimate reality and the question of the nature of human motivation so that it is not committed to either the materialism or the egoism of Hobbes. It should be open to the possibility that our human situation is best understood as one of communal solidarity under obedience to God; but, precisely because it is intended to regulate the relations of people with each other who may, for various reasons, not accept this account of the human situation, a sound human rights theory should be independent of such disputed religious views. Of course, as the example of Hobbes illustrates, a human rights theory may be embedded in a larger philosophical or theological system, important elements of which may be incompatible with Christian faith and tradition and thus open to criticism. On the other hand, it may be appropriate to incorporate a sound human rights theory into a theological system or to present it from a theological viewpoint which shows its compatability with or derivability from more basic values and norms in the Christian (or other religious) tradition. Thus, to take a specific example, Christians can argue for religious freedom not merely as an instance of freedom of thought and opinion or as a consequence of the dignity of the human person but also as a consequence of the freedom appropriate to the act of faith itself. They can also reject arguments for religious freedom on the basis of skepticism or agnosticism. On a deeper level, Christian thinkers may criticize alternative approaches to the understanding of human rights on the ground that these approaches make use of premises that are ultimately incompatible, not merely with Christian views but also with the principles of a sound human rights theory itself. Or they may argue that alternative approaches simply leave the principles of human rights theory ungrounded.

The position that I am taking here is one that acknowledges a relative systematic independence between human rights theory on the one hand and Christian ethics, anthropology and theology on the other. It allows the possibility of a variety of different ways of providing a systematic basis for human rights theory. Since these different ways may be contradictory to each other, this is an unsatisfactory and incomplete outcome for minds drawn to clarity about the ultimate truth of things; but it is, I believe, congruent with the incompleteness and lack of perspicuity characteristic of our affirmations in faith and also with the pluralism and diversity of belief characteristic of the actual situation in which we have to live together. It is also my belief, as I shall argue in a subsequent section of this essay, that religious forms of human rights theory can make a positive contribution to the proper understanding of the content of a sound doctrine of human rights.

The considerations that I have just advanced with regard to the view that in the human situation obligations are prior to rights apply also to the view that gift and grace are prior to rights, a view which is even more likely to rest on theological premises which are not acceptable to significant sections of civil society. But we should also be aware that secular forms of these views can be put forward for social, psychological and philosophical reasons. Thus there can be arguments that the experience of being loved is necessary for the development of benevolence and of the moral point of view or that there is an irreducible and inescapable element of obligation in our awareness of ourselves as moral persons. It is not my intention to reject such arguments, since I believe that they point to important truths about ourselves and that they bring with them both a deeper understanding of the context within which we advance rights claims and of certain limits to the practice of claiming and exercising rights. Such considerations can provide reasons for our renunciation of rights in certain situations. They serve to remind us of the non-absolute character of rights claims, the possibility that they can be overridden by more pressing claims and moral demands. For there are important and fundamental aspects of human life, having to do with family and religious community, with mutual love and ultimate hope, in which we are no longer in the circumstances of justice and to which the notion of rights has only a limited though important application.

These considerations, however true they may be, should not blind us to the essential function of human rights practices in establishing fences to protect the free self-determination of persons who are in the circumstances of justice[22] and in providing floors to ensure their minimal well-being, and to the parallel functions of human rights theory and political debate in determining where and how these fences and floors are to be maintained. Human rights of various types realized through institutional patterns are intended to provide minimal public protection for people precisely in those situations where reliance on generosity and goodwill, on communal solidarity and shared values and beliefs is or is likely to be inadequate. Therefore, they need to be conceived in relative independence from the beliefs and practices of communities that may be more fundamental or more ultimate but that are in our social experience particularistic and liable to be either exclusive or coercively inclusive. For this reason philosophers and social theorists as well as some theologians have usually based their theories of human rights either on the consent of individuals conceived in isolation from particular communities (as in social contract theories) or on a certain conception of human nature presumed to be applicable to all individuals (as in natural law or natural rights theories) or on some combination of these two. As I observed earlier, human rights theories may be incorporated in larger systematic wholes which may be of considerable theological or philosophical or social scientific interest and value. But the essential function of human rights practice and theory is jeopardized if acceptance of one or the other of these larger wholes is regarded as essential to the practice of human rights. Thus a theological claim that grace and gift are more fundamental than rights can be important for our understanding of human nature and destiny and for our living of the moral life in Christian terms, but it is not to be treated as essential to our acceptance of the practice and theory of human rights.

I suggest that the situation of human rights theory is comparable to the situation of the principles of what Alan Donagan refers to as common morality or Hebrew-Christian morality. Donagan observes that "the middle part of moral theory . . . is far better understood than either its application to highly specific cases or the establishment of its fundamental principles."[23] Clearly, there are numerous differences both in the effort of various thinkers to integrate notions of human rights into systematic world views and to provide a fundamental theoretical justification for them and in the application of human rights claims to the resolution of particular policy questions and to the transformation of political and economic structures. But we should keep in view the high level of support (even if we suspect that some of it may only be lip service) that the Universal Declaration of Human Rights along with previous and parallel statements has enjoyed. In an ideologically divided world in which national, racial and religious disputes continue with vigor, this sort of consensus, even without foundational agreement, is an important merit.

IV

A final source of Christian difficulty with human rights theory is that it seems to imply a mistaken order of values. Thus in the Universal Declaration one can point to guarantees for freedom of thought and of expression, freedom of assembly, the right to own property, and "the right to a standard of living adequate for the health and well-being of himself and his family, including food, clothing, housing and medical care and necessary social services." Now it is affirmed in most forms of human rights theory that claims to these goods have a special moral urgency. But it seems that these are not the most important human goods, which are such things as truth, morally virtuous activity, doing the will of God, love, communal solidarity and union with God. Not merely are the objects of various human rights of less worth than the most important human goods; they can even be obstacles to the attainment of these goods. For instance, freedom of expression and freedom of the press can promote the spread of false beliefs and of ignoble desires, as in Western consumerist and materialist societies. Thus the statement of human rights in most forms of human rights theory should be regarded as conveying a mistaken or at least misleading ranking of human goods, and the practice of human rights should be regarded as threatening to the attainment of the most important human goods.

Something like this line of argument has appealed to both religious and non-religious critics of liberal society who are distressed by its toleration of mediocrity and its withdrawal from heroic and sacred values. One should note that this line of objection assumes that we are able to make correct judgments about the relative importance and worth of values of different kinds. This assumption would not be shared by all secular defenders of liberal conceptions of human rights, many of whom have a non-cognitivist theory of value, but it would be shared by most Christian defenders of human rights. For such Christians, among whom I would count myself, it is not possible to overturn this objection by taking an agnostic approach to questions of value.

In reply to this line of objection to human rights theories, it is useful to recall the two tests for human rights that were mentioned earlier: namely, paramount importance and practicability. The paramount importance of a certain good does not by itself entail that people will have a human right to the good in question, unless that good is one which it is practicable for public acknowledgment and (if appropriate) public action to guarantee. For there are goods, however important they may be, whose attainment by human persons cannot be guaranteed by acknowledgment of them as objects of rights. Recognition of this point underlies Jefferson's inclusion of a right to "the pursuit of happiness" among the "unalienable rights" with which the Creator has endowed us. Happiness is a higher good than the pursuit of happiness (except perhaps for process theologians), but proposals to guarantee this higher good for all run afoul of the problem of practicability. The right to pursue happiness can be respected in both negative and positive ways, by forbearing from certain kinds of interference and coercion and by providing certain basic goods and services such as education. But it seems beyond the capabilities of both governmental action and private cooperation and forbearance to guarantee happiness as a human right.

One might also argue that public recognition of a right to a certain sort of good is not the undertaking of an unfulfillable commitment, but is rather an inappropriate extension of public power and responsibility and an interference with appropriate ways of attaining the good. This seems to be the line that Maritain follows with regard to religious freedom of conscience. Thus he writes:

The first of these rights is that of the human person to make its way towards its eternal destiny along the path which its conscience has recognized as the path indicated by God. With respect to God and truth, one has not the right to choose according to his own whim any path whatsoever, he must choose the true path, insofar as it is in his power to know it. But with respect to the State, to the temporal community and to the temporal power, he is free to choose his religious path at his own risk, his conscience is a natural inviolable right.[24]

Maritain wishes to maintain both existence and knowability of a realm of religious truths and the teaching authority of the Catholic church at the same time that he defends the human right to religious freedom; a right which he regards as having its roots in Christian philosophy.[25] His basic strategy for reconciling these views is to distinguish between two ways in which we are related to a good, one in which the good imposes an obligation on us and one in which we are free to pursue the good as we see fit, and then to hold that the first is appropriate in the religious realm and that the second is appropriate in the political realm. This is a strategy which would allow a combination of religious authoritarianism and political liberalism and would preserve traditional Roman Catholicism in the age after Christendom. It is also a strategy which builds on the traditional Catholic denial of the omnicompetence of the state and affirmation of the freedom of the church. It also proceeds not so much from an affirmation of the freedom of the individual as from an elimination of appropriate spheres of action for distinct institutions that are taken to be fundamental and irreplaceable aspects of the human situation. These are the state by reason of humanity's political nature and the church by reason of God's plan of salvation. This strategy is of particular interest since it does not proceed from the view that the highest goods are unattainable and/or unknowable, but it insists that it is not the business of the state or the public order to undertake to provide them. This approach would enable us to see the continued vitality of the church as a support to freedom of conscience and of religion rather than as a potential threat to these freedoms. It has the further attraction of making the protection of the rights of individuals at the same time a matter of institutional concern and interest. In our contemporary context we can see that this approach provides an interesting framework for understanding aspects of the defense of human rights in Poland and in Latin America. But at the same time it may obscure our understanding of situations where the religious freedom of individuals is threatened by religious institutions and by social pressures as well as the quite different situations where religious institutions do not have a pervasive influence on a culture or society. A more fundamental criticism of this approach is that in the understanding of human rights as properly universal, we should not rely on institutional developments and distinctions which are proper to the Western tradition.

The general line of argument with which we began this section has another important aspect to it beyond the charge that human rights theory protects values of lesser worth, namely, that it allows and condones damage to higher values. Usually this attack focuses on the misuse of human freedom which is protected by traditional civil liberties and the rights of the person. So the defender of human rights theory can reply by stressing the value of human freedom in a theological perspective, a value which is of central importance in a free-will theodicy, a theodicy which vindicates the benevolence and wisdom of God precisely by urging the greater worth of a world in which human beings freely choose to serve God and to act virtuously in comparison with a world in which both physical and moral evils are avoided.[26] More specifically, one can argue that freedom is an essential aspect of certain specific goods, such as faith, marital fidelity, sacrificial love and right action in general, which are unattainable without allowing the possibility of failure and the misuse of freedom. This consideration will not apply to such goods as truth and communal solidarity, in which there is no conceptual link between freedom of action and the realization of the good in question. Alternatively, one can point to the evils of coercion in bringing people to higher goods in general. Or more positively, one could offer a utilitarian argument that the benefits in protecting freedoms which can be misused outweigh the costs present in the evils that are brought about by the misuse of these freedoms. One can also argue that other means of preventing the misuse of freedom such as persuasion and various kinds of social change can achieve a better balance of good over evil than a resort to coercive methods, which deny or restrict those human rights, the exercise of which can involve a misuse of human freedom. It should be stressed that these arguments can be used without resorting to skeptical or agnostic premises about values, which we can presume are unacceptable to proponents of Christian ethics. It may be that those arguments do not yield clearly correct conclusions; but that is a difficulty they share with nearly all forms of theodicy which take seriously the multitude of evils in the world.

Those human rights which are claims for goods which are necessary for human survival (food, clothing, housing, health care) or for effective functioning in one's culture (education, information, economic security) are not to be understood as implying that these are the highest goods even in the material order. The case for rights of this type does not depend on the intrinsic worth of the goods claimed but rather on their universal necessity for human beings who wish to live fully human lives. For this reason the justification of these rights usually brings with it a demand for participation in social and political processes or for a basic equality or treatment and respect or for a real opportunity to exercise one's freedom in society. David

Hollenbach puts the matter in more negative terms in his study of the Catholic human rights tradition, *Claims in Conflict*, when he points to "marginalization or lack of participation" as a "primary criterion" in our judgments about violations of human dignity and then he proposes that the "lack of adequate nourishment, housing, education, and political self-determination" be seen as "a consequence of this lack of participation."[27] The goods that are claimed in demands for social and economic rights need not be prized for themselves, but are to be valued because they save people from evils that afflict them and enable them to strive for goals that are commonly taken to make human life worthwhile and enjoyable. It is a misreading of most revolutionary movements that demand basic economic necessities to see them as purely or even prodominantly materialistic in their aspirations. The materialist tendency in such movements is important, however, as a rebuttal of suggestions that the most valuable human goods are easily attainable without regard to a satisfactory provision of those material goods that are necessary for human survival with dignity and decency and that free persons from subjection to the wishes and whims of the powerful. The moral urgency of claims for such goods does not derive from a mistaken judgment that they are the most intrinsically valuable objects of human striving but from a sense of their indispensability for the attainment of intrinsically valuable objects by embodied and interdependent creatures such as we are. Christians should in fact be prepared to read such claims as compatible with acknowledgment of our creaturely situation of need and interdependence, even when this is not fully or clearly expressed by those making the demands.

In these ways it is possible to defend the principal claims of a comprehensive human rights theory from charges that such theories fail to evaluate properly or to respect the highest or most fully human goods.

V

Thus far we have concentrated mainly on potential challenges to human rights theory from Christian ethics, some of which have been made actual in the course of theoretical discussions or of ecclesial pronouncements. It may also be helpful to indicate at least some of the principal ways in which human rights theory can be attractive to and useful for Christian religious groups and those who formulate their stance toward social movements and institutions. Then we will also indicate some of the principal ways in which Christian ethics can influence and modify human rights theories. Many of the points to be made have been anticipated in our considerations of Christian challenges to human rights theory.

The principles of human rights theory first showed their attractiveness to religious communities that because of their minority status were in a position to regard religious freedom not as a challenge to Christian society but as emancipation from an inferior status. Thus the Catholics of Maryland and of Holland welcomed the legal establishment of religious freedom.[28] Of course, this acceptance was in the interest of the local religious community and its members; it could also be seen as a continuation of the church's demand for its own freedom from secular restraints and penalties. Thus acceptance of religious freedom could be seen as simply one moment of the notorious thesis-hypothesis distinction, in which Roman Catholicism would claim freedom for itself before proceeding under more favorable circumstances to restrict the freedom of others.[29] We should not, however, adopt an unduly negative attitude toward any church's acceptance of religious freedom because it is to its advantage. For one thing, it is implicit in any human rights approach to the organization of society that there be a general congruence between the rights of persons and their legitimate interests. Furthermore, the acceptance of religious freedom on grounds of institutional and personal advantage can provide an opportunity for further learning in a social situation structured according to human rights principles and for a deepened and more altruistic commitment to these principles as they are internalized and extended. Something along these lines does seem to have happened within American Catholicism.

Second, the principles of human rights theory commend themselves to Christians and others as an appropriate way of achieving a mutual acknowledgment of just claims in a pluralistic and largely secular society, in which appeals to the norms of one's own religious tradition are unlikely to be persuasive to a majority of one's fellow citizens. In this regard I find instructive the change from the reliance on a natural law of theory of an ideal society to a concern with human rights which David Hollenbach points to as occurring at the time of Vatican II and the issuance of John XXIII's encyclical, *Pacem in Terris* and which he regards as indicative of Catholicism's acceptance of a pluralistic world.[30] For the language of human rights, with its combination of secularizing demands and regard for human dignity, proves an apt vehicle for both Christian acceptance of a post-Christian world and a critical insistence of a humanizing political agenda. This way of thinking about the use of human rights language also accords with Hollenbach's characterization of the most recent development of the Catholic human rights tradition as "a dialogically universalist ethic rather than a natural law ethic."[31]

Third, human rights theory provides a way for Christian thinkers and religious communities to acknowledge and to share the moral claims being advanced by those who for various reasons have stood outside the Christian tradition and to enter into creative and collaborative praxis with these people in a way that breaks through previous religious and ideological divisions. Such considerations seem to me to be operative in the ecumenical character of church involvement with the cause of human rights in Latin America, a cause which has brought with it a sympathetic interest in many of the demands made by Marxists and a willingness to act in various ways for the protection of various dissident groups in defiance of military regimes dedicated to the cause of national security. Here we can see human rights theory along with such other crucial considerations as the Christian option for the poor helping to justify a historical reversal of social alliances for the Christian churches and particularly for Catholicism. Similar considerations in the arena of international economic affairs strengthen the churches' tendency to support Third World economic demands.

Fourth, as we have already hinted in several places, human rights theory is attractive to both religious and political dissidents, many of whom are now to be found in mainline denominations and established churches. It serves as an appropriate instrument for the criticism of both oppressive political regimes and traditional ecclesial institutions. One reason for this is that a comprehensive human rights theory articulates moral demands that have been of central importance to revolutionary and liberalist movements in the Western and westernizing world since 1789. Despite Marx's own dismissal of the language of human rights as bourgeois ideology, the content, especially of social and economic rights, has been an object of central concern to many Marxist movements and thinkers, and the content of civil and political rights has received at least lip service from many Marxist governments. Also, the language of human rights is implicitly internationalistic, a characteristic that it shares with classical Marxism and that can be used in criticism of traditional forms of colonialism and aggressive nationalism. At the same time, it retains its original use in liberal theory as a way of criticizing abuses of political power and religious intolerance. It is virtually impossible to find a government anywhere in the world that is immune from criticism on human rights grounds, when these are articulated in comprehensive terms. Treatment of refugees and of minority groups, of guest workers and dissidents all provide opportunity for human rights criticism of the performance of governments and of other social institutions even in advanced countries with social democratic governments. This should not cause us to overlook violations of human rights by revolutionary groups, especially those that use terrorist techniques and tactics. The crucial point is that the language of human rights, even when, as in the Marxist tradition, it is not the preferred vehicle for social criticism, or when, as in the Christian tradition, it is not the original language for the expression of social aspirations, is available as an instrument both for building coalitions across ideological and religious divides and for legitimating criticism of those who misuse power.

Fifth, beyond its critical use in political conflicts, human rights theory also holds out the promise of providing a means of communications with regard to moral and political values that can unite those who have previously been divided along lines of sex, race, class, creed, party, region or language in a common acknowledgment of their humanity and their shared situation of dignity and vulnerability. It offers the hope for restricting the savagery of those forms of oppression and conflict that involve the denial of the full humanity of the adversaries. By focusing our attentions on those just claims which persons make precisely by virtue of their humanity, it turns us from preoccupation with ancient wrongs and historic disputes to matters that can be discussed in a language that is in principle available to all. It offers the possibility of a higher viewpoint from which even the actions of conflicting religious and ideological communities can be assessed and of a language that does not bear the marks of a religiously divisive past. Accordingly, it makes a strong appeal to those tendencies in Christian thought which aspire to universal reconciliation and universal liberation, and which aim at the transcendence of historic conflicts and which are sensitive to abuses of political, economic and religious power. It also appeals to those tendencies and schools in Christian ethics which affirm the harmony of secular moral insight and moral values with the demands of the Gospel. The attractions of a higher or universal viewpoint expressible in secular terms are not, however, to be easily obtained by any form of Christian ethics that wishes to retain its religious distinctiveness and that wishes to do more with human rights theory than to acknowledge it as an external constraint or to endorse it as an external good.

VI

But, in order to avoid leaving you with the impression that such a systematic integration would be a one-sided accommodation of Christian ethics to an inherently secular human rights theory, I would like to conclude by indicating some of the major ways in which Christian ethics can complement or challenge human rights theory.

First, it can stress the limited and instrumental character of many human rights. This possibility is available to a sound human rights theory which acknowledges the possibility that rights can on occasion be overridden. But it is often true that advocates of civil liberties seem to urge their claims without regard to possible consequences for other important values. I am not suggesting that rights or liberties should be withdrawn when they are misused, but I do believe that the point of exercising human rights is to enable us to act rightly and to achieve our human (and Christian) destiny in a humane way. Christian ethics can strengthen and clarify our concern for the good to be achieved by action in a way that is normally open to forms of human rights theory that argue from skeptical premises. With regard to social and economic rights which are more obviously instrumental in their relationship to human dignity, Christian ethics can stand in opposition to reductivist and materialist understandings of human nature which might justify treating these rights as non-instrumental.

A second possible contribution that Christian ethics can make to human rights theory is to stress the full range of human rights as against partial and reductivist conceptions of humanity. To some extent, this points in the opposite direction to the previous point, but I believe that it is not contradictory to it. Even while Christian ethics cautions against the absolutization of specific rights, it can also insist that we pay serious regard to the full range of rights, especially for those who by reason of deprivation or discrimination are not in a position to make their own case. Christian ethics should provide us with the resources both to accept the curtailment of rights because of conflicting rights and in situations of emergency and scarcity, and at the same time to sustain a continued demand that rights be satisfied and that the goods and liberties necessary for the life and dignity of human persons be available to all. This requires an understanding of the life of the Christian as a person capable of both resignation and demand and endowed with the discretion to judge which is appropriate. It also requires that Christian ethics work with a wider and deeper understanding of the human person than is provided by those partial approaches to human rights theory which see the human person as autonomous will or as biological need.[32]

Third, Christian ethics can serve to provide links between the symbols and histories of a particular religious tradition and the universal values and claims of human rights theory. The elucidation of the universal significance of such basic Christian symbols as the covenant, the cross, the Eucharistic meal and the image of God is obviously of great significance for our understanding of how the Christian life is to be lived. It is also of considerable exemplary value for the treatment of particular symbols and events in other religious and national traditions. Christian thought has not been content to regard its symbols as of merely particularistic and internal interest, but has presented them as addressing universal human concerns and perplexities. The universal demands of human rights theory provide yet another matrix for developing the cognitive and emotive richness of the Christian symbols, but these symbols can in turn give a concrete dimension to the abstract and general claims of human rights theory.

Fourth, Christian ethical thought, which draws both on the sacred history of Israel and the tradition of the church from apostolic times on and which builds on a biblical understanding of God's action in history, can deepen the sense of history and the sense of community, both of which are often left in obscurity or taken for granted in liberal forms of human rights theory. Liberal forms of human rights theory have, from the time of Burke on, commonly been regarded as destructive of the traditional bonds of community. This is often linked to their reliance on the notion of a pre-social state of nature and to the critical attitude they inculcate with regard to premodern forms of authority and community. But these deficiencies of liberal human rights theory are not a matter of merely academic concern to historians and political theorists. The effort to achieve economic development is an effort which many nations see as their central project at the present time and for the forseeable future. Many nation-states, including both the new states of Africa and older states with long-smoldering regional or minority claims, face a task of nation building or of redefining a national community in new terms. These are tasks which require a sense of history and a sense of community, both of which will undergo significant changes as these tasks are carried out. These tasks can be carried out with a profound disregard for human rights (as in the collectivization of agriculture in the Soviet Union or the repression of minorities in many industrializing societies), or they can be carried out in ways that respect and fulfill human rights for all. In this situation, the sense of history as the field of saving action and the sense of a community that is open and inclusive, both important aspects of the Christian tradition, can contribute to the building of a social context in which it is possible to recognize and to meet the just claims to liberties and to goods that persons make by virtue of their humanity.

Fifth (and finally), the Christian ethical tradition, through its emotionally powerful symbols and the reality of the common life from which it grows, can contribute motivation and commitment to the long, uneven struggle for the realization of human rights in our world. This struggle by Christians is to be sustained through sharing in the mystery of life and death of the Christ who came that we might have life and have it more abundantly.

NOTES

1. For a brief introduction to the most influential works in this revival, see John P. Langan, "Rawls, Nozick, and the Search for Social Justice," *Theological Studies* 38 (1977).

2. Robert Nozick, *Anarchy, State and Utopia* (New York: Basic Books, 1974), p. 1.

3. John Rawls, *A Theory of Justice* (Cambridge, Mass.: Harvard University Press, 1971), pp. 202–5.

4. Ronald Dworkin, *Taking Rights Seriously* (Cambridge, Mass.: Harvard University Press, 1977), pp. 176–83.

5. Alan Gewirth, *Reason and Morality* (Chicago: University of Chicago Press, 1978).

6. A. I. Melden, *Rights and Persons* (Berkeley: University of California Press, 1977).

7. Joel Feinberg, *Rights, Justice, and the Bounds of Liberty* (Princeton, N.J.: Princeton University Press, 1980).

8. John Langan, "Defining Human Rights: A Revision of the Liberal Tradition," in *Human Rights in the Americas: The Struggle for Consensus*, ed. Alfred Hennelly and John Langan (Washington, D.C.: Georgetown University Press, 1982), p. 69.

9. Joel Feinberg, *Social Philosophy* (Englewood Cliffs, N.J.: Prentice-Hall, 1973), p. 86.

10. Maurice Cranston, *What Are Human Rights?* (New York: Basic Books, 1962), p. 39.

11. For a recent treatment of this duty, see Gewirth, *Reason and Morality*, pp. 217–30.

12. See Langan, "Defining Human Rights."

13. Bernard Plongeron, "Anathema or Dialogue? Christians' Reactions to Declarations of the Rights of Man in the United States and Europe in the Eighteenth Century," in *The Church and the Rights of Man*, ed. Alois Müller and Norbert Greinacher, Concilium 124 (New York: Seabury Press, 1979), p. 41.

14. Edward R. Norman, *Church and Society in England 1770–1970* (Oxford: Clarendon Press, 1976), p. 21.

15. Ibid., p. 83.

16. A valuable account of the complex and uneven acceptance of human rights norms by the largest Western religious group can be found in David Hollenbach, *Claims in Conflict: Retrieving and Renewing the Catholic Human Rights Tradition* (New York: Paulist, 1979), chapter 2.

17. Piux IX, *Syllabus Errorum*, 79; cited from *Church and State Through the Centuries*, ed. Sidney Ehler and John B. Morrall (London: Burns and Oates, 1954), p. 285.

18. John Paul II, Homily to Priests, Philadelphia, Pennsylvania, October 4, 1979, in *Pilgrim of Peace* (Washington, D.C.: United States Catholic Conference, 1980), p. 84.

19. Leo Strauss, *Natural Rights and History* (Chicago: University of Chicago Press, 1961), p. 181.

20. Ibid., p. 183.

21. Nozick, *Anarchy*, pp. 28–33.

22. Rawls, *Theory of Justice*, pp. 126–30.

23. Alan Donagan, *A Theory of Morality* (Chicago: University of Chicago Press, 1977), p. xv.

24. Jacques Maritain, *The Rights of Man and Natural Law*, trans. Doris Anson (New York: Charles Scribner's Sons, 1943), pp. 81–82.

25. Ibid., p. 81.

26. See, for instance, Alvin Plantinga, *God and Other Minds* (Ithaca, N.Y.: Cornell University Press, 1967), chapter 6, "The Free Will Defense," pp. 131–55.

27. Hollenbach, *Claims in Conflict*, p. 86.

28. Plongeron, "Anathema or Dialogue?", p. 41–42.

29. See John A. Ryan and Francis J. Boland, *Catholic Principles of Politics* (New York: Macmillan, 1941), pp. 316–21.

30. David Hollenbach, "Global Human Rights: An Interpretation of the Contemporary Catholic Understanding," *Human Rights in the Americas: The Struggle for Consensus*, ed. Alfred Hennelly and John Langan (Washington, D.C.: Georgetown University Press, 1982), p. 9.

31. Hollenbach, *Claims in Conflict*, p. 131.

32. For a critique of such views of the human person, see Iris Murdoch, *The Sovereignty of Good* (New York: Schocken, 1971).

8

The Limits of Politics: The Christian Clash with Radicalism

CHARLES DAVIS

I want to ask how far radicalism as a political option is compatible with Christian faith. But first, since radicalism is an unusually vague term, I must make clear the meaning I have in mind.

In the widest sense, "radical" is used of those political and religious views that push to an extreme their demand for change in the existing order. It is generally associated with a movement for fundamental change, but the exact change desired has differed from period to period. Moreover, although most often used of left-wing democratic movements, "radicalism" does sometimes designate right-wing oligarchical movements calling for a regeneration of society.

My concern is with a more precise meaning. By radicalism I mean the belief that human reason and will are powerful enough to overcome the present imperfection of the human condition by basic social and political change and thus to create a completely new social order of liberty, equality and fraternity. There are several elements in the definition.

First, there is the idea that social and political change, if thorough enough, can remove the present evils of the human condition. This reflects the gradual weakening and loss of belief in the doctrine of original sin. From the Renaissance onwards, there was a reluctance to accept that human beings were intrinsically implicated in a reign of sin and thus in permanent need of a supernatural redemption. Human nature was regarded as good, and men and women as capable of improving their condition. It was Rousseau who first pointed to society as the source of human misery, so that the present evils of the human condition were due to a corrupt social organization. He himself did not think that the situation could be righted by political action, but this was the conclusion drawn by a line of radical thinkers. Hence, radicalism, according to this first element, is the view that the evils of the present human condition are due to a bad, unjust organization of society and that these evils can be removed and human potentiality fully released by social and political action.

The second element is already implied in the first. To make it explicit, it is that reason and will are sufficient of themselves to bring about the changes required in the social order to perfect society, remove present evils and thus achieve fulfillment for human nature. On this point secular radicalism differs from apocalyptic, which in its extreme demand for fundamental change is the religious counterpart of political radicalism. Apocalyptic, however, looks not to human power, but to a divine intervention to accomplish the change. Nevertheless, the two may coincide if radical reformers see themselves as instruments of a divine purpose. At the same time, the optimistic confidence in human reason for effecting human improvement and creating a new social order links radicalism to the liberal tradition and the Enlightenment. From that standpoint, for example, John W. Derry in his book, *The Radical Tradition*, can include such unquestionably liberal thinkers as Jeremy Bentham and John Stuart Mill.[1] Radicalism, however, as distinct from liberalism, derives less from the reasonableness of bourgeois thinking than from the vivid example of the practice of the French revolutionaries, who showed that sweeping changes could indeed be brought about in the social order by human action. According to the second element, then, radicalism is the confidence that men and women can devise and construct an ideal social order to meet the needs of human fulfillment.

The third element further distinguishes radicalism from liberalism. The radicals were those who refused to go along with the liberals in their individualist stress upon freedom, because the liberals ignored or regarded as inevitable the economic inequities of a liberal social order. The radical interpretation of freedom placed it in the context of equality and, in the political order, of democracy. Although the push toward extreme change has often led radicals to the acceptance of dictatorial power on the part of a charismatic leader or select group, the radical vision of the ideal society is egalitarian, and this creates a reluctance to grant that human fulfillment may be mediated by a traditional authority. So, according to the third element, radicalism is an insistence that the essential equality of human beings should result in an equal participation in the economic, social and political life of the ideal social order.

How do each of these elements stand up when compared with the Christian understanding of the human condition and its need for salvation? I take it for granted that the Christian tradition, like any other religious tradition, is not a static deposit, but is open to change and modification within the historical process. Thus, we should not canonize as immutable truth Augustine's view of original sin, despite its dominance of Western culture for centuries. There is no valid objection to loosening up our interpretation of the myth of the Fall, to taking it as a set of symbols, provoking and facilitating reflection upon the human situation in regard to evil, but without its providing a definitive theoretical answer. It would therefore be an exaggeration to argue that human sinfulness excludes the radical aspiration after a fundamentally new social order. There is no reason why the human race should not learn to create institutional checks against the worst manifestation of human waywardness. Indeed, unless this is not merely possible but also actually accomplished in the near future in respect of war, the human race will be exterminated in a nuclear holocaust. The present stress by Christian theologians upon the universality of grace does not allow us to regard the majority of the human race, with Augustine, as a *massa damnata*. Even if the final kingdom, with its elimination of sin, is not to be fully realized in this historical order, men and women with the help of grace should be able to create a social order closer to the ideal than present society. Christians indeed will differ among themselves in determining how this is to be done and what reforms are practicable in a particular concrete situation. Not all Christians will make the same political option.

To give an example where the Christian outlook straddles the political options, Edmund Burke,[2] the great conservative thinker, argued that revolutions achieve the opposite of what they intend. They begin by promising freedom, equality, justice and democracy, and end in a tyranny that negates all four. The reason is that revolution threatens or produces anarchy. Now, the basic social need is for law and order, for security. Most people, however low their state, fear disorder. They therefore distrust the radicals, who make great promises, but who will probably bring chaos. Consequently, radicals usually end by despising the people and imposing their new social order by force. It is difficult to be a radical and a democrat, because extreme measures are usually unpopular. Hence, the law put forward by Burke, which states that revolution or the practical implementation of radical political theory, necessarily leads to tyranny via anarchy. Radicals are led into tyranny, because they want to change society fundamentally and fast. But they are also acting, according to Burke, on inadequate knowledge. Radicals have an excessive trust in their theories. There is never in fact enough sufficiently reliable knowledge about the social order with its complexity to justify tearing down an existing order and constructing something entirely new. Politically we must always act with restraint because of the inevitable limits of our knowledge.

There is a great deal to be said in support of Burke's argumentation against revolution. Its weakness is that the scenario Burke presupposes is not always verified in fact. His scenario is that of a stable, if unjust society, which is threatened by anarchy because revolutionaries are acting to overthrow the existing order and replace it by a new and more just order. But the factual situation may be that the social order has already disintegrated through the misrule of the governing class, who in the absence of a rule of law are clinging to their privileges by terrorism and uncontrolled oppression. The ordinary people may be deprived of the basic security, which any society is intended to supply, because they are subject to arbitrary arrest and the lack of the basic material necessities of life. Revolutionary action in those circumstances is not the overthrow of the social order, but an attempt to restore social order by action from below. In extreme situations only extreme measures may work; moderate action may not even be possible.

In any particular instance the situation will rarely be crystal clear. Hence it will be differently assessed by people whose fundamental political attitudes differ. In brief, there will be the political conservatives, urging moderation, and political radicals, insisting that matters have become intolerable. There may be Christians in both groups. It is a mistake to suppose that the differences can be settled by appealing to traditional Christian teaching or by an authoritative decree of the ecclesiastical hierarchy. A factual assessment and a practical judgment are involved here. These will be influenced by a person's hold upon Christian meanings and values, and Christians in the local community affected by the situation should endeavor to reach a sufficient consensus for some degree of common policy and action. This may not always be possible, but Christians have to learn to differ from one another in practical social and political affairs without immediately labeling their opponents un-Christian.

All the same, if Christian faith is not to be emptied of content, the meanings and values it carries with it must at times clash with those implied in one or other political option. Where differences are rooted in a divergent factual assessment and in estimating the probable effects of action, Christians fully unified in faith may differ. But this is not so where the differences are differences of fundamental outlook. If political radicalism is not taken simply to mean the advocacy of revolutionary action in extreme situations, but is made explicit as a fundamental political theory, consisting in the elements I have analyzed, there is cause to ask about its compatability with any recognizable version of the Christian understanding of the human condition. That kind of questioning should not be raised only in regard to radicalism; it is in place concerning liberalism and conservatism as basic political options. But it comes to the fore with radicalism, because for some the radical option has taken on the lineaments of a secular religion, and some Christians, judging rightly that being a Christian in the present un-Christian world involves social and political action to change the world, have been tempted to identify Christianity with political radicalism.

Political radicalism does, I suggest, clash in several fundamental respects with Christian principles. I am indeed treating radical ideas in the abstract. How far they are actually held by political radicals will have to be determined in particular instances. The ideas, however, are sufficiently current to call for a theoretical clarification. The various ways in which radicalism clashes with Christian principle may be summed up by saying that radicalism transgresses the limits that Christianity imposes upon political action.

Take the first element of radicalism, namely, the conviction that the evils of the human condition can be removed and human potentiality fully released by social and political action. Since Christian faith relates human beings to God as transcendent reality, the subject of Christian faith and the recipient of Christian salvation must be seen as transcending any historical social and political order.

The subject of Christian faith is, from one standpoint, the individual person, actualized in his or her individuality by the response to God's call that every individual must make for himself or herself, because it cannot be made vicariously by another. That is the essence of Christian individualism, which places each individual in a personal relationship with God. From another standpoint, the subject of Christian faith is the community constituted by persons who, in opening themselves to a relationship with God, have thereby opened themselves to one another. Faith in actualizing the individual constitutes the community or Kingdom of God. It is, however, a community that cannot be fully identified with an institutional community. From a sociological viewpoint, it is a community-forming principle rather than a community. The recipient of Christian salvation is the communal individual as freed from sin and as immortalized, that is, as having overcome death, however that victory is more precisely interpreted.

But if such is the subject of Christian faith and salvation, that subject, that faith, that salvation, cannot be brought within the confines of any temporal social order. No matter how ideal may be a society, it cannot in its own temporal terms provide faith to ward off ultimate meaninglessness and salvation to overcome sin and death. I say "in its own temporal terms," because social and political institutions and action may, especially when sacred and secular have not yet been clearly differentiated, have a function in mediating faith and salvation. Again, because of the interdependence of the various levels of human existence, it is not true to say that no matter how bad and unjust a society may be, men and women in it may still always meet God in faith and receive salvation from him. The evils of society may and often do block people's access to the higher levels of human existence. What is true is that faith and the conscious acceptance of salvation do not demand an ideal order of society and can be found even in a high degree where social conditions are far from ideal. In brief, society on the level of social and political organization is neither the cause nor the remedy for the fundamental ills of the human condition, and it is not the source of human fulfillment at its deepest level, even though it may act negatively to block or positively to mediate access to that source.

Admittedly, then, there is an extrinsic dependence of faith and salvation upon social and political conditions. If a person is starving, one must first give him or her food before talking about saving souls. In general, the injustice of a social and political regime in depriving people of the satisfaction of their basic needs—for self-esteem and community, not just for food and shelter—will, apart from a miracle of grace, block the emergence of the higher needs and aspirations proper to a developed human life. The establishment of basic social justice and of a political order free from stark oppression may be the necessary path in the bringing of faith and salvation. Again, it is a mistake to suppose that religious activity is necessarily private and personal. Actions embodying religious meaning and values are as appropriate in the public realm as in that of private existence. All the same, human society in the variety of its historical forms and in the different degrees of its success in satisfying human social needs does not belong to the deepest level of human existence, where human beings are related to a transcendent order. In making society the root of human evil and the place of human fulfillment, political radicalism distorts politics by disguised religion.

The second element of political radicalism, namely the confidence in human ability to construct an ideal social order, likewise offends against political modesty. Let us suppose that the social order has been brought to a peak of perfection. As a temporal order, it will remain subject to change, which if perfection has indeed been reached will be in the direction of disintegration and corruption. The historical process does not allow eternal permanence. But the more striking defect of any utopia built by human hands is that it provides for the fulfillment only of the generation that achieves it and for those subsequent generations that precede its eventual collapse. It has nothing to offer the victims of generation after generation of preceding history. More than that, it would seem that the ideal social order, made immanent in history without transcendence, can offer human fulfillment only at the cost of a complete forgetfulness of the victims of past history. To remember them would be to evoke a frustrated sense of human solidarity, which would either mar with sadness the utopian fulfillment or be repressed with a blunting of human sensibility. There is indeed an inherent absurdity in a secular radicalism, which calls for generation after generation to work for a fulfillment they themselves will never enjoy, while at the same time repudiating the self-transcending faith that alone would ground such selfless action. If, as a radical, one is dissatisfied with the politics of enlightened self-interest and yearns for the achievement of human solidarity, one is led to hope for a communion among human beings that transcends both space and time. We cannot forget the victims of the past. As Walter Benjamin noted, people are moved "by the image of enslaved ancestors rather than that of liberated grandchildren."[3] But however envisaged, such a transcendent communion is not within the range of political action. Hence, though hope for it will transform political action away from self-interest toward concern for others in justice and love, it will inculcate an acute sense of the limits of political action that will moderate the urge to create a new social order by political means.

The alternative to consciously reconstructing radicalism as a religious rather than a political hope is to turn it into a tragic vision of human history, according to which human beings can only find fragments of human meaning by working for the ideals of freedom and justice with the realization that the human enterprise is in any event destined to end in extermination, meaninglessness and nothingness. Radical politics without any ultimate meaning! It is indeed a possible option, but it is essentially a religious not a political option, to be assessed accordingly.

The third element of political radicalism is its egalitarianism. Insofar as this was historically an uncovering of the brutal economic inequality that was veiled by the bourgeois ideology of freedom, it was a legitimate political demand. But insofar as equality is erected into a universal political principle, it implies an attempt to extend human control beyond its appropriate range. Human beings are unequal in the endowments of nature and in the gifts of God's grace. Although the limited human control over nature may do some-thing to offset the inequalities of natural endowment, it is questionable whether this should be done in the name of equality. That, as experience shows, is most likely to lead to a leveling down rather than a leveling up, an impoverishment rather than an enrichment. In any event, human beings have no control over the gifts of the Spirit and over the utterly free distri-bution of God's grace. Undoubtedly, for the Christian, human beings are essentially equal in the sense that each person stands before God as having eternal, individual worth. Hence, each person is an end and cannot ever legitimately be treated as a mere means. Moreover, personal worth is not to be measured by the function of place the human occupies in earthly society. For that reason, radicality has fundamentally relativized social and political inequalities. All the same, the radical vision does not see human beings as equal, either by nature or by grace. It allows, therefore, a place for authority or legitimate power over others in both political and religious institutions. The drive for equality, religiously assessed, is an arrogant claim by human beings to total mastery over their destiny. So often its conse-quence is the urge to destroy what persists in eluding human control.

To bring these remarks to some conclusion, if radicalism is understood in a broad, vague sense as the conviction that in a particular situation the existing order of society must be fundamentally changed, it is a practical judgment and decision that is not merely compatible with Christian faith but may also be based upon its values. Our present society is both struc-turally un-Christian and headed for annihilation. Christians, therefore, are called upon to work for its fundamental change. But radicalism may be viewed as more than a practical response to a particular situation, as a theoretical political option, a set of political principles, determining a con-ception of society, of human perfectibility, of human destiny. The three elements I have analyzed constitute a political theory, present in various forms on the political scene since at least the French Revolution. As such it forms a political outlook incompatible with Christian faith for reasons I have stated. If I have stressed the incompatibility of radicalism rather than of, say, bourgeois liberalism, it is to make clear the distinction between a firm Christian commitment to social and political action in favor of the oppressed and exploited and its deceptive similitude, namely, a political radicalism that identifies human fulfillment with the establishment of an ideal social and political order.

NOTES

1. John W. Derry, *The Radical Tradition: Tom Paine to Lloyd George* (London: Macmillan, 1967).

2. I am dependent here upon the interpretation of Burke in Michael Freeman, *Edmund Burke and the Critique of Political Radicalism* (Oxford: Basil Blackwell, 1980).

3. From the "Theses on the Philosophy of History," in Walter Benjamin, *Illuminations*, ed. and with an intro. by Hannah Arendt (Glasgow: Fontana/Collins, 1973), p. 262.

PART III

ISLAM

9

Islam and Political Action: Politics in the Service of Religion

FAZLUR RAHMAN

When Muhammad began his prophetic career in Mecca in 610 C.E., a central part of his mission was social reform in terms of strengthening the socio-economically weak and depressed classes—the have-nots in general, orphans, women, slaves, and so on in the prosperous, mercantile Meccan society. Both he himself and his opponents knew that social reform on this scale would require his assumption of political power, and there is no doubt that the source of a good part of the opposition to him came from this situation. In part, this opposition was rooted in fierce interclan rivalry: the Prophet being from the clan of Banu Hashim of the large tribe of Quraish, other clans feared that recognition of Muhammad as the political head could involve rule by Banu Hashim.[1] Short of recognizing him as the absolute religio-political head, they offered him an effective share in the decision-making city council of Mecca, an offer which he refused.[2] In his later years in Mecca (before emigrating to Madina), the upper-class Meccan merchants offered to accept his faith provided he got rid of his poor and weak followers. The Qur'an condemned such offers and warned against them; he, of course, refused to accept them.[3]

After his arrival in Madina in September 622 C.E. (the year of the beginning of the Islamic Hijra—lunar calendar) at the invitation of that town, Muhammad assumed his position as its religio-political head. He was able to carry out his program of social reform (apart from promulgating worship of the one and unique God, Allah), imposing the Zakat tax upon the well-to-do to ameliorate the condition of the poor, to rescue the poor who were under chronic debt, to improve the defense effort and other social services, allotting shares in inheritance to women, regulating marriage and divorce, and so on.[4] He contracted peace agreements, conducted wars, legislated and decided cases as the supreme judge. In 630 C.E. Mecca fell to him without opposition; this was followed by a constant flow of representative delegations from Arab tribes. When he died in June 633 C.E., Muhammad was the effective prophet-ruler of virtually the whole of the Arabian peninsula.

The outline presented here should make clear the relationship between "religion" and "state" under the Prophet. It is not the case that "religion" and "state" were sisters; nor can it be said that they "co-operated" with one another. The state is nothing at all by itself; it is a reflex of those moral and spiritual values and principles called Islam. The state is not an "extension" of religion; it is an instrument of Islam, a transparent instrument which vanishes when one tries to regard it per se. The Prophet never claimed to be Prophet *and ruler*; he never even claimed to be a ruler whose rule was under this Prophethood; he only claimed to be a Prophet. His rule was the way in which he performed his Prophetic office. The adage is fairly well known by now that "in Islam there is no separation between religion and state." The actual case is much stronger: ideally, the state per se cannot exist in Islam where it is only a reflex or a transparent instrument of "religion." Religion (Islam), therefore, is that which directly permeates and directs all spheres of human life. Islam is just as much to be found in the market place, in the school, in the legislative chamber as in the mosque and the battlefield, for all these loci manifest and interpret Islamic values.

Given this, we shall have to say that political action is a part of, a manifestation of and a necessary instrument of Islam and the values it stands for in the public sector of life. Leaving the Prophet's lifetime, we would now like to know what the Qur'an, the Word of God revealed to Muhammad during the approximately twenty-three years of his mission, had to say to Muslims for the future conduct of affairs, since the Prophet's revelatory experience was by definition irrepeatable. As the basic instrument of the implementation of the divine message, the Qur'an had established the Muslim community, which it called the "brotherhood of the Faithful." This community was asked by the Qur'an to regulate its internal conduct on the basis of active mutual goodwill (*tawasi*),[5] and cooperation (*ta'awun*).[6] Being brothers, they all stood as equals before God and before the law. Exploitation, political, social or economic, was forbidden. In his Farewell Pilgrimage Address, the Prophet talked of "all men being children of Adam and Adam being from dust ... there being no superiority of an Arab over a non-Arab or of a white or brown man over a red or black man." In any case, distinctions based on origin and physical provenance had been decisively repudiated by the Qur'an itself.[7]

The task of this community was formulated as "believing in God, establishing prayers, effecting Zakat, commanding good and prohibiting evil,"[8] to establish a viable ethical sociopolitical order by "reforming the earth and rooting out corruption from the earth."[9] For the achievement of this global task, the community was provided with the necessary tool called "*jihad*."[10]

Jihad means total and unrelenting effort "in the cause of Allah," that is, the task with which it was charged and which we have briefly described just now.

In order to "reform the earth," however, the members of the community have to be properly formed as individuals. Without such formation, it is inconceivable that the kind of community capable of bearing this task could be brought into being. The individual is to be formed, then, on the basis of what the Qur'an calls "*taqwa*." *Taqwa* is that attitude, or rather quality of mind, whereby a person becomes capable of discerning between right and wrong and makes the necessary effort to do so. It assumes that the human task is to discern and to act with the full awareness that the law whereby people are finally judged is not of their making and is, in this sense, external to them. *Taqwa* could be translated as "conscience," provided conscience is not conceived of subjectively but fully recognizes the objectivity or "externality" of this law of judgment. In other words, a notion of effective transcendence is central to *taqwa*. It is the exit point from moral subjectivity into objectivity, from individuality into society: "There is no private talk of three people but that God is the fourth, nor five but that God is the sixth, nor of any lesser or greater number but that God is present there" (Qur'an, 58, 7).

Without individuals with the kind of sense of responsibility that *taqwa* brings, there is no hope of building a worthwhile community. Muhammad was able to train a good nucleus of people with this moral equipment, whom the late Professor H.A.R. Gibb describes as "the leaven which was to leaven the whole lump."[11] What thwarted and distorted the development of Islamic polity on proper lines was ironically the astonishingly rapid political success of the Muslim Arabs in terms of swift conquests which put them in charge of a large empire within a matter of a few years, also swelling the numbers of the community by literally millions of people. First, it was inconceivable that the kind of effective moral training required by the Qur'an and actually imported by the Prophet to his inner circle during a period of more than two decades could have been successfully transposed to the large and almost sudden influx of new converts. Secondly, with the erection of a big empire almost overnight, the newly formed Muslim intellectual class (the 'Ulama') had to face the immense task of working out and perfecting a system of Islamic law for the administration of this empire. These early legists were not only brilliant men but models of devotion and piety and, for their time, they performed their task extraordinarily well. But as it happens, law is not the same thing as morality! And, although Islamic law developed a peculiar nature (whereby it sought to preserve within itself certain major moral elements which rendered much of it unenforceable through a court of justice but suitable only for the bar of conscience), still law by definition deals with overt behavior. Because of this development, inner moral training of the kind envisaged by the Qur'an necessarily suffered recession. A century or so later, when the impulse of inner spiritual development re-asserted itself, it did so with a vengeance in the form of Sufism. Sufism chalked out its own course independently of, and sometimes in conscious and even willful opposition to, the law for some time until the process of deliberate integration began seriously about the tenth century C.E.

Let us resume the story of Islam and politics. When the Qur'an established the Community of Believers and required them to work through mutual cooperation, it also gave a basic procedural principle to regulate the process of decision making. This is the principle of *shura* or "mutual consultation": "Their [the faithful's] affairs shall be decided by their mutual consultation" (Qur'an, 42, 38). The Qur'an did not create this principle; it was the democratic principle of decision making among the Arab tribes which the Qur'an confirmed. When deciding upon momentous questions like war and peace or migration, and when settling such major internal and external disputes as would affect a tribe as a whole, the tribal chief could not proceed by himself but convened a council of elders, which had the final say on such matters. The Qur'an considers it of such importance that, in spite of the Prophet's exercise of absolute authority, it asks him to "consult them in (the decision) of affairs" (Qur'an, 3, 159). The basic change that the Qur'an effected was to turn *shura* from a tribal institution into a community institution since it replaced blood ties with the bonds of faith.

The first test of *shura* came immediately after the death of Muhammad over the question of succession. Although he was looking for an appropriate opportunity to settle this fateful matter before his death, in view of the delicate balance of forces in the community—particularly as between the Meccans who had settled in Madina after the emigration and the original Madinese population who had given him and his Meccan followers a haven—he had no opportunity to decide. After a protracted debate in the Hall of Banu Sa'ida, the Meccan elder statesman and an old faithful companion of Muhammad, Abu Bakr, was elected the first caliph (successor), despite a certain amount of covert dissent from 'Ali, the Prophet's cousin and son-in-law and his kinsman supporters who thought that rule should remain in the Prophet's household (he left no male issue). This group and their later followers became the Shi'a.

This test was successful, but this is the first and last time in Islamic history that the community as a whole, that is, its decision-making representative elements, met and saved the community from disintegration which the frailties and vagaries of history may well have perpetrated. *Shura* continued to function informally for some time during the time of the first four caliphs until the Umayyad rule. With the introduction of dynastic rule under the Umayyads, *shura* was naturally replaced by those cliques that supported the regime. It was, in fact, never developed into an institution. If it could have been so developed, the history of Islam, both political and religious, would have been radically different, with important consequences for the non-Muslim world as well. What happened instead was that a concept was evolved called "Ahl ah-Hall Wa'l-'Aqd" or "people of loosening and binding." These were people of public influence and confidence who were co-opted by the ruling authority for consultative purposes with regard to formulation of internal and external policies. These men could be from the military cadres, learned men ('Ulama') or other influential personalities, including, of course, ministers charged with various responsibilities.

This was undoubtedly better than purely despotic rule. Despotic absolutism in any case could not develop in Islam because, as we shall see presently, the ruler was always regarded in Islam as being under the sacred law, the Shari'a, and not above it. There were, therefore, concrete limits to his exercise of power, limits that he could not violate flagrantly or frequently except on pain of losing power entirely through rebellion. Nevertheless, this situation was a far cry from the Qur'anic ideal which demanded rule through *shura*. In the view of the Qur'an, *shura* does not mean that a single person (the ruler) seeks advice from a certain number of people he deems fit for the purpose of consultation, and then he may or may not accept their advice. Obviously, the Qur'an is thinking first of all in terms of the *community's affairs or business (amruhum* = their affairs), not in terms of the business of a single person or an elite. Rule is, thus, the community's joint affair. Secondly, and this is equally important, the words of the Qur'an are "shall be decided by their mutual consultation (*shura bainahum*)." This evidently repudiates a situation where one person (the ruler) "consults" others, others whom he himself has appointed and who do not represent the community by being appointed or elected by them. The interpretation of the Qur'anic verse on *shura* given here is not only that required by the words of the Qur'an, but is further corroborated by what we know of the process of tribal decision making referred to above. There is no doubt, therefore, that the medieval practice of Islam constituted a grave departure from and an utter distortion of the Qur'anic teaching.

But although the principle of democracy as embodied as the Qur'anic *shura* fell derelict, Sunni Islam, at least in theory, never gave up the twin principles of the election of the caliph and the positive acceptance of his rule by the people through the oath of obeissance (*bai'a*). There was no agreement on the number of the electoral college, "the people of loosening and binding," nor on the mode of election, but the principle of election was never let go. What further retarded the progress of the political process was, of course, the weakening of the caliphal institution at the center and the rise of emirs and sultans in neighboring or outlying regions. These were very often self-made political adventurers, outstanding in their daring and intelligence and full of cynical wisdom who, from the tenth century C.E. onwards, were de facto rulers of different regions of the Muslim world and who, while they reduced the political efficacy of the caliph to zero, nevertheless preserved and used his spiritual authority for legitimizing their own rule. With the emergence of this semi-autocratic class of conqueror-rulers, there could be hardly any talk of rule-by-*shura*.

There is no question that the sultans were effective rulers, they kept law and order and dispensed justice. But their ideals of rule and justice were progressively permeated by ancient Iranian notions. From these came the notion of the "God-supported king" (*farr-i izadi*); from these came the doctrine that "one day of political chaos and lawlessness is worse than thirty years of tyrannical rule,"[12] which even the Islamic orthodoxy absorbed with gusto due to the frightening early experiences of the civil wars and rebellions of the Khariji-idealist fanatics who stubbornly held that the political authority must be upset if it committed one single major mistake. From this evolved the idea that "effective seizure of rule even by force was legitimate."[13] And, finally, the ancient Iranian view of justice was not the Qur'anic one; it could not, of course, speak of participation by the community in rule, let alone of "reforming the earth." That view, called "The Great Circle of Justice," was primarily concerned with maintaining equilibrium among social classes—the military, the peasants, the artisans and the clergy; it laid particular stress on the well-being of the peasants, who produced food for the rest of the society.

With all this, however, the Sunni constitutional theorists insisted that the ruler must rule in accordance with the canons of the Shari'a and a ruler who gravely violated the Shari'a might be deposed. The fourteenth-century Indian strong-man ruler, 'Ala' al-Din Khilji, wanted to tax his subjects severely, particularly Hindus whom he suspected of rebellious attitudes. His shaikh al-Islam (the head of religious affairs) did not allow this on the ground that overtaxation was improper according to the Shari'a, upon which the sultan complained that whenever he wanted to build his rule on strong foundations, he was told that this was against the Shari'a! And when the early sixteenth-century Ottoman sultan Selim I wished to order his Christian subjects to convert to Islam by force (in order to make his realm more homogeneous, à la Charlemagne's treatment of the German tribes), his shaikh al-Islam prohibited him from doing so on the ground that Christians and Jews were protected people (*dhimmis*) and therefore could not be forced to accept Islam.

Particularly in opposition to each other, it seems, did the Shi'a and the Sunnis push their respective positions further and further toward their respective logical conclusions. Thus, while the Shi'a pushed, through their idealism, their infallible imam literally out of this world and started awaiting his "return" (a position of which we shall see below the reaction in Khomaini's peculiar concept of rule), the Sunnis retorted by stressing more and more the consensus of the community ('ijma'), even though no machinery could be ever brought into being for that consensus to materialize, and insisting that the ruler is responsible for discharging his duties or his "trust" (*amana*) to the community which can wrest its rights from him by force if he will not listen to advice and warnings.[14]

We hinted earlier at the development of the Islamic law at the hands of certain brilliant personalities during the first two and a half centuries of Islam. Now, Islamic law developed at the hands of these private individuals because without the development of *shura* into an institution of the people, the state could not legislate and people did not trust the heads of governments or their administrations to legislate. By the tenth to eleventh century C.E., this private evolution of law came more or less to a stop because the fiction gained ground that the "gate of new legal thought" (*ijtihad*) was no longer open. Since, however, societies kept on moving, under later Muslim rulers, governments promulgated their own laws. This governmental legislative activity was particularly systematically pursued by the Ottomans. Although their law cannot be said to be secular law because sanctions for it were found within the body of the principles of the Shari'a law, nevertheless it paved the way in Turkey at least for the emergence of secular law. The 'Ulama' stopped new thinking on law, *shura* did not exist and, therefore, the only way open to the governments was to promulgate law on their own, something which was impossible even for a ruler like the Abbasid Harun al-Rashid in the earlier centuries. We shall see the effects of this legal dualism shortly when we come to modern times and see the controversy over Islam and democracy and as to who has the right of legislation in an Islamic state.

Before we come to that, however, we should note the emergence of a major trend in Islamic political thought after the destruction of the Islamic caliphate at Baghdad by the Mongols in 1257 C.E. The two most important political thinkers in Islam since that event are the Arab Ibn Taimiya (d. 1328 C.E.) and the Indian Shah Waliy Allah of Delhi (d. 1763 C.E.). Since Muslims no longer had any central government, in the thought of both of them, the Shari'a and the Muslim community gained prominence rather than any particular government. Ibn Taimaiya states that it is not necessary for the Muslims to have one global government under a caliph; it is essential, however, that various Muslim governments cooperate closely with each other. But he puts special emphasis on the Muslim community and the implementation of its constitution, the Shari'a of Islam. Shah Waliy Allah's emphases are slightly different; nevertheless, his central point of stress is also the Shari'a and the community, although he does emphasize the necessity of an international world political order of Muslims, to which the national or regional Muslim states will be subordinate. It is this stress on both the community and the Shari'a which rendered these two thinkers so influential with many Muslim modernist reformers in recent times. This is because this emphasis on the community was naturally helpful to the reformers who wanted to introduce democratic forms of government in Muslim societies.

The process of Muslim modernist thought began around the middle of the nineteenth century. The pioneers in this direction were Jamal al-Din al-Afghani (d. 1897) and the Turkish thinker Namik Kemal (d. 1886). Namik Kemal in particular wrote a series of articles on *shura*[15] which he, and the other Modernists, correctly interpreted as meaning an adequately representative form of government embodying the will of the people and ensuring the people's effective participation in deciding their affairs. His efforts played a major role in the actual introduction of constitutional democracy in Ottoman Turkey; similarly, Jamal al-Din al-Afghani contributed materially, directly and indirectly, to the institution of constitutionalism in Iran and Egypt. Turkey, however, went secular, after the model of the West in 1924 under Atatürk, thus removing Islam and the Shari'a as the basis of the state. No other Muslim country has followed suit; on the contrary, during the past few decades Islamic fundamentalism has been vastly strengthened everywhere in the Muslim world, including Turkey, and has resulted in a spectacular revolution in Iran. Indeed, this fundamentalism has, at least temporarily, drowned Islamic modernism itself. Before taking account of this phenomenon, we would do well to outline briefly the controversy over Islam and democracy and the achievement of Islamic modernism in this field.

First of all, it should be noted that Islamic modernism is not equivalent to secularism, even though so many Western social scientists, particularly political scientists, partly through ignorance but, I suspect, largely through wishful thinking, identify the two. They assume that all modernization is secularization, which is palpably untrue in the case of Islam. A Muslim modernist is every bit Islamic. Indeed, it was the Muslim modernist who consciously reformulated the idea that Islam is applicable to the whole gamut of life and is not confined to certain religious rites, family law and certain penal provisions of the Qur'an as the 'Ulama' had come in practice to accept, and by so doing had become quasi-secular. What is true is that Muslim modernism represents Islamic liberalism: it has accepted certain key liberal social values from the modern West and has interpreted the Qur'an to confirm those values and not just to "legitimize" them as a social scientist is so fond of putting the matter. For in this process of re-understanding the Qur'an and the legacy of the Prophet, it is not just the intellect of the Muslim but even more so his faith that is certainly involved. In the face of this situation, I cannot understand what "legitimation" means. The Muslim modernist certainly does not accept the entirety of Western social values. He rejects certain very important ones. While he espouses the cause of the emancipation of women, for example, he is not blind to the havoc that is being produced in the West by its new sex ethics, not least in terms of the dilapidation of the family institution.

In the case of the introduction of democracy, the modernist was also convinced that democracy subserves the requirements of the Qur'an much better than medieval forms of Islamic rule—be it caliphate or sultanate—which he regards at best as working solutions for those days and at worst as deviations from and distortions of Islam, which kept the Muslim community backward. He is right, for earlier we have brought evidence from the Qur'an to show that it puts the burden of the Islamic task on the shoulders of the community and not a single individual or a class of individuals, no matter what pretentions any class or self-styled elite may have. Furthermore, the Qur'an requires that the community (or its representatives) must decide matters by mutual consultation. The adoption of democracy, therefore, is not "legitimation" but a genuine rediscovery.

The opposition which the modernist faced in his democratic reform from the Islamic conservatives was of two kinds. The first and most formidable argument against democracy—and, as we shall see, this question is far from settled—has been that since the masses are ignorant and immature and lack proper discernment between right and wrong, governance of an Islamic state cannot be left to them. Nor will they be able to choose representatives fit to legislate and rule. Legislation, in particular, is a delicate issue because judging a certain proposed law in the light of the Qur'an requires an expertise which neither the masses nor their representatives will possess. Hence, legislation must be entrusted to the 'Ulama' who are experts in Islamic teachings. The second objection, which has progressively become less important, is that the presence of non-Muslim minorities, sometimes large ones, will complicate the governance of an Islamic state. This objection has been more or less settled now by the modernist argument that certain encumbrances to which non-Muslims as minorities were subject in the past (for example, the *Jizya* or poll tax) need not exist now, for whereas in the past non-Muslims were not expected to fight wars for Islam and had to pay this tax instead, all the citizens of a modern state are equal in all respects, and there is no reason to suspect the loyalty of minorities if they are treated equally with Muslims. This has been accepted even by most religious conservatives. In fact, the Qur'an espouses the protection not only of the Jewish and Christian revealed documents (5, 48), but also of their places of worship, whose defense it regards as the prime cause of *jihad*:

Today those [Meccan Muslims] who have been attacked are given permission [to fight back] because they have been expelled from their homes without reason—except that they said "Our Lord is God [alone]" and God is surely powerful in coming to their aid. But for the fact that God repels some people through others, monasteries, churches, synagogues, mosques and all places of worship where God's name is regularly mentioned, would be destroyed" (22, 39–40).

It was only later, after the establishment of the Islamic imperium, that the law was enacted which disallowed the construction of non-Muslim places of worship except with government permission. On the freedom of the profession of religion, the Qur'an has uniquely declared, "There is no compulsion in matters of faith, for truth and falsehood have become clearly distinguished [through the Qur'an]" (2, 256). It is true that the Qur'an regards Prophethood as an indivisible office, proclaims that one may not believe in some prophets while rejecting others and considers *mutually exclusive* religions as a form of polytheism, but it is equally true that it stresses religious tolerance and allows pluralism in its midst.

As to the argument from the masses' ignorance, Namik Kemal replied to it by saying that in Turkey one could find people with enough wisdom to understand questions of peace and war, of taxation and education, who could run the government, thus implying that no technical knowledge of theology was necessary to govern a society. This answer appears correct to the present writer. If the Qur'an—which calls itself "guidance for people"—had been such a difficult technical matter, it would not have addressed humankind in general. The essential aim of the Qur'an—which is hardly a book of law—is to create proper conscience in people, to maximize moral energy and use that energy through appropriate channels. It can be effectively argued that the more you turn the Qur'an into a technical work, the more your conscience is dulled—witness, for example, the unconscionable and uncontrolled spree of killings unleashed by the clerical government of Iran on all sorts of groups among its citizens in the name of Islam. And this is called by Khomaini "the divine rule" or "rule by the clergy."

And if the mass of the Muslim community is in one sense ignorant of Islam, whose fault is it? The blame must be laid at the door of the Muslim governments and the Islamic religious leadership, particularly the latter for their grave neglect of educating Muslims at large. Let us repeat that the Qur'an recognized no elites, no specially privileged classes but recognizes only the community of believers. The Qur'an specifically states that certain people from every group or part of the community should learn the faith with understanding and insight and then teach others, so that the whole community develops an adequate understanding of Islam (Qur'an, 9, 122). This is because, as said before, the bearers of the responsibility of the Qur'an are Muslims at large, the community, and if this community is ignorant of the tasks of the Qur'an and unable to distinguish between right and wrong, then one must frankly admit that the Muslim community is not in existence. Then the first task that devolves upon those who claim to be repositories of Islamic learning and wisdom is that they try to enlighten the Muslims at large by teaching and preaching and raise their standards of understanding and motivation, rather than claim for themselves the right of absolute leadership and obedience. For, it is absolutely certain that, so far as the Qur'an is concerned, there is no way that any single person or a self-styled clan of elites can arrogate to himself or themselves the rights and duties vested in the community, unless one wishes to change Islam into something quite different.

The extent to which deviation from Qur'anic standards has occurred is perhaps nowhere so palpably and sensationally illustrated as in Khomaini's Iran. It is true that Shi'a political theory, probably under the influence of ancient Iranian concepts of the Divine Ruler, had formulated the doctrine of the infallible absent imam. It should be noted, first, that this doctrine was formulated only after the occultation of the last and twelfth imam: for at least beginning with the sixth imam, ja'far al-Sadiq, all Shi'i imams had eschewed pursuit of political power and had regarded their function as purely religious and educational and no imam in actual history had ever claimed infallibility. During the absence of the imam, which, according to Khomaini, "may well last another hundred thousand years,"[16] the office of the deputy imam was envisaged. But all the personalities upon whom this title was bestowed in history were purely religious personalities and none of them had any direct political role. Khomaini's teaching, therefore, is a grave heresy even from the point of view of historical Shi'ism. His justification for the 'Ulama's rule, is that these, being the "inheritors of the Prophet," must possess that inheritance *in toto*, including political power. Since his doctrine of clerical rule has little basis in the Qur'an, he relies on a few Hadiths or traditions of the Prophet. By now, it is well known, not only among the Western scholars of Islam but among many educated Muslim circles as well, that both Shi'i and Sunni Hadith is suspect and that all political Hadith on both sides is forged. But even apart from this, classical Islamic authorities had laid it down as a principle that in cases where a Hadith blatantly contradicts the Qur'an, the former must be rejected or interpreted in conformity with the Qur'an.

Now, Khomaini's position of "rule by the clergy" is in patent contradiction with the Qur'an and even in grave violation of traditional Shi'i religio-political thought. It is truly astonishing how Khomaini, with this kind of narrow (and distorted!) basis, has been entertaining hopes of "exporting" the Iranian Revolution to Sunni Muslim countries. What he has essentially done is to arouse the Shi'a 'Ulama' to political action—and, indeed, to violence—in reaction to the late shah's oppressive and suppressive policies: "The seats of religious learning should become alert and should equip themselves with organizations and the necessary power to be able to control matters."[17] Again, "The 'Ulama' enjoy the same trust as the Prophets in matters of executing laws, military command, governing the society, defending the country, judging cases and dispensing justice."[18] And finally, here is Khomaini's philosophy of dealing with the political opposition: "Therefore, Islam has killed many people in the interests of social weal and has destroyed many people in order to safeguard the larger interests of society. It has annihilated whole groups because they sowed corruption and were injurious to society."[19] Khomaini gives no examples of such incidents. Certainly, his own massacre of so many groups inside Iran contrasts oddly with the general declaration of amnesty by the Prophet Muhammad when in 630 C.E. he triumphantly entered his own hometown of Mecca which for two decades had persecuted him, tortured his followers and fought several battles against him. When some of his followers wanted to avenge themselves against some of their enemies, the Qur'an intervened, saying, "Let the enmity of a people not determine you upon an unjust course of action; be fair, for justice is nearest to piety" (Qur'an, 9, 8).

This critique of Khomaini's concept of the Islamic state and of others who reject democratic participation of the community in the governance of the state in favor of some kind of elitism, whether religious or other (as, for example, General Zia al-Haqq of Pakistan has explicitly done on several occasions) is only intended to show how difficult it is to understand and appreciate the Qur'an on its own terms and without the coloration of centuries of tradition, vested interests, wishful thinking, and so on. There is little doubt that the Qur'an wants a certain sociopolitical order established on earth, that for this it wants to prepare a community whose nature and constitution we have described in this essay and that political action is, therefore, of the essence of Islam and unthinkable without its being subservient to the Islamic ideals. This is called *jihad* or "total effort in the cause of Allah." This *jihad* can be peaceful, but, if necessary, fighting is not to be shunned: Islam is far from being a religion of violence; its aim is to establish a just and peaceful social order on earth; therefore, it cannot raise violence to the order of a moral principle in itself. Yet, if such an order cannot be set up without resort to some violence, it will not shirk violence. It should be pointed out that when, in the nineteenth and twentieth centuries, the greater part of Muslim lands fell under Western colonial domination, the anti-colonial liberation movements in many of these countries effectively invoked the principle of *jihad* to regain independence, the Algerians losing 10 percent of their population fighting for it.

NOTES

1. Ibn Ishaq, *Sirat Rasal Allah*, vol. 1 (Cairo, 1963), p. 208.
2. Ibid, pp. 189 ff.
3. A. Yusuf Ali, ed. and trans., *The Holy Qur'an* (Lahore, 1934, 1959), 18, 28; 6, 52. All further quotations from the Qur'an are from this edition and are indicated by *sura* and verse.
4. Qur'an, 9, 60.
5. Qur'an, 90, 17; 103, 3.
6. Qur'an, 5, 2.
7. Qur'an, 49, 11–13, particularly verse 13.
8. Qur'an, 3, 104, 110, 114; 22, 41.
9. Qur'an, 26, 152; 27, 48; 2, 11, 193, 251, and passim.
10. Qur'an, 22, 39–40; 2, 193.
11. H.A.R. Gibb, *Mohammedanism* (London: Oxford University Press, 1964), p. 30.

12. For one version of this, see Fazlur Rahman, *Islam* (Chicago: University of Chicago Press, 1979), p. 239; also, the entire analysis of political Hadith in chapters 2 and 3 of idem, *Islamic Methodology in History* (Lahore, Pakistan: Islamic Research Institute, 1965).

13. Rahman, *Islamic Methodology*.

14. Rahman, *Islam*, p. 259.

15. I have translated some of these into English and hope to complete the translation at the earliest possible opportunity.

16. *Wilayet-i-Faqih* (in Persian), (n.p., n.d.), p. 30.

17. Ibid., p. 85 and passim.

18. Ibid., p. 91.

19. Ibid., p. 111.

10

Islamic Resurgence: Religion and Politics in the Muslim World

CHARLES J. ADAMS

A great deal of attention has been attracted in recent days by the phenomenon that is variously known as Islamic resurgence, Islamic revivalism, militant Islam, integralist Islam or fundamentalist Islam. All of these terms, whatever may be their merits or their limitations as descriptions of what is happening, point to the same thing: the greatly increased role that Islam and Islamic factors seem, all at once, to have come to play upon the world stage, both in the internal affairs of the Muslim countries and in the relations of those countries with others. That role has been dramatically emphasized by such events as the Iranian revolution, the hostage crisis, the assassination of Anwar al-Sadat, the attack on the great mosque in Mecca, and the terrorist assault on American marines in Lebanon, all of which have drawn worldwide attention.

It will assist to make one distinction from the beginning. There are many things which people have in mind when they speak of Islamic resurgence, but two basic notions emerge: (1) the increased political and economic importance of certain Muslim-majority countries in recent years, and (2) the greatly enhanced influence of Islam and specifically religious factors on public life across the Islamic world.

We may deal with the first of these views of Islamic resurgence quickly, since it is not the matter of primary concern here. The growing political and economic weight of parts of the Muslim world are due almost entirely to the discovery of abundant petroleum in the countries concerned. As a fuel, as a raw material and as a strategic military resource, petroleum is an indispensable commodity for the industrial world, and those in a position to control supplies of petroleum have found themselves in a highly favored position. Although some of the Muslim oil-producing countries—such as

Kuwait, Qatar, Bahrain and the Arab Emirates—are tiny in area, and others— such as Saudi Arabia and Libya—have small populations, and all of them relatively underdeveloped, they exercise great influence in the international arena.

The possession of oil has brought with it also great wealth. Oil revenues have risen and accumulated at such a rate that the decade between 1973 and 1983 has witnessed what is perhaps the greatest transfer of liquid wealth in the entire history of the world in a comparable period of time. It has been of vital importance to the industrialized countries to recycle oil wealth back into the industrialized economies from which it has been drawn, either through the sale of goods and services or through investment. The result has been to consolidate and extend the already considerable prestige and power of the oil producers and, indeed, to change the structure of the entire world economy. The miracle of oil has also enabled the producers them- selves to introduce measures of immense and enormously rapid social change that are transforming the lives of their own people. When Islamic resurgence is mentioned, often there is not more in mind than the fact that certain Muslim peoples, formerly impoverished and of little significance in world affairs, are now riding the crest of a wave of great good fortune.

This change for the better in worldly fortunes is not without relationship, however, to the second sense of Islamic resurgence, for accompanying the growth in power, prestige and wealth has also been a psychological change, a shift in the mood of Muslims, that is of incalculable importance. It has affected not only the Muslim populations who directly benefit from recent developments but others as well, who share in the exultation, if not the wealth, brought by oil. The Qur'an teaches Muslims that they are the "best of communities," holding out the expectation that life in obedience to the will of the sovereign God will be one of fulfillment both here and hereafter.[1] Early Islamic history bore out the divine promise, by giving rise to one of the most powerful, brilliant and creative civilizations the human race has known. For several centuries now, however, and more especially in the past 150 years, in spite of its glorious heritage the Muslim community has been subjected to encroachment, disruption and domination by others. Among intellectual leaders there has emerged a pervasive sense of decline bordering on despair and a virtual obsession with the reasons for it and the ways to reverse it.[2] However, with the recent great access of prestige and power matters seem to be righting themselves, at least so it appears from a Muslim perspective. Gone is much of the depression and sense of intellectual and religious crisis that arose from the frustration of the expectations Islam posed for the faithful. In their place have come anticipation and an ebullient optimism. After a long period of trial, the upswing in Muslim fortunes seems both to vindicate the truth of Islam once more and to substantiate its philosophy of history. The consequence has been not only an easing of tensions in many Muslim minds but also a renewed sense of the validity of the faith and a vigorous assertiveness. There can be little doubt that improvement in Muslim fortunes has contributed in a decided way to the renewed and powerful expressions of Islamic religiousness.

We may turn now to the second sense of Islamic resurgence, the apparently greater role of Islam in public life in Muslim countries, or to put it another way, the greater visibility of Islam in recent times. Here we may distinguish between the personal and the social use of Islamic symbols.

At the personal or individual level there are a number of ways in which an apparently closer tie to Islam manifests itself in many different countries across the Islamic world. Among them, for example, is the tendency of increasing numbers of young men to wear beards in accord with the requirements of Islamic law. One of those most remarked upon by outside observers is a return to the veil or to some other kind of dress that can be identified as specifically Islamic on the part of large numbers of women. Not only in Iran, where the full weight of the regime has been thrown behind more traditional modes of dress for women, but elsewhere in the Islamic world also this trend is quite marked. In Egypt, which is in many ways the most Westernized and most sophisticated of all the Arab countries, the effort of swelling numbers of women to meet Islamic standards of dress is quite noticeable. This may be seen among university students to a marked degree, and also among older women of the relatively well-to-do and Westernized middle classes. Such a phenomenon, however, is not necessarily a sign of greater personal piety on the part of the wearer of the veil. Here we have a fact of great importance that points to the diversity and complexity of the so-called Islamic resurgence. The use of religious symbolism is ambiguous; it may have non-religious meanings as well as religious ones and perhaps—even most often—a mixture of the two. In addition to giving religious reasons for their behavior, Egyptian girls who have been questioned about their adoption of Islamic dress have replied in terms of its appropriateness for the cultural milieu, of its traditional nature and of its authenticity as a symbol of their own identity as Egyptians and Muslims.[3] They reject Western fashions as a betrayal of what they are, preferring a mode of dress that stems from their own culture. Such a way of dressing, they affirm, makes them feel more comfortable.

Women's dress is also a form of political protest, a way for a woman to indicate her adherence to the tenets of one of the Islamically oriented sociopolitical protest groups that have become so prominent a feature of politics in some Muslim countries. When worn for this reason, the veil is among other things the symbol of a political stand, much like the Afro hairdos familiar in American culture. In Iran prior to the revolution any woman university student who wore a *chador* was identified automatically as a dissenter against the policies of the regime, and in the University of Isfahan where the writer taught for a time, such women were excluded from eligibility for scholarships or other forms of assistance from the university. Nonetheless, there were many *chadors* on the campus, since their very ambiguity made them one of the few safe ways in which a public statement of dissent could be made. The *chador* had special appeal as a symbol, no doubt, because of the ruthlessness with which Reza Shah had tried to suppress this practice of the old, pre-modern Iran and because of the sense of cultural alienation so widely felt in Iran, but at the same time it represented a religiously approved, if not mandated, form of dress. It would be difficult to think of another symbol that so effectively brings the weight of religious sentiment to bear on the political situation, though there were a number of other powerful religious symbols employed in the Iranian revolution.[4] The presence of hundreds of thousands of veiled women in the demonstrations against the shah was a dramatic statement of the torment created in many Iranian souls by the policies of the regime, especially the headlong adoption of foreign models that seemed to threaten the very existence of a distinctive Iranian culture. Again at the personal level one can also point to a greater visibility of Islam in terms of attendance at the mosque, practice of the ritual prayers, observation of the month of fast, and participation in other religious observances or ceremonies of the community.[5]

The upsurge of Islamic observance at the personal level is all the more striking in the light of the general lines of development in the Islamic world in the past one hundred years. There have been strong trends toward the progressive urbanization, modernization, Westernization and secularization of the Islamic societies, and these trends have wrought incalculable changes in the nature of the societies at issue. In spite of the strength and persistence of these trends, however, they have not succeeded in displacing or significantly weakening the religious ties of the great majority of persons.[6] This is especially true of the vast bulk of the lower strata of these societies who are scarcely touched, if at all, by the transformations in world view that have accompanied the emergence of the modern age. The judgment holds true as well, however, in varying degrees, for the elite groups, educated and semi-educated, of the Muslim societies. The leadership responsible for the modernizing and secularizing course of most Muslim countries is drawn from this class of people, many of whom have lived, studied and worked in the Western world. While there may be much less of deeply felt personal piety and a looser observance of religious duties among them than in the lower classes, there are very few who have turned their backs on the religious tradition altogether. Islam is too closely bound up with the culture and the past glory of the Islamic peoples for it to lose its meaning completely as a symbol of identity and as a basis for dignity even among the highly Westernized—and sometimes irreligious—elites. Given a climate that is favorable, the sometimes hidden, perhaps dormant, impulse to Islamic expression has come surging to the surface. On their face these outbursts of pious behavior may seem purely religious, but at another level they also give vent to the manifold discontents, fears and frustrations of the modern Muslim intellectual.

The social uses of Islamic symbols in the present day Islamic world have also increased in number and in frequency. This is equivalent to saying that Islam and its principles have exerted an increased influence on the politics and public life of the Muslim world. This is the matter that has captured headlines, that has attracted the interest and awakened the fear of people outside the Islamic lands, which is, in fact, the nub of the concern for Islamic resurgence. A very large number of examples of Islamic impact on political life could be cited. They range from concession by the highly secularist Bourguiba government in Tunisia to provide more religious education in schools, for example, to prohibitions of the public consumption of alcohol by Muslims in Egypt and the banning of dancing acts in nightclubs in Kuwait.

The most persistent such manifestation, however, is the demand to recognize and enforce the provisions of the Shari'a or Islamic law. The very heart of religious duty as the majority of Muslims understand it lies in submission or commitment to obey a set of rules and prohibitions laid down by the sovereign will of deity and called collectively by the name Shari'a. In theory this Shari'a or divinely marked out "path" contains provisions that suffice to give guidance for every aspect of human activity. In the course of Islamic history, however, many—indeed, most—of those provisions have been neglected, forgotten or replaced by other kinds of law. The sole part of the Shari'a other than religious ritual to have escaped this process of evolution and erosion is that which deals with so-called personal law, such matters as marriage, divorce and inheritance.[7] The personal law forms as it were the core of the Shari'a, at least as most present-day Muslims see it, and for much of recent history when thinkers have called for protecting or reinstating the Shari'a, they have meant only this personal law with perhaps the addition of some elements of traditional Islamic criminal law. Muslim spokesmen in virtually every Islamic country have been insistent upon the necessity to preserve the Shari'a as the actual law of Muslim society. Many, however, go beyond the somewhat limited understanding of Islamic law indicated above to insist that the law must serve as an ideology which controls the life of the individual, the society and the state in every particular. Thus they would enforce portions of the law that have long been in abeyance and would seek generally to extend the control of the law into ever-expanding areas of life.

Moves to strengthen the role of Islamic law in public life have been taken in a number of countries. In Egypt, for example, there was an attempt a short time back, much to the alarm of the Coptic minority, to enforce the death penalty for religious apostasy as specified by the Shari'a. In 1979 a referendum in the country to change the constitution made the Shari'a the source of *all* legislation; it had previously been only one among many

sources. In Pakistan the *hadd* punishments, that is, those punishments specifically laid down by the Qur'an for certain offenses such as theft and
adultery, have been officially instituted,[8] and squads of police have been
sent into public places to carry out the floggings decreed for some of these
offenses. Similar steps to accord with clear Islamic provisions in respect to
criminal law have been taken in Mauritania, Libya and Abu Dhabi.[9]

By far the most significant of the intrusions of Islamic elements into public
life have come in the political arena, however. In one instance, that of Iran,
a movement led by a religious figure, relying upon the active support of
the religious class, and making maximum use of an elaborate religious symbolism in its propaganda and its political activity, has succeeded in destroy-
ing a powerful and long-established regime and instituting in its place one
that is self-consciously Islamic. The Iranian revolution is perhaps the most
notable example in our time of Islam as politics, but it is far from the only
one. In many other countries also there have arisen religious-cum-political
movements, a number of which antedate the Iranian revolution by many
years, seeking either to influence the political process or more typically to
gain outright political power. Unlike the Islamic Republican party in Iran,
which has been successful, however precariously, in establishing itself in
the seat of power, elsewhere these movements usually take the form of
protest and present themselves as alternatives to systems, governments or
regimes that are deemed to be inadequate, wrongful, corrupt or unIslamic.
The attraction which an appeal to Islam exercises upon the generality of
Muslims is profound and powerful; parties making such an appeal constitute
a tangible and immediate danger to established systems and rulers. In consequence, the resurgence movements have been feared by those in power
and wherever possible, as in Syria, Pakistan and Saudi Arabia, for example,
have been suppressed; in other instances where it seemed unwise or impossible to exercise outright suppression, ruling groups have made concessions to resurgence movements, even co-opting or incorporating them into
government as in Sudan or in the early days of the Zia al-Haqq regime in
Pakistan as a way of blunting their criticisms. No observer of the international
scene can have missed the reactions of Islamic governments in other places
to the Iranian revolution or the steps which these governments have taken
to prevent the rise of similar tendencies in their own territories. As movements of political protest, the Islamic resurgent groups carry the potential
of disrupting the political arrangements of the entire Muslim world and of
reversing many of the important trends that have characterized it in recent
times.

The element of newness in the contemporary situation that has excited
so much interest is precisely the self-conscious encroachment of religion
upon the political sphere, indeed, the insistence of the spokesmen of Islamic
resurgence movements that politics should become no more than an expression of religion. While the call for dominance of religion in and over the

political sphere is everywhere the same for these movements, they differ from country to country in their social bases, the specific goals they pursue, the strategies adopted, the programs espoused, and the details of the ideological stances upheld.[10] In these respects the resurgence movements are not monolithic, but they have enough in common that they may be viewed as constituting one important type of Muslim reaction to the modern world. We may now look briefly at some of what they share with one another.

First, these movements are characterized by their view of Islam as an all-embracing ideology, an integral system that provides the norms not alone for an individual life, but also for the state and for society as a whole. They operate, therefore, on the basis of an articulated, well-rounded and rigid set of ideas, drawn from the Qur'an and prophetic tradition, which purport to provide ready answers to most of the problems—varied as these may be—of Muslim societies and to relate those answers to an ultimate basis. The claim that Islam is an ideology is itself a very recent notion among Muslims and is one index of the extent to which these movements, despite their aim to resurrect and restore the pure Islam of the Prophet and his immediate successors, are the products of the age in which they have appeared. Like other committed ideologists, the upholders of Islamic ideology are intolerant of points of view that differ from their own. The choice which they hold out to those whom they address is that between complete and absolute good on the one hand and irredeemable error on the other, there being no in-between ground and no possibility for an evolution of perspectives or for the discovery of new, heretofore unknown, truths that may affect the vital issues of human life. In their understanding Islam is a seamless whole of revealed truth, a total way of life, whose ordainer is God and which needs only to be unfolded from the infallible divinely inspired sources. Islamic truth must, therefore, be accepted in its totality or not at all. Such an absolutist view of the duties of Muslims is the element which causes these movements to be perceived as anti-modern, anti-Western and anti-liberal.

In accord with traditional Islamic thinking the resurgent movements do allow a place in the ideal societies toward which they strive for non-Muslim minorities. These minorities, however, would occupy a special status as protected groups not enjoying full political rights and living under certain restrictions. Neither members of religious minorities nor dissenters of any other kind, including Muslims of divergent views, might be allowed to frustrate the full implementation of the Islamic ideology and the realization of the society it aims to build. The exercise of power but especially the right of decision making would have to remain in the hands of upholders of the Islamic ideology. In practice the stand of the Islamic resurgence movement in Iran has been extremely harsh toward religious minorities; the Baha'is in particular have been subjected to a bloody and relentless persecution, and others, such as Christians, have seen their places of worship desecrated and closed.

Based as they are upon a belief in the sufficiency and authority of certain decisive revelatory events in the past, the resurgence movements are committed to a static view of truth. The ideal standard of truth and model for the just and upright sociopolitical order are located in the era of the Prophet and his four rightly guided successors or caliphs. There is no place either for innovative thought or for social experimentation in order to solve the pressing problems of the Islamic world or modern society more generally, no matter how much the world may have changed or may continue to change. In the view of the movements to which we refer the guidance which the Muslim community has possessed from the very beginning of its history is sufficient and unimpeachably authoritative; the call of these movements is for the Muslims to follow the clearly given guidance and in so doing to transform the world. Hence, they are anti-intellectual, seeing all questioning, probing or speculation outside the limits of what they consider to be the proper Islamic views and methods to be implicit attacks upon the one true Islamic "system."

The resurgence movements are also vigorously apologetic, coming strongly to the defence of Islam against rival ideologies or criticisms. This is not to say that they are necessarily reactionary in the sense of opposing or rejecting the technical and even some of the social changes which modernization has brought about in the lands of Islam, for, in fact, they incorporate many of these innovations into the vision of the ideal society which they seek. In this respect they exhibit the same ambiguity toward change and adaptation that may be seen in almost every strain of modern Muslim thought.[11] Such changes are, however, through one device or another explained and justified on Islamic grounds, whatever their historical origins may have been. Thus, for example, the resurgence movements use the terminology and profess to preserve the forms of liberal democracy while, in fact, the political and social systems which they aim to establish are thoroughgoingly authoritarian, even totalitarian. It would be a complete misunderstanding to view the political initiatives of the resurgence movements as a protest against the authoritarianism of existing regimes in the name of a more open and free society, no matter what the content of the political rhetoric they may employ. Quite to the contrary, they are efforts to substitute one type of authoritarianism, perhaps even more thoroughgoing, for another type.[12] Conspicuously lacking in the ideological perspective is any recognition of the possibility, not to speak of the need, to adapt basic religious perspectives to accommodate the radically different world view of the modern world. Also lacking is any accommodation to divergent opinions about the basic structure of an Islamic polity and the principles it should follow.

In the instances of certain movements, such as the Muslim Brothers of Egypt and the Arab world or the Jama'at-i Islami in Pakistan, these Islamic political protest movements have been highly organized and highly effective in their ability to mobilize opinion to support the causes in which they believe. Except when governments have interfered with their operations, which has often happened, they have developed trained cadres of full-time workers, have recruited sympathizers and supporters, and have built up organizations that touch not only every separate town and city but distinct neighborhoods within the towns. When allowed to operate, they publish literature, hold meetings, set up schools, organize labor unions and engage in charitable activities. Most important of all, they also field candidates and contest elections, carrying on a generalized political activity and propaganda. In spite of opposition, even repression, by governments the survivability of the resurgence movements is remarkable; they have in some instances suffered greatly but have nonetheless remained active, sometimes clandestinely and sometimes by spawning other organizations which allow the same activities to be pursued under different names. The latter is the case with the Jama'at-i Islami in Pakistan at the present time.

The tendency of such movements is also to be puritanical, to insist upon a strict discipline for those who constitute the actual membership of the group and to argue for a strong public morality, backed by the police power of the state, in the society at large. Their unbending discipline applied to their own people has, in fact, been one of the great elements in their organizational effectiveness and in the appeal that such movements have exerted on many Muslims. In societies where public life has been riddled with corruption, or at least been perceived to be so by the majority of citizens, the presence of a body of pious, upright individuals who not only proclaim a lofty moral ideal but adhere to it in their personal lives is a factor of much impressiveness. Their moralism, however, is both a weakness as well as a strength, for as ideologically oriented groups, these organizations tend to pay more attention to broad principles than to specific problems. The whole thrust of their politics can in certain cases be reduced to moral criticism of those in power, who, it is held, must necessarily be in error, no matter what their actions, since they do not adhere to the single set of true principles for the governance of a state as enunciated by Islam. This attitude breeds a high degree of unrealism in their political rhetoric. The purpose of politics from such a perspective becomes that of replacing morally bad leadership with a morally good one, and no need is felt to spell out the details of the measures that will be undertaken or the policies that will be pursued. Politics is necessarily, therefore, always aimed at the overthrow and replacement of entire regimes and political systems, not only at the alternation of specific policies or party orientations. It should be small wonder then that governments take the resurgent religious protest movements with great seriousness or that they act decidedly to attempt to blunt their effect.

Perhaps most alarming to people both within and outside the Muslim world, some of the resurgence movements have also adopted violence as a means to achieve their ends. The notable case is Iran, and it is the more telling because it is the one instance of an Islamic movement actually gaining power and being able to put its convictions more or less into practice. The existence of the paramilitary secret arm of the Muslim Brothers was revealed in the attempt of the life of 'Abd al-Nasser in 1958 and led to the suppression of that organization and the imprisonment and execution of some of its leaders.[13] We have been reminded more recently of these violent potentialities by the assassination of Anwar al-Sadat, whose murder was accomplished precisely by a group drawn from one of the more radical Egyptian Islamic movements, and also by the occupation of the great mosque in Mecca. The most devastating incidence of violence in connection with one of the Islamic resurgence groups, however, was the action of the Syrian government to thwart an apprehended insurrection among the Muslim Brothers in the city of Hama. The military steps taken against the brotherhood resulted in destruction of a large part of the principal Syrian cities and the deaths of hundreds, if not thousands, of Syrian citizens.

There are no doubt many reasons why religious political movements of the kind we have been describing should have appeared at this particular point in history, and to give an adequate account of their antecedents and what has created them would involve us in the lengthy business of examining them one by one against the background of the time and place in which each arose. As we have said, some have existed for years and others are of more recent origin; each exhibits important differences in comparison with others. While insisting that detailed study of the individual movements is ultimately necessary, we must be content here with pointing to three of the background factors that have formed the climate from which these movements have sprung. These factors are not in themselves sufficient to account for the rise of particular movements and organizations, but they will help to understand the milieu which the resurgent Islamic political movements presuppose.

The first thing which all of these movements, from the Iranian Revolution to the Jam'at-i Islami, implies is a strong sense of social crisis in the Islamic world. Wilfred Cantwell Smith, one of the most sensitive students of contemporary Islam, has said that the premise of all else in modern Islamic thought is the feeling that something has gone wrong with Islamic history and the need to put it right.[14] For more than a century and a half the Islamic world has been preoccupied with an awareness that its former greatness has slipped away and that it is afflicted with a debilitating but poorly understood malaise.[15] It is not necessary to dwell at length on the nature of the crisis in the Islamic lands, for its dimensions are well known. It is related on the one hand to centuries of weakness and the experience of being dominated on every level, political, economic, military and cultural, by colonial powers and the representatives of an alien civilization. The humiliation and injury which Muslim peoples have felt in consequence of this long period of decline is deep-seated and enduring. On the other hand, the crisis is also related to disruption within the Islamic societies themselves, the collapse of traditional modes of social organization and behavior, the frantic experimenting with social readjustments and political forms, the loss of ancient cultural values, the paucity of distributive justice, and the growing sense of bewilderment over identity and purpose. The stimulus for much of what has happened has come from the outside, but its effects have been worked out within the Islamic societies, and they have almost always been destructive. Even the recent explosion in the wealth of some Islamic states and its secondary effects on their neighbors, while it might seem to offer new hope and pride, has also contributed significantly to the disuption and malaise. Wealth has provided the means for governments to initiate and carry through schemes which have altered the social fabric of certain Muslim countries almost beyond recognition, all within a very short span of time. Far from solving the problems of the oil producers and making their people happy, wealth and what it has been used to do have exacerbated the dis-satisfactions of many parts of the population, creating near, if not outright, revolutionary tendencies. The widespread unhappiness with the state of society has provided a fertile seed-bed for the Islamic political movements we have talked about. Their appeal is the stronger in direct proportion to the insecurity, frustration, puzzlement and humiliation felt by their fellow citizens around them.

A second element that contributes to the milieu favorable to Islamic resurgence movements of a political and ideological nature is the manifest failure of the other experiments that have been undertaken in the Islamic world to find a synthesis that would integrate the Islamic societies and given them vitality in the radically changed conditions of modernity. Along with the disillusionment about such forces as nationalism and socialism has gone an even more significant disillusionment with the Western civilization that is their inspiration and source. No longer for most Muslims is the West an ideal to be emulated; rather it has been revealed as itself inherently weak and unstable, unable to solve its own problems or even to ensure its survival. Perhaps most forceful of all is the sense of the West being corrupted and morally degraded. In spite of great intellectual effort by Muslim thinkers and a series of social upheavals that have come with bewildering rapidity, there remains a sense of failure and frustration, a continued groping for the approach that would preserve the best in the tradition while appropriating the dynamic of the modern age. In the early part of this century, but es-pecially in the period at the end of the Second World War when most of the Muslim world threw off the yoke of colonialism, there was all but universal confidence in the promise held out by nationalism, constitution-alism, republican institutions and liberal democracy. When subsequent to the war in country after country, along with the achievement of independ-ence the hopes based on the democratic experiment turned to ashes, there was then an attempt to find the justice, stability and strength that the Muslim

peoples seek in various forms of socialism and more recently in increasingly
authoritarian forms of government. What has, in fact, been the result of this
development of political forms and social experiments is the emergence of
military dictatorships in much of the Muslim world. Only a decade ago the
prevailing ideology in the Arab world and the rallying cry of its various
national groups was a virulent revolutionary nationalism; today there are
perhaps some dying voices still upholding the elan of the Arab nation as
the answer to the problems of society, but those voices grow faint and are
steadily giving way to others that now proclaim the solution to lie in turning
or returning to an Islamic commitment.

The failure is no less marked in the intellectual sphere. Islamic modernism
which had its origins in the recognition of something radically amiss and
lacking in the traditional Muslim approach to the world has also been unable
to provide the answers and the conditions that would satisfy the yearnings
of the Muslim populations. In its beginnings the modernism of thinkers such
as Sayyid Ahmad Khan or Muhammad 'Abduh, al-Tahtawi and others was
frank in admitting the shortcomings of the community's historical heritage
and in advocating change, even where that change meant adopting the
institutions and the ways of thinking of others. With the passage of time,
however, analysis and criticism of Muslim problems degenerated into apologetics, and the advocacy of change gave way to the romanticization of the
Islamic past. Instead of being an impulse to seize and remake Muslim des-
tinies—a spur to dynamism—modernism has for some time now been a
source of bland assurances that divert Muslim attention from the real problems of the time and blunt the thrust of the intellectual enterprise. The
need for a thorough rethinking of the role of the tradition in relation to the
accelerating change of the modern age is no less today than it was one
hundred years ago—it is, in fact, much greater—but the Islamic modernists
have failed to carry through the task.[16] Almost everywhere today the modernists are in disrepute and of little influence. The vacuum that they have
left in intellectual life has been filled by the anti-intellectual authoritarianism
and broad, general, moralizing formulae of the Islamic resurgence movements which claim to offer an ideology so complete and so perfect that it
answers all questions and deals with all problems.

The third element in the milieu that favors the militant Islamic movements
is the strong and unbroken hold that Islam exercises upon the minds of the
majority of Muslims despite the inroads of modernity and all its minions.
The social, political and intellectual experiments that have been conducted
in the Muslim world in response to the demands of the modern age have
all occurred through the initiative of a relatively small elite of leaders, many
of whom are highly secularized and alienated from their own social origins
and many of whom have also received their personal and intellectual formation in Western universities. These leaders have led their compatriots
along pathways that have to a large extent been marked out after the pattern

of alien, Western models, and in doing so have left their fellows behind. Undoubtedly one of the reasons why both liberal democracy and socialism have floundered in the Islamic context is the fact that both are institutions of a foreign origin which the majority of the Muslim populations do not understand or find ultimately to be legitimate. The course that the Muslim world has followed has raised the twin questions of identity and legitimacy in a most acute form, and there is quite clearly a strong preference among many for what can be seen without question as being familiar and truly their own. Modernization is not necessarily to be equated with Westernization, there being other possibilities, but Westernization is the mode or form of modernization that most Muslim countries have pursued. To the extent they have done so, they have alienated a large portion of their own people and thereby undercut their own policies. Even for the elite leadership groups themselves the course followed has been a difficult and painful one, not without a profound ambiguity. Had the power relationships between the dominant Western world and the Islamic countries been different, as they were once in the past, the process of cultural borrowing that the elite leadership felt it necessary to undertake in order to recoup the fortunes of their lands would have been much easier. There is little trauma for one in a superior position when he adopts or takes on some of the characteristics of those whom he dominates as the Muslim in the classical period had done, for instance, with Greek thought. But consider the psychological pain that ensues when the dominated must borrow from the dominator, must in part take on the qualities of the hated other and forsake his own, in order to counter the evil effects of domination. Such is the dilemma in which the Muslim leadership has often found itself, and therein lies much of the explanation for the apologetics that is so characteristic of modern Islamic religious thought. One great strength of the Islamic resurgence movements is the fact that they escape this dilemma and all of the ambiguities that it poses. They speak in terms of something that is familiar to the populations among whom they work, and they appeal to values which the Muslim peoples instinctively embrace and recognize as ultimate. Their stance does not pose, at least initially, the same troublesome problems of legitimacy and identity that liberals, modernizers, Westernizers, secularists, socialists, communists, republicans and military dictators all must face and deal with. The proposed Islamic solution to the social crisis is, therefore, immediately both better understood and more acceptable than its rivals. For many Muslims the resurgence movements have come like a person speaking their own language after a long period of trying to cope with a foreign political and social idiom.

In the space that remains we shall offer some brief comments on the Islamic resurgence in respect to three countries, Saudi Arabia, Iran and Pakistan. The discussion in this regard will be more clear, however, if we first distinguish several types of relationships between Islam and the state as currently exemplified in the Muslim world.[17] We may then use these types as a means of locating the countries to be discussed in a systematic scheme.

There are, we may suggest in agreement with 'Ali Dessouki, three principle kinds of relations between the state and Islam at the present moment. There are first of all situations where states have consciously allied themselves with the Islamic cause and claimed to base their policies on Islamic principles as they see them. Among states with long-standing relationships of this kind to Islam may be numbered Morocco and Saudi Arabia while Iran has joined their ranks more recently. Second, there is a kind of relationship in which states call upon Islam as a means of legitimizing both their policies and their very existence. The Egypt of Anwar al-Sadat and of 'Abd al-Nasser, as well as Pakistan, Libya and numerous others may be considered as exemplifying this type. The last manner of relationship is one in which Islam stands against the state; presenting itself as a judge of the existing system and an alternative to it. Such a relationship is that which characterizes the attitude toward the state of most of the Islamic resurgence movements that we have tried to describe a few paragraphs above. These movements are found universally in the Islamic world, as we shall soon see, even in those countries where governments consider themselves the upholders and purveyors of an Islamic world view. 'Ali Dessouki characterizes the first two relationships as "Islam from the top down" and the latter as "Islam from the bottom up."

We may begin then with Saudi Arabia. In the eighteenth century in the province of Najd in the north central part of the Arabian peninsula there arose a religious movement of great vigor centered upon the teachings of a certain Muhammad ibn 'Abd al-Wahhab. The essence of his religious message was the need to purify Islamic religious life and practice of accretions which over the centuries had corrupted it and stolen its vitality; he sought a return to what he considered to be the pristine and simple Islam of an earlier time, believing that the dynamic of the early generations of Muslims would thus be regained. The movement was strongly puritanical and fundamentalist; it was also militant. Taking root among the Bedouin tribes of the Najd, it acquired sufficient strength and following to establish a Wahhabi regime in the Arabian peninsula in the nineteenth century that had to be put down by a Turkish military expedition sent from Egypt. In the present century, however, Wahhabi fortunes rose once again when the sect found a champion in the Sa'ud family, who through a combination of military operations and tribal diplomacy were able eventually to extend their control over most of the peninsula.

From the very beginning, therefore, the Kingdom of Saudi Arabia has been identified with militant Islam, and there is probably no other country in the world except possibly Iran in recent times where at the official level Islam pervades every aspect of life to the extent that it does in the Saudi kingdom or where Islamic symbols are exhibited so frequently. There is a strict enforcement of the injunctions of Islamic law in respect to such things as the consumption of alcohol, the mixing of the sexes, punishments for crime, observance of the fast and the like, and Saudi Arabia is the only country I know where police have gone about the streets at the time of prayer to ensure that all those in public places render their devotions. Saudi Arabia has within its boundaries the sacred territories of Mecca and Medina, the cities where the Prophet lived and foremost holy places for all Muslims. It is therefore eternally the homeland of Islam and sees itself in consequence as having been naturally vested with the leadership of the Muslim world. The government has lavished attention as well as huge sums of money on improving and embellishing the shrines themselves and the facilities within the sacred territories. Every year at the time of the pilgrimage enormous numbers of persons from other parts of the Islamic world descend upon Saudi Arabia for the obligatory rites, and the government has considered it a special obligation to see to the facilities for the transport, protection, provisioning, and well-being of these pilgrims.[18] The arrangements for the pilgrimage are the single greatest and most important activity of the Saudi government.

Not only does Saudi Arabia give its resources to the promotion of Islam within its own territories; it has also been the most generous of the Muslim states in promoting the cause of Islam elsewhere. Saudi money has financed international Muslim organizations such as the Rabitat al-'Alam al-Islami, has built mosques, Islamic religious centers and libraries in many places, including the United States and Canada, has provided student fellowships, has encouraged Islamic organizations such as the Muslim Students Association of North America and so on through a long list of religious and charitable activities. Saudi money is also one key to the very considerable missionary effort now being mounted on behalf of Islam, not the least of the centers of its attention being North America and especially its black community. In this case Islamic resurgence would almost seem capable of being equated with the expansion of possibilities and activities that the money from its oil has opened to the Saudi Arabian kingdom.

All, however, is not as simple as it seems, and that is one of the more important themes in regard to Islamic resurgence that must be emphasized. Although the Kingdom of Saudi Arabia rests its claim to sovereignty and legitimacy upon its role as the defender and promoter of Islam, the government of the country is, in fact, a kingship where all power rests in the large and decidedly autocratic royal family. Now kingship can in no way be justified or upheld on the basis of the classical Islamic political theory nor in terms of the principles of Islamic law. The reality of the situation is that legitimation in Saudi Arabia has two bases, one of them tribal and the other Islamic, and the two are plainly in conflict with one another. The rulers of the country, therefore, face a difficult dilemma. To the extent that they may attempt to strengthen the tribal basis of their rule, that is, to ensure and protect the position of the royal family, they invite the opposition and resentment of the orthodox religious authorities and the general population. If on the other hand they make the effort to strengthen their position by appeal to Islam, they undercut the claim to rulership as the Sa'ud family. If the operative priorities in the country are examined, not in terms of the professed ideology—which, to be sure, is Islam—but from the perspective of a student of politics, they are revealed to be as follows: first, the protection of the position of the royal family; second, the political and economic interests of the kingdom as a whole; third, Islam; and fourth, the interests of the other Arabs, then other Muslims, in that order. There is nothing in the Saudi outlook, regardless of its long alliance with a vigorous militant Islamic sect, that gives it sympathy with the Khomaini regime in Iran which so many others have seen as the initiator of a new Islamic era. On the contrary, it has shown unremitting hostility to Iran's Islamic revolution for fear of the havoc that such impulses would wreak with the situation of the royal family. The fears are increased and given real substance by the fact that Saudi Arabia has a large Twelver Shi'a minority of about 250,000 persons, most of whom are concentrated in the rich agricultural and oil-producing Hasa Province along the Persian Gulf. Agitation in favor of a Khomaini-style revolution had to be put down by military force among these Shi'i Saudis in 1979, and this was only one incident of a number in the past few years that have threatened the regime.

The ambiguity of the role of Islam is shown also by at least three other things in Saudi life. One is the incident in the great mosque in Mecca, which was seized by a group of armed religious dissidents in the autumn of 1979. The dissidents were dislodged by military means only after considerable loss of life and great physical damage to the sacred building and its precincts. Not a great deal is known about these dissidents because of the strict censorship that the Saudi authorities have maintained around the entire affair, but some things are clear. Those who invested the mosque were all members of a militant fundamentalist Islamic organization which has grown increasingly dissatisfied with the course of Saudi national development. Convinced that the country was being led away from Islam and that its resources were being squandered, the dissidents wanted to overthrow the regime. That is to say, their objectives were political, the displacement of the Saudi royal family and a restructuring of the polity. Their purposes were religious only in the individual sense of seeking a greater devotion to Islam or of trying to purify Islam in some way but had a strong social dimension. The objective of the operation was to shake the system and, if possible, to bring it tumbling down. Thus, this group conforms to the description of a militant resurgence movement in protest against the established system. The movement had acted in the name of Islam, but it was nonetheless ruthlessly suppressed by an outraged Saudi government.

Another matter of importance about the dissidents is the fact that the majority of them were apparently Saudis. Much has been made of the presence of large numbers of foreigners in the labor force in Saudi Arabia, their status as second-class residents of the kingdom and the potentiality which their presence holds for disruption and future trouble. Although there were foreigners among the dissidents and although the base from which their actions were planned and prepared was outside Saudi Arabia in Kuwait, the seizure of the great mosque was largely a Saudi show. It was a vivid illustration of the diversity and ambiguity—one may also say vitality—within the body of present-day Islam, indeed, within what we have called resurgent Islam.

A second and related matter that is revealing of the Saudi attitude is its treatment of resurgent groups such as the Muslim Brothers or the Jama'at-i Islami within the confines of the kingdom. Contrary to what one might expect from a regime assiduous in the cause of Islam, these organizations are simply not allowed to exist, no doubt because they would be possible sources of criticism directed against the state policy and the royal family. The Saudi authorities and the various religious organizations they have sponsored do, however, make much use of the ideologies espoused by these movements. The writings of Mawdudi, leader of the Jama'at-i Islami, and of Sayyid Qutb, the popular martyred (in Egypt) spokesman of the Muslim Brothers are translated, printed and distributed on a large scale both inside and outside the country. That such activity should occur in government-sponsored agencies is ample evidence of the authorities' approval of the resurgent ideologies per se. The resurgent organizations, however, are quite another thing. As potential sources of opposition, subversion and perhaps even armed resistance, they must be suppressed. In other countries, however, the Saudis have been open-handed in their support of such organizations in those instances where their foreign policy dictated such support. In Syria, for example, where the Muslim Brothers have been the most effective opposition to Hafiz al-Assad's government, whose radicalism the Saudis strongly oppose, large amounts of money have come for the Brothers' activities from Saudi sources. As mentioned earlier, this major dissident group has gone as far as staging an armed uprising in a major Syrian city, and it was put down only with much destruction and loss of life.

The third and perhaps the most important thing in Saudi life that demonstrates the true place of religion in the order of things is the policy toward the religious class. In the expansive phase of modern Saudi history between 1902 and 1924 when the territories now comprising the kingdom were being brought under the control of the Sa'ud family, the most effective instrument available to Ibn Sa'ud was the religious organizations known as the Ikhwan. These were groups of Bedouin living in settlements and receiving religious instruction from teachers especially appointed for the purpose.[19] With Wahhabism as their ideology and a firm belief in the need for *jihad* to subject the world to Islam, these Bedouin warriors were a devoted, even fanatical, fighting force without which the Kingdom of Saudi Arabia would never have come into existence. Once the consolidation of Saudi territory had taken place through the conquest of the Hijaz in 1924, however, and the struggle to create institutions to assure proper rule and stability had begun, the uncompromising strictness and militancy of the Ikhwan became embarrassments for the Sa'ud family. Ibn Sa'ud was finally forced to take up arms against them in 1929 and to abolish the Ikhwan settlements and organizations completely. When militant religious convictions came into conflict with the interests of the ruling family and began to undercut the stability of the kingdom, the religious elements had to be sacrificed to the interests of the state.

The case is not dissimilar with the religious class, that considerable group of men learned in the traditional Islamic sciences and known as the 'Ulama'. The religious class is one of the elite elements of Saudi Arabia, the other two being the royal family and the tribal leaders, and they have played a most important role in the life of the kingdom. As Saudi Arabia has developed more and more of the institutions of a modern state, however, the tendency of government has been increasingly to restrict the functions of the 'Ulama' and to bring them within the state bureaucracy. On almost every occasion when the system faces a threat or the government becomes involved in controversy because of some policy or the other, the 'Ulama' are called upon to lend sanction and legitimacy to what is being done. For example, during the height of 'Abd al-Nasser's popularity in the Arab world after the Egyptian union with Syria, the Saudi government mounted a campaign to discredit the nationalism, socialism and radicalism which were the bases of Nasserism. The 'Ulama' wrote books and articles to prove that these foreign ideological notions were contrary to Islam and that sympathy with them was a dereliction of the Muslim's religious duty. So long as they support the state and the royal family, the authority and prestige of the 'Ulama' are given full recognition, but they are allowed little real autonomy and have no independent voice. There is as good as no possibility for them publicly to criticize the regime on religious grounds. The co-option of the religious class by the Saudi regime has been relatively easy to achieve because of the close tie between the Wahhabi shaikhs and the royal family, although there has been some 'Ulama' opposition to the modernizing policies of the state, but for the most part expressed directly to the king and not publicly. Saudi Arabia maintains its appearance of a state system devoted to the preservation and spread of Islam in part by keeping its religious class within well-defined limits and under close control.[20]

We may turn then to Iran. One writer (Fred Halliday), who has treated the Iranian revolution has said, with as much truth as wit, that the Iranian case offers evidence to support almost any theory of revolution one may care to espouse. It is not the purpose here to sort out the many factors that figured in the overthrow of the Pahlavi regime, nor are we interested in trying to fix where the responsibility for what happened might lie. We should like instead to elicit some of the things which the Iranian revolution tells us about resurgent Islam.

One of the first things which the Iranian revolution underlines as does no other event in recent times is the depth and the power of the appeal that an Islamic movement has for a broad spectrum of people in the Islamic world. An aspect of the revolution to which almost every observer has called attention was its character as a mass movement. Once it was launched, the revolution reached into and drew support from almost every segment of the Iranian society, and it forged a great national synthesis of many classes and styles of people without which its victory would not have been possible. Even those persons in Iran who had benefited most from the policies of the shah—and they were both many and powerful—lent their weight to the agitation against the regime though their ultimate economic and political interests would have been better served by the regime's survival. Today that social solidarity in the country has seriously broken down as the interests of different sections of the population again reassert themselves, but it is doubtful that a movement launched on any basis other than religion and with any other ideology could have mustered such broad support.

This judgment must be tempered to some degree by the peculiarly advantageous position enjoyed by the religious class in Iran as the revolution began and gained momentum. The various non-religious opposition groups—nationalists, leftists, secularists, and others—had been so successfully repressed by the shah's government that no one of them and no individual among them was in a position to exercise effective leadership.[21] The religious class, however, had retained its—admittedly somewhat loose—cohesiveness and maintained its institutional bases in the great shrine cities of both Iran and Iraq. It was in a position, therefore, to take the lead in the revolutionary movement as no other group was. Khomaini's role was beyond any doubt greatly enhanced by his membership in the religious class, indeed, would have been inconceivable without it. Even though he was in exile, he had access to the 'Ulama' of Iran and through them could influence events in the country in a decisive way. Under the circumstances it was inevitable that the Iranian revolution should have a strong religious flavor.

The call of Islam forged a unity among Iranians as has no other force in the course of the nation's long history. But the pull of the revolution was felt not only in Iran. Almost everywhere in the Islamic world, Islamic groups and parties welcomed the revolution as a great victory for Islam and hailed Khomaini as a noble hero who had done away with a corrupt and evil regime. The bitter Sunni-Shi'i differences of the past were apparently forgotten in the enthusiasm for Islam victorious. The Iranian revolution has become a symbol of the hopes and expectations of Muslims in many places for the transformation of their own societies into an Islamic order. In Egypt

the Muslim Brothers were and have remained enthusiastic about developments in Iran despite President al-Sadat's disapproval and despite the specifically Shi'i nature of many of the Iranian revolutionary symbols. There
was originally similar approval for the revolution expressed by the Jama'at-
i Islami in Pakistan and by much of the Pakistani public at large, though
strong doubts are now entertained in that country about the genuineness
and the Islamicness of the revolution because of the continued series of
executions in Iran. The Iraqi-Iranian war has contributed to this disillusionment with the revolution. There was excitement also in Iraq and the
states of the gulf region, all of which contain large Shi'a minorities for whom
the language of the revolution had an especially strong attraction. Even as
far away as Montreal, as a recent study of Syrian immigrants in the city has
shown, the events in Iran were admired and seen as a model for the changes
which these people, disaffected from the Ba'ath regime at home, hoped to
see take place in Syria.[22]

The case of Iran also teaches another lesson, however, for what has occurred there has not been simply the triumph of traditional Shi'ism over
the secular power of the shahs. There are strong elements of novelty in the
revolution as, indeed, there are in all of the Islamic resurgent movements
regardless of their claims to be reviving or resurrecting a pristine Islam
exemplified in the lives of the earliest generation of Muslims. One of the
most daring new aspects of the Iranian situation is the claim, made by
Khomaini in his well-known book, *Wilayat-i Faqih*, of the right of the
religious class to rule. Since the establishment of Shi'ism as the official
religion of Iran under the Safavid Shahs in the seventeenth century, the Shi'i
'Ulama' or religious class have maintained a relationship with the shahs that
was at times uneasy and strained but which basically recognized and supported the shahs as rightful rulers. It seldom dared to oppose the shahs and
certainly not to challenge their right to rule. Under the Qajar shahs in the
nineteenth century the dependence of the 'Ulama' upon the shahs and their
courts grew much weaker than it had been in the era of the great Safavids
because the rulers themselves were weaker, and at the time of the Tobacco
Boycott at the end of the century and the Constitutional Movement of the
present century the religious class began to play a definite political role in
Iran. The influence of the religious class in Iran today, however, goes far
beyond anything that this previous history has witnessed. There are elements in the traditional Shi'i teaching about the imamate that provide a
basis on which political prerogatives could be asserted for the religious
class, but Khomaini is the first to have put these claims strongly and bluntly
and then to have acted on them.

Another factor of novelty in the Iranian situation with far-reaching significance is the role played by the people at large. Not only has traditionally
elitist Twelver Shi'ism in effect been democratized in Iran, but the passivity
that was the characteristic attitude of the religious outlook in its classical

forms has been swept away. No more in Iran is the Shi'a believer urged to contain himself in patience and piety, hiding the true nature and import of his faith, to await the coming of the Imam Mahdi who will sweep away tyranny and injustice and initiate a reign of peace upon the earth. The eschatology that created passivity has been transformed into a realized eschatology, and the Iranian people are presented as the active, furious and vengeful instrument who hasten the coming of the Expected One by their own will to abolish tyranny and injustice. The divine truth and the destiny of this world are linked to the wrath and the passion for righteousness of the Iranian people as a whole. What happened in Iran is not a revival or even a revitalization of religious forms and emotions that existed in a previous age but rather the creation of quite a new and unique religious dispensation, offering ideas and forms of religious expression previously unknown to the tradition. The most important of these is the now broadly accepted principle that Islamic faith must issue forth into political activity that seeks to build the kingdom of the imam even before his coming.

Pakistan is almost an ideal case for studying the complexities of the relationship of Islam and the political process. The country came into being as the climax of a long and bitter political struggle that was conducted in the name and on behalf of the Muslim population of the Indian subcontinent. That struggle was three-cornered, involving British colonial power from which all the Indians wanted their independence, a party of Indian nationalists that comprised the majorities in all the various communities of India save for the Muslims, and a party of Muslim nationalists who upheld the view that India was not one nation but two, a Hindu nation and a Muslim nation. Thus, when the view of the Muslim nationalists prevailed and Pakistan at last came into existence, it was already closely and inextricably linked with Islam. The fight for a separate state had been carried on by Muslims in order to protect Muslim interests, and it was perhaps only natural that the majority of individuals in the new country should have considered that Pakistan must be conquered as an Islamic state.[23] In any event, soon after the partition of India a vigorous movement arose in Pakistan in favor of the Islamic state. The Islamic state issue rapidly became the most prominent question in Pakistani public life, overshadowing the war in Kashmir and the difficulties posed by the refugees pouring into the country. The agitation was related to the discussions in the Constituent Assembly relative to a constitution for the new country. Almost everyone was agreed that the constitution must reflect the culture and the religious values of the Indian Muslims, that is, that it must be an Islamic constitution, but there was great disagreement about the nature and content of an Islamic constitution. The public debate that ensued over this question is the most thoroughgoing investigation of the meaning of Islam for the political order that has been witnessed in the modern era.[24]

As it turned out, the provisions that Pakistanis eventually devised and accepted in their first constitution in 1956 were a compromise in which the liberal, Westernized bureaucracy and political leadership had the upper hand. The basic model of the state was that of a parliamentary democracy guided by certain statements of Islamic intent and restricted by some Islamic provisions. The most important of the Islamic elements, however, in particular the provision that no law should be passed which is contrary to Qur'an or Sunna, were made non-justiciable. The 1956 constitution was swept away in 1958 by the rise of a military government in the country. With the exception of the Bhutto years Pakistan has continued to be governed by its military until the present time. The early passionate interest in the character of an Islamic state has not returned, the politics in Pakistan, to the extent that it is permitted at all, revolves around the desire for power and the forwarding of mundane social and economic interests of various groups.

Despite what might be called the failure of Pakistan to give real substance and content to the notion of an Islamic polity, the successive governments of the country have found it important to maintain Islamic symbolism in a place of prominence, and none more so than the present one. The stated objective of Zia al-Haqq's regime is the fostering of the Nizam-i Mustafa, that is, the establishment of the system of government and social order that were advocated by the Prophet of Islam. The government has taken a number of steps that give high visibility to its Islamic intentions, such things as the prohibition of the sale of alcohol in public places, and the enforcement, though on a very limited scale, of the harsher punishments decreed by the Shari'a. Pakistani radio and television have filled their schedules with religious programs; the numerous shows and films of foreign origin that once were shown there are no longer available. The most important Islamic measures the government has taken are its efforts to codify the Islamic Shari'a, a task being carried through by the Council on Islamic Ideology, and the attempt to establish an interestless banking system in accord with the Islamic prohibition of usury, though the results achieved are not yet very impressive. There is no question that the government—and others—have greatly increased their resort to Islamic symbolism.

What lies behind these appeals to Islam is the government's quest for legitimacy. Recognizing the hold which religion exercises upon the minds of its people, it wishes to associate itself with the most basic values of the population. This quest is especially important for a military government that has imposed itself by sheer force. It cannot lay claim to authority on the basis of the popular will—it is, in fact, very unpopular—and it cannot point to legal constitutional modes of investiture. Yet it must have some way of justifying its existence and some ground upon which to extend its authority over the people whom it rules. These things it has sought to provide by presenting itself as the champion of Islam and its policies as exemplification of Islamic principles. Its attitudes toward militant resurgent

Islam and its principal spokesmen in Pakistan may, however, be judged by the government's having prohibited the activities of the Jama'at-i Islami very much as in the Saudi case. One is faced with the paradox of a government that professes Islamic objectives but that interdicts the work of the most vigorous and effective Islamic organization on its territory.

What conclusions may one draw from all this too brief discussion of Islamic resurgence? I would suggest at least the following:

1. Islamic resurgence is not monolithic, one single and uniform thing across the whole of the Islamic world. It is rather complex and multiform, different in each context in which it occurs. It, therefore, cannot be explained by a single principle but requires to be investigated in depth and in detail, case by case, before an adequate approach to understanding will be possible. It differs in respect to the factors that have evoked it in different countries, in the social bases upon which it rests, in its understanding of the nature of Islam, and in the strategies and tactics that it may adopt in its various settings. It also clearly differs in its relationships to governments and states, sometimes providing them with support and at other times posing a significant opposition to them.

2. Islamic resurgence is not merely the resurrection or revival of an older form of Islamic piety but contains genuine elements of novelty. These new factors in the interpretation of Islam are exemplified in such things as the adoption of the concept of ideology with all that it implies, in the content of the apologetics directed at other Muslims and at outsiders, and in the unprecedented claims to authority made by Khomaini.[25] The resurgence movements must thus be seen as but the latest steps in the continuing evolution of the Islamic perspective upon the world. They represent the grappling of an organically developing religious perspective with a changed set of circumstances. The resurgence movements are a distinctively modern phenomenon that must be described and judged against the background of the modern milieu that has provided the conditions for their existence.

3. Essentially the Islamic resurgence movements are a continuation, though in a new phase, of the questioning and discussion that have preoccupied Muslim minds throughout the whole of the modern period. Though the forms of approach may be new, the vital questions to which the resurgence movements address themselves remain the same. Stripped of their details the issues at stake have been and are, those of: identity, legitimacy, of dignity and of purpose.

NOTES

1. See Yvonne Y. Haddad, *Contemporary Islam and the Challenge of History* (Albany: State University of New York, 1982), preface. The best statement of Muslim expectations of history and the consequences of their frustration may be read in

Wilfred Cantwell Smith, *Islam in Modern History* (Princeton, N.J.: Princeton University Press, 1957).

2. Haddad, *Contemporary Islam*, p. 1.

3. See John Alden Williams, "Veiling in Egypt," in John Esposito, ed., *Islam and Development* (Syracuse, N.Y.: Syracuse University Press, 1980), pp. 80 ff.

4. See Peter Chelkowski, "The Shi'a Symbolism and Ritual as demonstrated in the Iranian Revolution," in Richard Martin, ed., *Approaches to Islam in Religious Studies* (Phoenix: University of Arizona Press, 1985).

5. Jean-Claude Vatin, "Revivalism in the Maghreb," in 'Ali E. Hillal Dessouki, ed., *Islamic Resurgence in the Arab World* (New York: Praeger Publishers, 1982), p. 242 footnote.

6. See Daniel Crecelius, "The Course of Secularization in Modern Egypt," in John Esposito, ed., *Islam in Transition* (Syracuse, N.Y.: Syracuse University Press, 1980), p. 70.

7. See J.N.D. Anderson, *Islamic Law in the Modern World* (New York: New York University Press, 1959).

8. See "News from the Country," *al-Mushir* 24, no. 3 (Rawalpindi, Pakistan: Autumn 1982), pp. 123 ff.

9. 'Ali E. Hillal Dessouki, "Islamic Resurgence," in Dessouki, ed., *Islamic Resurgence*, p. 10.

10. Ibid. Although this volume deals only with the Arab world, the introductory chapter by its editor, who is professor of political science at Cairo University, is the best discussion of the problems that arise in connection with the study of Islamic resurgence known to the present writer.

11. See Charles J. Adams, "Tradition and Legitimization of Social Change," in Jessie G. Lutz and Salah El-Shakhs, eds., *Tradition and Modernity* (Washington, D.C.: University Press of America, 1982), pp. 115 ff.

12. See a series of three articles by the French orientalist, Maxime Rodinson, published in *Le Monde* (Paris), December 6–8, 1978.

13. The best study of the Muslim Brothers is Richard Mitchell, *The Society of the Muslim Brothers* (London: Oxford University Press, 1969).

14. Smith, *Islam in Modern History*, p. 41.

15. Haddad, *Contemporary Islam*, Part I.

16. For a full discussion of this see Fazlur Rahman, *Islam and Modernity* (Chicago: University of Chicago Press, 1982).

17. Dessouki, ed., *Islamic Resurgence*, p. 14.

18. See David Edwin Long, *The Hajj Today* (Albany: State University of New York Press, 1979).

19. On the Ikhwan see John Habib, *Ibn Sa'ud's Warriors of Islam* (Leiden: E.J. Brill, 1978).

20. See "Religion and Foreign Policy in Saudi Arabia," by Ayman al-Yassini, Discussion Paper No. 2 of the Centre for Developing Area Studies, McGill University, 1983. The role of the religious class is treated at greater length in the same author's Ph.D. dissertation submitted to McGill University in 1982, "The Relationship between Religion and State in the Kingdom of Saudi Arabia."

21. See Mangol Bayat, "Islam in Pahlavi and Post-Pahlavi Iran: A Cultural Revolution?" in John Esposito, ed., *Islam and Development*, pp. 87 ff.

22. The study was done by Professor Yvonne Haddad of the Hartford Seminary

Foundation. See Yvonne Haddad, "The Syrian Muslims of Montreal," in Earle H. Waugh, Baha Abu-Laban and Regula B. Qureishi, eds., *The Muslim Community in North America* (Edmonton: The University of Alberta Press, 1983).

23. This history and background are traced in Wilfred Cantwell Smith, *Modern Islam in India* (London: Victor Gollancz, 1946).

24. Probably the best survey of this controversy is Leonard Binder, *Religion and Politics in Pakistan* (Los Angeles and Berkeley: University of California Press, 1961).

25. See R. Hrair Dekmejian, "The Anatomy of Islamic Revival: Legitimacy Crisis, Ethnic Conflict and the Search for Islamic Alternatives," *The Middle East Journal* 34, no. 1 (Winter 1980); and Yvonne Y. Haddad, "The Islamic Alternative," *The Link* 15, no. 4 (September/October 1982).

11

How Useful Is "Islam" as an Explanation of the Politics of the Middle East?

MARVIN ZONIS

The success of the Iranian revolution was an achievement of staggering proportions. The common denominator which fed the revolution of 1978 was a drive to oust the shah and his vision of the *Tammaddon-e Bozorg* or Great Civilization. By the time of his departure from Iran on January 16, 1979, virtually the entire Iranian people shared that goal.

There was far less agreement on the shape of post-Pahlavi Iran. Many of the revolutionaries were so outraged by the shah that they expressed the optimism of the desperate: "Why plan for the new order; anything would be better than the shah." But other than this flight from responsibility—a flight of which the Western-trained intelligensia of Iran were especially guilty—there were three basic political positions among the opposition.

The middle and upper sectors of the Iranian population still clung, however tenuously, to fragments of the legacy of the late Prime Minister Mohammad Mossadegh, who had been ousted in the August 1953 coup. Widely believed to be the responsibility of the Central Intelligence Agency (CIA), popular wisdom in Iran has it that the coup demonstrated that the United States "stole" the independent nationalism of Iran and vested power in a dependent "tool" of American global interests, the shah. That view has been cemented in recent years by the publication of an account of its perpetuation by the chief CIA officer charged with its responsibility.[1] Not surprisingly, that account elevated the role of the United States at the expense of indigenous forces.

But a more recent study by an Iranian and former aide to Mossadegh presents a "revisionist" view.[2] He shows how the late prime minister had almost systematically eliminated one after another of his domestic bases of support, so that by the summer of 1953 he stood alone, holding power through his desperate attempts to monopolize it and his ever more strident rhetoric. In this view, the American and British intelligence agencies are seen to play an almost minor role, stimulating processes which would have independently led to Mossadegh's ouster as they matured in late 1953. Whatever the truth between these conflicting accounts, the CIA and the British did play a role, and the shah was never able to shake the legacy of his returning to power through foreign assistance. The upper and middle sectors of the opposition, then, were committed to a democratic, republican Iran, far more nationalist and independent of the United States than was ever the case under the rule of the shah.

The second major sector of opposition was led by the Mujahedin-i Khalq and the Fedayin-i Khalq, and composed of diverse groupings of armed urban guerrillas and their more numerous sympathizers. They were committed to more (in the case of the former) and less (in the case of the latter) Islamically inspired versions of socialist political and economic orders. The depth of the Islamic content of their ideologies determined their political alliances. The Mujahedin, infused with a commitment to an Islamically just egalitarian society, were an offshoot of the secular political movement which had grown around Mossadegh.[3] As a result they claimed many allies among secular opposition leaders sympathetic to Islam as well as among Islamic clerics, in particular Ayatollah Mahmud Taleghani. The Fedayin were ruthlessly secular but committed to many of the same "socialist" goals of the Mujahedin. Both groups fought for a republic—and fight they did during the 1970s through guerrilla-style attacks against the Pahlavi police and symbols of the Pahlavi political order, including American military and civilian advisors.

The third major sector of the opposition, the Islamic Shi'ite clerics, their secular allies, and their "troops," essentially the lower middle and lower sectors of Iran's city dwellers, were equally committed to a different vision of an Iran without its monarch. They sought to establish an Islamic republic, one in which the tenets of Shi'ism provided the ideology and the representatives of the faith enacted these tenets to achieve an Islamic political order.[4]

The principal political dynamic of Iran from the flight of the shah to the fall of 1979 concerned the break-up of the winning revolutionary coalition into these two tendencies, with victory going to the Islamic forces.[5] The charismatic leadership of Ayatollah Khomaini, who had long since become the symbolic counterpoint to the shah, the organization and financing of the clerics through their country-wide networks of mosques and ties to the bazaar merchants, and their armed strength, provided first by the political/terrorist organizations, the Fedayin-i Khalq and Mujahedin-i Khalq, and later by the Pasdaran or Revolutionary Guards, guaranteed victory in the post-revolutionary struggle.

With the seizure of the U.S. Embassy and its American diplomats by students motivated by and loyal to Ayatollah Khomaini and the dismissal of Prime Minister Bazargan, his foreign minister, Dr. Ibrahim Yazdi, and other so-called "secular moderates," the fate of the post-revolutionary struggle was sealed. Victory went to the Shi'ites and was institutionalized in the new Islamic Constitution and the Islamic Republic of Iran.

That victory of the Shi'ite leaders—Ayatollah Rouhollah Khomaini foremost among them—expressed a loathing and repugnance for the West, and especially the United States. Moreover, the overthrow of the shah and the seizure of the U.S. Embassy and its diplomats by "Students in the Line of Imam Khomaini," seemed to initiate a series of Islamically inspired events throughout the Middle East which struck at Western interests. Almost immediately following the capture of the diplomats, the Grand Mosque of Mecca—the symbolic center of the Islamic faith—was seized by zealots demanding a return to "pure" Islam and the overthrow of the "pro-American" rulers of Saudi Arabia.[6] In turn, rioters attacked the U.S. Embassy in Pakistan to protest alleged American involvement in the desecration of the most holy of Islamic holy places. What came to be known as the "Islamic Revival" seemed an immediate and threatening reality to the United States.[7]

Following that period of intense confrontation in the fall of 1979, political forces acting explicitly in the name of Islam moderated. The Islamic Revival appeared to be fading. But since that period, there have been enough dramatic events to indicate that the virulently anti-Western forces which had been unleashed by the Iranian revolution were still at work. The murder of President Anwar al-Sadat of Egypt in October 1981 was one such event. The uprising of the Muslim Brotherhood in the Syrian city of Hama in February 1982 was another. That effort to establish an Islamic republic in Syria was crushed by forces commanded by Rifaat al-Assad, the brother of Syria's president. His "Defense Forces" leveled whole areas of the city, killing some 70,000 people in the process. The uprising and its aftermath seemed to demonstrate not that the processes unleashed by Islam were necessarily hostile to the United States but rather that those processes were driven by deep passions which could motivate Muslims to perform extraordinarily zealous acts.

The next series of dramatic events which struck at the United States seemed to confirm what for Americans had become the two central features of Islamically inspired political action: its implacable opposition to American interests and its capacity to generate or unleash consuming passions. The suicide bombings in Lebanon began in April 1983 after the United States had sent marines to Beirut. First, an explosives-laden van was blown up in front of the U.S. Embassy in Beirut. Many were killed, including the entire Beirut CIA station and the chief CIA Middle East analyst, who had been sent from Washington to brief his colleagues. Then two buildings being used by the Israelis in their occupation of southern Lebanon were blown up. The first, with great loss of life, was apparently destroyed by the accidental leaking of natural gas. But the second installation was decimated by another truck bomb, apparently exploded in kamikaze style by a Shi'ite zealot.

The Shi'ite capacity for zealotry did not hit home for the American public until the fall of 1983. Then on the same morning in October, Shi'ites dispatched themselves and over 250 marines and 75 French soldiers by driving garbage trucks laden with explosives into their respective barracks in Beirut. Those acts of martyrdom demonstrated that terrorism does pay; that is, that it can be effective in accomplishing significant political goals. The death of so many marines in a venture whose goals had been ill-defined and even more poorly communicated to the American public proved decisive in leading to an American withdrawal from Lebanon.

But there was more terrorism to come. In December 1983, seven explosions damaged installations in Kuwait: French, American and Kuwaiti buildings were all targets. And, in the last of these dramatic and destructive series, the newly relocated American Embassy on the outskirts of East Beirut was badly damaged by another truck bomb in 1984.

What must be determined in contemplating these acts of awesome destruction is whether they can legitimately be grouped with those other phenomena which have come to be labeled as the "Islamic Revival." That revival, or more aptly, resurgence, of Islam does appear to entail a resurgence of Islamic piety insofar as more Muslims appear to be more faithfully adhering to the religious dictates of their faith. In addition, more Muslims appear to have adopted what have come to be identified as authentically Islamic customs, although there is nothing in Islamic doctrine which specifies the particular content of these customs. (The clothing which has come to designate a woman as dressed in an appropriately modest, "Islamic" fashion, is not, for example, the product of Islamic doctrine but rather, of the practice of Muslims.) Finally, accompanying these changes, there has been a resurgence of activist political movements, finding their justifications, purposes and goals in Islam. Together, these changes constitute the Islamic Resurgence of the 1970s and 1980s.

This phenomenon whereby personal, social and political behavior has come to be infused with the spirit of vigorous action in the name of Islam is not about to disappear from the Middle East scene. The processes which brought it into existence remain vital throughout the region. There are states committed to its perpetuation and willing to commit resources to its expansion. In different, but frequently complimentary ways, Iran, Libya and Saudi Arabia have used state prestige as well as state resources to insure that the processes underlying the Islamic Revival will remain vital and result in further organized political manifestations of those processes.[8]

Four essential processes which intersected in the 1970s served as the basis for the Islamic Revival. No one of them was sufficient to produce the political revolutions and violence, the renewed emphasis on cultural integrity and distance from the West or the restoration of religious practice to its central place in the lives of so many of the faithful. But the confluence of those four processes proved decisive. The first process grows from the ideology of Islam. While there are important differences of detail between Shi'ite and Sunni Islam, the two sects agree in essentials on the political nature of Islam.[9] The faith is not seen as having political implications but as being essentially political. Islam claims to provide its followers with a life of morality and justice. But the principal goals of the faith are not to be achieved primarily by its followers adhering to the prescribed standards of conduct in their daily lives. Although like other great religiously based ethical systems, Islamic ideology is replete with instructions to govern even the most minute aspects of the behavior of the faithful, it is not ultimately from the fulfillment of its ethical codes that Islam purports to realize morality and justice.

Rather, Islam has never relinquished its essential political claim. For all practical purposes such a claim has been relinquished by all but the most Orthodox Jews, with whom Islam shares the most similarities of the three monotheisms emanating from the Middle East. That claim centers on the communal aspects of Islam and argues that Islam cannot achieve justice by individuals living "justly" but only through an Islamic community, that is a community whose social and political relationships are organized according to Islamic beliefs.[10] Put another way, Muslims have never abandoned their original beliefs that an Islamic political order is as much a part of Islam as is an Islamic ethical system. "Render unto Caesar what is Caesar's and unto God what is God's" is a dictum that has characterized much of Islamic history but only as a regrettable recognition of the political reality of the weakness of Muslim vis-à-vis non-Muslim or even Muslim secular authorities. The religion itself, in the minds of Muslims, has always centered on the establishment of an Islamic political community, thoroughly permeated with an Islamic ethos.

The shah strived, with apparent success, to achieve a political system that separated the communal and personal aspects of Islam. He frequently spoke of the need to establish Islam according to his definition of its proper sphere, the personal.[11] In his own life, he tried to demonstrate personal commitment to that vision. At official state functions, Islamic clerics (widely disparaged in Iran as "kept *mullahs*") would bless the proceedings. The shah would frequently be photographed observing major Islamic holidays with his family. Annually, he and Empress Farah would make the pilgrimage to Meshed where he would be photographed kissing the grill over the tomb of the eighth Shi'ite imam.

Otherwise, however, the shah pursued a secular vision of the organization of the political system, a secular vision which inexorably relegated Islamic authority to ever less signficiant areas of Iranian life. Perhaps the watershed in that regard was the adoption of the Family Protection Act of 1975 which assured women of progressive and liberal rights in matters of marriage, divorce, child custody, inheritance and like.[12] Most women, especially the Westernized upper strata, welcomed the new law, but the clerics saw it as one more in a series of threats—perhaps the ultimate one—to the legitimacy of their authority, even in the dramatically restricted sphere of personal morality.

More fundamentally, the shah not only struck at even the domain of the clerics in matters of personal morality, but he created political and economic systems which vitiated the communal aspects of Islam in more fundamental ways. As Amin Saikal notes,

The increasing oil wealth enabled him *the Shah* to finance ambitious economic and military programs, subsidize every basic commodity, and create an economic atmosphere in which the Iranian people became deeply preoccupied with their own personal pecuniary gains. This gave a new dimension to the acquisitive instincts of many Iranians, who from different points of the social scale, interpreted everything in terms of a status based on wealth. Money became the central theme of many Iranians' activities under "government controlled capitalism."[13]

As Iran's hyper-boom of the 1970s grew with mounting intensity—even in the face of a downturn in oil revenues which began in 1975—even more Iranians became engulfed in the individualistic, competitive atmosphere of capitalist acquisition. Clearly, the shah had struck a deeply resonating value in Iranian culture.

But equally clearly, that competitive, acquisitive capitalism violated other values deeply felt by the Iranin people—values of harmony, asceticism and community as embodied in Islam. In the very act of acquiring wealth and accumulating material possessions, many Iranians felt lessened for forsaking other important and cherished values. One crucial basis of Ayatollah Khomaini's appeal for Iranians at all levels of the social scale was his capacity to represent those very values which the shah was seen as forsaking. The ayatollah and his clerical supporters were also successful in convincing the Iranian people that the shah was to blame for their having violated many of their own values. The shah's entire system had to be destroyed and replaced by Islamic rule if the individualism fostered by capitalist modes of acquisition was to be countered and the communal harmony of Islam restored.[14]

A similar tension between the individualism of capitalist acquisition and the social harmony within the community of the faithful exists in most Islamic states of the Middle East. In some, Saudi Arabia, for example, the royal family seems to have recognized the political danger which that tension poses. The rulers allow the pursuit of wealth to continue unabated but strive to minimize its deleterious effects by the authoritative (many would say forced) imposition of an Islamic community from above. By espousing Islamic values and using state power to enforce Islamic institutions, they struggle to reduce the tension; to make individualism only an incidental rather than a central feature of Saudi life.[15] Other Islamic states propound indigenous notions of "socialism," notions heavily influenced by Islamic thinking which also stress communitarian values. Still other states, especially those of the Persian Gulf, seem to follow the Iranian pattern more closely, hoping to minimize tension through many of the same mechanisms followed by the shah: rigorous political control, co-opting the clerics, free or highly subsidized state services and wealth for many.

A second process which has fed the Islamic Revival of the Middle East takes the form of an Islamic response to the creation of the State of Israel and its success in winning four wars against coalitions of nearly all Arab and most Islamic states of the region. That response takes many forms of which two are of major concern here.

Many Muslims understand the success of the State of Israel in terms of its Jewish character.[16] By adhering to the bedrock of Judaism, in institutionalizing the state around the notion of a homeland for the Jews, Israel is seen as having institutionalized a spirit or ethos which has given the state extraordinary power. That ethos motivates citizens to valor in war and industriousness in peace. The point here, of course, is not the accuracy of this understanding. That all but a minority of Jewish Israelis celebrate the relatively secular character of their state does not lessen the significance of an alternative observation on the part of many Muslims. For they find few other explanations to account for their defeats and the victories of Israel.

The Arabs believe that they have adopted Western technology as have the Israelis. They have armed themselves with modern weapons as have the Israelis. And they have their Soviet or Western patrons or friends as the Israelis have the Americans. And yet the combination does not seem to work for the forces of Islam as it does for the Israelis.

Many of the more Westernized Arabs, especially Arab ruling groups, understand their defeats in terms of some special Israeli relationship with the West. In their view, Israel is an "outpost of Western imperialism." As a result, it was not Israel alone which defeated the Arabs but the West. While such claims continue to be heard with great frequency, especially from the more secular groups in the Arab world, such as the leaders of Fatah, especially Yasir Arafat, the claim seems lately to have worn thin. "Western imperialism" has become more of a ritualistic cant, uttered with less conviction that previously.

With a decline in the power of the metaphor of "Western imperialism," the power of the Islamic vision has been enhanced. Leaders more oriented toward Islam successfully point to the Jewish basis of Israel while drawing the obvious moral that success will be visited upon the Arab world when it puts its Islamic house in order. While many understand such claims more as last-ditch rationalizations than as explanations for Arab defeats, they seem to have found a receptive audience among many, especially among those Muslims who have also been subject to the other processes described here.

The third process which feeds the Islamic Revival is the use of Islam as a language of political discourse, and especially of political opposition to established ruling groups.[17] There is no explicitly Islamic state in the Middle East which is democratic in the sense of allowing untrammeled party politics. Political opposition to authoritarian governments is not allowed a legitimate place. Rather, the states of the region strive to incorporate all hierarchical structures within the overarching structure of the state. This is true of Islamic institutions as well.

Where the Sunni sect of Islam is dominant, the states have been largely successful in converting the clergy into an appendage of the state bureaucracies: the schools, to the ministries of education; the courts, to the ministries of justice; and the Islamic welfare functions to the ministries of social services.[18] In Shi'ite Iran, despite years of effort, the shah never succeeded in controlling the Islamic institutions, a result of both Shi'ite ideology and the nature of the organization of the Shi'ite religious institutions.

Thus, in Pahlavi Iran, Shi'ite institutions were the only organizations which geographically and socially reached the entire population of city dwellers.[19] They naturally served as the only available focus for anti-regime activity because structurally they were the only available national institutions which were not part of the ruling system. Their clergy, through their network of mosques and other Islamic institutions, were able to claim the center of the organized opposition in the revolution of 1978.

But the incorporation of Islamic institutions into public bureaucracies results in a different role for the forces of Islam in Sunni states. For insofar as Islamic institutions are part of the ruling structures, they are less useful centers for political opposition to those structures. In states which have experienced this pattern of Islamic incorporation, Islamic organizations have arisen outside the mainstream of the conventional religious system. In Egypt and Syria, for example, the Muslim Brotherhoods, quasi-fraternal religious organizations distinct from the clerical structure of Islam, serve as the center of Islamic opposition to secular rule.[20]

But even in Egypt and Syria the incorporation of the formal Islamic institutions has been neither complete nor completely successful. Those states have been more successful in eliminating or controlling secular opposition. As a result, even formal Islamic institutions can serve as useful loci of political opposition. As long as Islam itself cannot be eliminated or Muslims prohibited from organizing for religious purposes, Islamic institutions will always be at least partially available for opposition political activities.

Those aspects of Islam as an ideology which are politically relevant increase the likelihood that those available structures will be used for narrowly political goals. This can be most clearly seen in Shi'ism, according to whose rhetoric, "Muslims have since the time of the Battle of Karbala been subjects of oppression and injustice."[21] The most holy day of the Shi'ite calendar is a dramaturgical re-enactment of the martyrdom of Hussein in that Battle of Karbala on the plains of Iraq in 680 C.E. at the symbolic hands of the Sunni

Caliph Yazid. Yazid has come to embody illegitimate political oppression for the Shi'ites. When Shi'ite ayatollahs spoke of the tyrannical Yazid and the martyrdom of the just Hussein, their listeners understood the parallels with the shah and their own perceived unjust fate.[22] Built into Shi'ite ideology, then, is the central concern with standing against unjust authority and the elimination of tyranny. Ayatollah Khomaini and his Islamic allies had at their disposal both an institutional and an ideological basis for the pursuit of revolution.

Sunni Islam does not center on these themes of illegitimate political authority. But as has been suggested above, the persistent dynamic of Sunnism is the urge to create an Islamic political community which will allow Muslims "to enjoin evil and foster the good."[23] As such, Sunni Islam has a different but nonetheless compelling ideological basis for seeking political action in this world.

Both Shi'ite and Sunni branches of Islam, then, provide both structures and ideologies conducive to this-worldly political action. But like all great ideological systems, the content of that political action is not precisely defined. Indeed, it would be impossible to imagine any profound system of thought with universal and historical claims which did specify the content of such action, for the appropriateness of the system would be immediately called into question by the lack of fit between the content of the specified action and actual historical circumstances. With few exceptions, Islam does not specify the content of political action. The single major source of disunity in the Islamic world is disputes over that content. (For Muslims, the problem of disunity is especially troublesome in that Islam purports to supersede all other significant identities in the creation of the domain of "Islamdom."[24] The inability of contemporary Muslims to achieve unity of political action is a constant source of discontent.)

Since the religion is relatively content-free, at least in terms of its political program, its dictates have had to be interpreted to elicit a specific plan for political action. Since there is no center of interpretation recognized by Muslims as legitimate for all of the Islamic world, various and competing centers of interpretation, increasingly defined by existing political boundaries, have come into existence. But even with individual Muslim states a single center for authoritative interpretation can hardly be said to exist. The secular rulers of Egypt, for example, have tried to elevate that center of Islamic education, Al-Azhar, into a center of authoritative interpretation and then to control its inner workings so that only clerics acceptable to the ruling authorities would reach positions of importance.[25] But even in Egypt where Al-Azhar is widely recognized for the legitimacy of its Islamic purity, alternative centers of interpretation have grown up, independent of and hostile to the secular rulers. Most recently, the blind cleric, Shaik Abdel Hamid Kishk, known as the Ayatollah Khomaini of Egypt, has staked out such a role and was an important voice in stimulating the Islamic opposition which succeeded in assassinating President al-Sadat.[26] A similar pattern persists even in Saudi Arabia. The Sa'ud family not only claims political legitimacy but also legitimacy in the religious sphere, both through its extraordinary efforts to advance the faith and through the alliance in 1744 between Muhammad 'Abd al-Wahhab, the founder of the fundamentalist interpretation of Islam now known as "Wahhabism," and Muhammad Ben Sa'ud, the founder of the House of Sa'ud.[27] Nonetheless, clerics operating outside the formal religio-political synthesis occasionally achieve great public repute and mass followings. The regime is then faced with the task of incorporating the cleric and his interpretations into the officially sanctioned body of doctrine or challenging the legitimacy of his interpretations and running the risk of offending his followers.

Interpretation presents a challenge not only to all Muslims seeking specific content to their political longings but more seriously to the political authorities attempting to control, in their own interests, their own populations. The results are frequent threats to the authoritative rule of the secular authorities, renewed efforts to manipulate the sources of interpretation by those authorities, and ever new sources of divisiveness for the community of Islam.

Furthermore, as that community of Islam has undergone divergent political and economic changes, especially in the twentieth century with the collapse of the Ottoman Empire and the rise of independent Muslim states, there is no longer a single, unified Islamic experience to serve as the basis for interpretation. Insofar as interpretation emanates from historical experience and Muslims no longer share a common experience, the interpretations which allow Muslims to make sense of their world differ.[28] The content of interpretation, in other words, is ever more likely to differ from country to country within the Islamic world as national boundaries increasingly come to define historical experience.

Thus both the Egyptian and the Syrian versions of the Muslim Brotherhood pose grave but divergent threats to the political regime of each country. The Brotherhood in Egypt was an important source of Islamic fervor which contributed to the atmosphere resulting in the murder of President al-Sadat. In the Egyptian case that fervor stressed the threat to Islam which President al-Sadat represented—his opening to the West and encouragement of capitalist economic development and, in particular, the peace treaty with Israel.

In Syria, the Muslim Brotherhood has also demonstrated remarkable political vitality. But it challenges the rule of President Assad on the grounds that his reliance on his fellow Syrian Alawite Muslims has been at the expense of the welfare of the majority Sunni population of Syria. Given President Assad's larger political commitments, Brotherhood opposition in Syria has railed against President Assad's alliance with the Soviet Union and his fostering a state socialist route to economic development. Thus in Egypt and Syria, and in many other cases, the content of the interpretations differ on the basis of various historical experiences. But the underlying theme is the same. In country after country Islam serves, for a variety of reasons, as the most persistent and most authoritative language of opposition to ruling political authorities.

A fourth process contributes to the Islamic Revival, a process which grows out of a basic aspect of the Islamic ethos. Islam, more than either Judaism or Christianity, is predicated on the notion of this-worldly success. The early historical experience of Muslims is understood by Muslims to testify that adherence to Islam results in great territorial expansion and grandeur for the faithful. The century-long expansion in the domains of Islam which followed upon the receipt of the message of the Prophet Muhammad is held as proof of God's favor to those who submit to Him. God's reward for such submission is manifest for many Muslims in the victories which he provided the armies of his earliest followers.

In the past two centuries, however, the this-worldly failures of Islam have been more manifest than its successes. The rise of the West and its political control over most of the Islamic peoples and the economic and cultural backwardness of Muslim societies are seen as having culminated in the Western-imposed creation of the State of Israel. The perceived backwardness and weakness vis-à-vis the West has been experienced as an embarrassment at best, and more often as a humiliation. One result was the fostering of a sense of rage by Muslims against the West that had inflicted such narcissistic injury on the Islamic world.[29] Muslim reformers and others who argued that parity with the West could be achieved through greater emulation of its practices increasingly fell into disfavor.

More recently there is evidence that God's grace has returned to Muslims. The initial successes of the Egyptian army in crossing the Suez Canal in the 1973 war and holding on to the Sinai before the United States imposed a truce on Israel has allowed many Muslims to define their "Ramadan War" as victory. More tellingly, the fifteen-fold increase in the price of petroleum since that war is widely understood as a tangible demonstration of the return of God's grace to those who submit to His will.

In short, previous attempts to emulate the West are seen as having produced failure. But the return to pristine Islam of recent years has brought with it a return of sacred grace. This perception then has strengthened those who argue for an Islamic Revival which is faithful to the practices followed at the establishment of the faith. Moreover, that argument is strengthened by the continued presence of rage against the West as well as against those Muslims who are seen as serving Western interests. This combination of anti-Western rage with the perception of the return of God's grace to Muslims as Muslims has been a powerful stimulus to the Islamic Revival in its fundamentalist form.

Four processes, then, nurture the Islamic Revival: a commitment to the establishment of an Islamic political order, an understanding of the successes of the State of Israel in terms of its religious character, the use of Islam as a language of political opposition, and a return to fundamentalist Islam as a means of achieving this-worldly success and dealing with the rage stemming from past humiliations.

The point has been made that these four processes are likely to persist throughout the Middle East. But it is essential to understand that future manifestations of these processes need not be similar to their past ones. They may, indeed, be quite remote from the manifestations of these processes in the immediate past. The consequences of a persisting Islamic Revival in the future may be quite different from the consequences witnessed in the 1970s and early 1980s. Social scientific theory has long distinguished between social processes and their behavioral manifestations, as psychoanalysts differentiate character structure from behavior. Similar processes can result in quite different behaviors (just as different processes can result in quite similar behavior).

There are two reasons for assuming that future manifestations of the Islamic Revival will be different from those of the past. Americans tend to focus on the extent to which American interests or American citizens have been victimized by the Islamic Revival. But, in fact, the states most menaced by vigorous infusion of Middle Eastern life with Islamic themes have been the states of the Middle East. The ouster and death of the shah of Iran and the assassination of President al-Sadat of Egypt are but two of the most obvious examples. In every instance in the Middle East where the Islamic Revival has had a political manifestation, the institutions of local states have been powerfully affected. Those states have, by now, learned that lesson and taken steps to co-opt or control their own indigenous Islamic movements.[30] Saudi Arabia is, perhaps, the foremost example of a state's successfully co-opting its Islamic clergy, co-optation which has resulted in the incorporation and control of clerical activism. Syria, with the leveling of Hannah, is a prime example of the control which can result from ruthless repression. Egypt under President Mubarak is a state which uses both instruments—co-optation and control—to manage the political manifestation of the Islamic Revival.

In short, while public life in the Middle East will continue to be infused, perhaps even at an accelerating pace, with the spirit of resurgent Islam, the political manifestations which follow are likely to be less severe than was the case in the past. The destabilization of individual states, of the Middle East as a whole, and of international politics which flowed from the first years of the Islamic Revival is unlikely to be repeated. As Middle Eastern states have learned to cope with the demands of the forces of Islam, they have become more successful in channeling those forces in less destructive directions.

Several other points follow. First, the Islamic Revival is sustained by many and diverse processes which have their roots in historical phenomena. As a result, these processes have a beginning—however difficult it is to identify such beginnings with precision—and an end—however impossible it is to predict when that end will be reached. As such, the Islamic Revival itself has to be understood as a historical phenomenon which is rooted in the nature of the Islamic experience and will, ultimately, constitute merely another phase in the history of that experience.

Second, the processes which principally feed the Islamic Revival are complementary but, nonetheless, diverse. Depending on the relative strength of each process within any given context, the Revival can be expected to take different forms and emphasize different themes.

Third, this is all the more likely because Islam itself is a rich body of doctrine whose specific applicability can be established only through interpretation. The nature of interpretation will differ according to the experiential contexts in which the interpretation occurs. The result is different interpretations producing different kinds of Islamic revivals.

Fourth, there have been clear differences in the political manifestations of resurgent Islam among Shi'a and Sunni Muslims. The former have been characterized by far more widespread acts of violence and far more successful political acts. The success of the revolution in Iran and the probability of the conversion of Lebanon to a Shi'ite state are the two most prominent examples. Shi'ite successes can be accounted for both by Shi'ite doctrine and by the energizing of that doctrine by Ayatollah Khomaini. The Sunni world, for a variety of ideological and political reasons, has not yet witnessed the rise of a comparably charismatic leader.

Fifth, the Islamic Revival is now generally atavistic. The forces of Islamic fundamentalism are dominant while those of Islamic reformers are equally in retreat. The tradition of Islamic modernism which were so vital in the late nineteenth and early twentieth centuries are, nonetheless, still in existence and still intellectually vital, if not currently of political significance. Given the diversity of processes detailed here and the array of interpretive bases, there is every reason to assume that Islamic modernism will once again dominate.

Sixth, the Islamic Revival, in general, poses a threat to the immediate interests of West. It results in a weakening of the position of the West in the Islamic world and of those Muslim politicians who seek closer ties with the West.

Seventh, the attack on the immediate interests of the West does not necessarily mean a strengthening of the position in the Islamic world of the Communist Bloc. But insofar as communist states are perceived as officially atheist, they are seen as hostile to the interests of Muslims, especially those Muslims living under communist regimes. And insofar as communist states are seen as based on Marxism, they are subject to the same anti-Western enmity, for Marxism is understood to be as much a Western system as are socialism, democracy, parliamentary rule and all those other secular ideologies which stem from the West and dominate so much of the non-Islamic world.

Eighth, while the immediate interests of the West are threatened by the Islamic Revival, the long-term interests of the West and of the Muslim peoples can only be positively served by it. Insofar as the Islamic Revival is understood as a search for cultural authenticity and personal integrity, the long-term effects of the Islamic Revival will, if successful, provide a new synthesis for Muslims. By establishing Muslim identity firmly in their centuries-long collective experiences, the Revival will do much to establish a new Muslim identity. And a new Muslim identity will make it possible, once again, for Muslims to embrace fully the contemporary world in all its scientific, intellectual, artistic and political manifestations.[31] A new identity will foster the role of the Islamic world as a full contributor to world civilization.

Ninth, and finally, the Islamic Revival cannot most usefully be considered the reflection of a religious revival narrowly conceived. Rather, those diverse processes which result in what is collectively and somewhat misleadingly labeled "the Islamic Revival" more appropriately should be considered as using Islam for various purposes. Islam is such a rich and complex body of beliefs that it lends itself to a variety of uses. One may speak of a revival of Islam, although there is certainly no evidence that it had ever even remotely approached extinction. More aptly, however, it should be said that Muslims have come to use Islam in a variety of ways to achieve a variety of purposes. In this sense, there is an Islamic Revival with major implications for the politics of the Middle East.

NOTES

1. For a recent work which maximizes the role of the CIA, see Kermit Roosevelt, *Countercoup: The Struggle for the Control of Iran* (New York: McGraw-Hill, 1979).

2. See Stephen Zabith, *The Mossadegh Era: Roots of the Revolution* (Chicago: Lake View Press, 1982).

3. For an account of the origins of both the Mujahedin and Fedayin, see Ervand Abrahannan, *Iran Between Two Revolutions* (Princeton, N.J.: Princeton University Press, 1982), pp. 480–95.

4. See Ayatollah Rouhollah Khomaini, *Islamic Government* (New York: Manor Books, 1979).

5. The best treatment in English of the victory of the Islamic forces after the flight of the shah can be found in Shaul Babhash, *The Reign of the Ayatollahs* (New York: Basic Books, 1984). For this author's review of that work see *The New York Times*, October 21, 1984.

6. For a brief account of the Mecca mosque incident see William B. Quandt, *Saudi Arabia in the 1980's: Foreign Policy, Security, and Oil* (Washington, D.C.: Brookings Institution, 1981), pp. 93–96. See also Robert Lacey, *The Kingdom* (New York: Harcourt and Brace, 1982), pp. 478–86. Also see *The New York Times*, February 25, 1980, and *The Financial Times* (London), April 28, 1980.

7. Since the Islamic faith has never been moribund, it hardly could be said to have been revived. A more apt term, but not one which captured popular fancy, is the "Islamic Resurgence." On the subject, irrespective of labels, see Ernst Gellner, *Muslim Society* (Cambridge: Cambridge University Press, 1983); John Obert Voll, *Islam: Continuity and Change in the Modern World* (Boulder, Colo.: Westview Press, 1982); Ali E. Hillal Dessouki, ed., *Islamic Resurgence in the Arab World* (New York: Praeger, 1982); James Piscatori, ed., *Islam in the Political Process* (Cambridge: Cambridge University Press, 1983); Edward Mortimer, *Faith and Power: The Politics of Islam* (New York: Vintage Books, 1982).

8. This point has been made most convincingly by Daniel Pipes. See his "Oil Wealth and Islamic Resurgence," in Dessouki, ed., *Islamic Resurgence*, pp. 35–53, as well as his *In the Path of God: Islam and Political Power* (New York: Basic Books, 1983).

9. For works that stress the political nature of Islam see the following: L. Gardet, *La cité musulmane: vie sociale et politique* (Paris, 1954); E.I.J. Rosenthal, *Islam in the Modern World* (Princeton, N.J.: Princeton University Press, 1957); J. Harris Proctor, *Islam and International Relations* (New York: Praeger, 1965); E. Kedourie, *Afghani and Abduh: An Essay on Religious Unbelief and Political Activism in Modern Islam* (New York: Humanities Press, 1966); Leonard Binder, *The Ideological Revolution in the Middle East* (New York: John Wiley, 1964).

10. See Bernard Lewis, "The Return of Islam," *Commentary*, January 1976, pp. 39–49.

11. Speaking of his faith in Islam, the shah wrote in his memoirs:

My faith has always dictated my behavior as a man or as head of state, and I have always considered that one of my most important duties was to preserve our religion and to give its rightful place. An atheist civilization is not truly civilized and I have always taken care that the White Revolution to which I dedicated so many years of my reign should, on all points, conform to the principles of Islam. Religion is the cement which enables the social structure to stand up. It is the very basis of family life and the life of a nation.

Mohammad Reza Pahlavi, *An Autobiography* (London: Michael Joseph, 1980), p. 39.

12. See Princess Ashraf Pahlavi's memoirs, *Faces in a Mirror from Exile* (Englewood Cliffs, N.J.: Prentice-Hall, 1980), pp. 155–56.

13. Amin Saikal, *The Rise and Fall of the Shah* (Princeton, N.J.: Princeton University Press, 1980), p. 189.

14. In particular during the first year of his return to Iran, Ayatollah Khomaini stressed such themes during his speeches. "The Iranian people did not make the revolution in order to buy cheaper melons," he argued as a preface to his assertions of the importance of achieving Islamic community.

15. Lacey, *The Kingdom*. See especially the chapter entitled, "As God Wills," pp. 514–23.

16. For a discussion of Islamic views of Israel in terms of its Jewish character see Fouad Ajami, *The Arab Predicament: Arab Political Thought and Practice Since 1967* (Cambridge: Cambridge University Press, 1981), pp. 55 and 67–70. Ajami discusses the view of Muhammad Jalal Kishk and Ahmad Baha'al-Din. See especially al-Din's *Thalath Sanawat* (Beirut, 1970).

17. See Jean-Claude Vatin, "Revival in the Maghreb: Islam as an Alternative Po-

litical Language," in Ali E. Hillal Dessouki, *Islamic Resurgence in the Arab World*, pp. 221–50.

18. See M.G.S. Hodgson, *The Venture of Islam*, 3 vols. (Chicago: University of Chicago Press, 1974), vol. 3: *The Gunpowder Empires and Modern Times*, chapter 3, "The Ottoman Empire: Shari'ah Military Alliance, 1517–1718," pp. 99–133. On Egypt, the State and Islam, see chapter 4, "Egypt and East Arab Land: Revival of the Heritage," pp. 272–302. On Egypt, see Nadav Safran, *Egypt in Search of Political Community* (Cambridge, Mass.: Harvard University Press, 1961); C. C. Adams, *Islam and Modernism in Egypt* (London: Oxford University Press, 1933); J. Heyworth-Dunne, *Religious and Political Trends in Modern Egypt* (Washington, D.C.: n.p., 1950).

19. See Farhad Kazemi, *Poverty and Revolution in Iran, The Migrant Poor, Urban Marginality and Politics* (New York: New York University Press, 1980), pp. 62–63.

20. See I. M. Hausaini, *The Moslem Brethren* (Beirut: Khayat's College Book Co-operative, 1956); Christina Phelps Harris, *Nationalism and Revolution in Egypt: The Role of the Muslim Brotherhood* (The Hague: Mouton, 1964); Mohammad Amien Rais, "The Moslem Brotherhood in Egypt, Its Rise, Demise and Resurrection" (Ph.D. dissertation, University of Chicago, 1981).

21. See Michael J. Fischer, *Iran: From Religious Dispute to Revolution* (Cambridge, Mass.: Harvard University Press, 1980), p. 7.

22. See Marvin Zonis, *The Political Elite of Iran* (Princeton, N.J.: Princeton University Press, 1971), pp. 151 ff.; and Hamid Algar, "The Oppositional Role of the Ulama in Twentieth Century Iran," in Nikki P. Keddie, ed., *Scholars, Saints and Sufis—Muslim Religious Institutions in the Middle East Since 1500* (Berkeley: University of California Press, 1972), pp. 231–55.

23. See Fazlur Rahman, "The Islamic State: Politics in the Service of Religion," paper presented at the University of Chicago Divinity School Association conference, "Religious Conviction and Public Action: The Life of Faith in a Pluralistic World," March 31-April 2, 1980.

24. For a discussion of the concept of "Islamdom" as one of unity, see M.G.S Hodgson, *The Venture of Islam*, vol. 1: *The Classical Age of Islam*, pp. 57–60.

25. In reference to Egypt's elevation of Al-Azhar and attempts to control it, see Chris Eccle, "Some Theory Considerations for the Study of Religious Elites and Social Change During a Period of Rapidly Increasing Societal Change" (Ph.D. dissertation, University of Chicago, 1976).

26. See the forthcoming Ph.D. dissertation on Islam and Egypt by Patrick Gaffney, University of Chicago.

27. Muhammad Ben Sa'ud is generally counted the first ruler of the House of Sa'ud (1745–65) who forged his alliance with al-Wahhab in 1744.

28. See, for example, Maxime Rodinson, *Islam and Capitalism* (Austin: University of Texas Press, 1978).

29. For a basic statement of the issues of narcissistic injury and rage, see Heinz Kohut, *The Analysis of the Self* (New York: International Universities Press, 1971) and *The Restoration of the Self* (New York: International Universities Press, 1978). For applications of these ideas, see Group for the Advancement of Psychiatry, Committee on International Relations, *Self-Involvement in the Middle East Conflict* 10,

no. 103 (November 1978) and Marvin Zonis, "Self-Objects, Self-Representation, and Sense-Making Crisis: Political Instability in the 1980s," forthcoming.

30. Bernard Lewis has made this point on numerous occasions, most recently, perhaps, at the conference on "Shi'ism, Resistance and Revolution," held at Tel Aviv University in December 1984.

31. See V. S. Naipaul, *Among the Believers: An Islamic Journey* (New York: Alfred A. Knopf, 1981), especially the chapters on Iran (pp. 3–58) and on Pakistan (pp. 85–210) and the conclusion (pp. 391–401).

12

Islamic Values and Radicalism in the Islamic Near East

KHALID BIN SAYEED

Interest in Islamic countries is currently greater in the West largely because of the enormous oil-based wealth that the Muslim countries of the Middle East possess and also because some of these countries are subject to social ferment—revolution in the case of Iran. Muslim countries are also understood to be experiencing an Islamic resurgence. We propose to examine the nature of this resurgence at the intellectual level. In terms of a specific geographical area, our analysis will concentrate mainly on Pakistan and partly on some of the developments in Iran.[1]

Since Islamic thought does not constitute a monolithic entity, we must first delineate the several forms in which Islamic resurgence has emerged in countries like Pakistan, Saudi Arabia and Iran. All schools of Muslim thought agree that Islamic ideology has to be derived from (*a*) the Qur'an, and (*b*) the Sunna or the Traditions of the Prophet. There is a controversy as to how the Qur'an and the Traditions are to be interpreted in the ongoing life of the community. Ernst Gellner, in *Muslim Society*, has arranged in a spectrum the three central elements in any Islamic ideological framework. These are, from left to right: Communal Consensus; the Book; Organization, Leadership, Ancestry.[2] The Saudi regime lies on the right of this spectrum. Deriving its ideology from the Qur'an and the Sunna, this regime has used its ancestral leadership, its ties with the Wahhabis and the modern organizations of the civil service and the military to maintain its conservative character. Almost unparalleled infusions of petro-dollars into the Saudi economy, together with the basically capitalist nature of its development, have posed certain serious problems to the regime; but so far it has been successful in persuading the majority of its citizens that its Islamic character remains unimpaired. The Saudi regime can argue that, because of its commitment to Islamic values of social justice, it has moderated the inequalities created by the market system through a policy of subsidies in areas such as housing, health and food prices.

General Zia al-Haqq's regime in Pakistan is similar to that in Saudi Arabia. Zia's regime is basically conservative because the Islamic policies that he is espousing and implementing—such as Zakat (state-administered assistance to the poor), the setting up of Shari'a judicial benches or of the Shari'at faculty at the University of Islamabad, the institution of prayer breaks during working hours, the revision of textbooks, and the holding of Islamic conferences—are all measures that do not threaten the power structure of the present dominant social and economic groups.

Even though there are certain Islamic principles that can be interpreted in favor of private property and the maintenance of certain social and economic differences among Muslim *darajat* (or "ranks"), and which these regimes can therefore use to justify their policies, there are nevertheless other precepts gleaned from the lives of the Prophet and the four Caliphs who succeeded him which stress social equality. Indeed, our interviews with Muslim intellectuals in these countries have suggested that the Islamic emphasis on social equality may assume concrete forms of redistributive justice that are quite radical. A well-known Egyptian intellectual, Hasan Hanafi, who has been banned several times from teaching at Cairo University, identifies a tradition of the "Islamic Left" which runs all the way from Muhammad 'Abduh and Muhammad Iqbal through such recent Islamic revolutionary thinkers as 'Ali Sheri'ati, Khomaini, Uman al-Mukhtar of Libya to the League of the Algerian 'Ulama'. "The Islamic left combines revolution in actuality against imperialism with a revolution of thought against backwardness."[3]

How should one classify Muhammad Iqbal (1876–1938), the national poet and philosopher of Pakistan? Iqbal's writings make it clear that he reckoned that the modern problems faced by Muslim communities throughout the world should be tackled by some form of communal consensus. For Iqbal, this communal consensus should be institutionalized in a legislative assembly, but any *ijtihad* (innovation) emanating from such an assembly would have to be inspired and guided by the principles of the Qur'an and Sunna. Therefore, it would not be quite proper to classify Iqbal as a Muslim liberal or socialist, because for him fundamental guidance and inspiration flow from the Qur'an and the Sunna and not from Western secularism, liberalism, or socialism. The basic difference between Iqbal and modern Muslim socialists or Marxists like the Mujahedin-i Khalq in Iran consists in the fact that the latter are in favor of tailoring or even modifying certain Islamic ideas to bring them into conformity with Marxist or socialist principles. Thus, one can see that although Iqbal lies on the left of Gellner's spectrum, his leftist position is quite different from that of other leftists or socialists.

Iqbal is admired in conservative circles for his passionate advocacy of an Islamic Renaissance. In some radical circles he is admired for the anti-imperialist and anti-capitalist thrust of his lyrics. In one of his most famous poems, "The Mosque of Cordoba," he discerned that the world of Islam was astir and that it could tear asunder the domination of the West.

> Now in the soul of Islam tumults like those are astir,
> Working God's secret will: tongue cannot tell what they mean.
> Watch from that ocean-depth what comes surging at last!
> See how those colours change, there in that azure vault.
> Destiny's curtain till now muffles the world to be.
> Yet, already, its dawn stands before me unveiled;
> Were I to lift this mask hiding the face of my thoughts,
> Europe could never endure songs as burning as mine![4]

The sense of outrage against Western domination and Muslim humiliation that Iqbal expressed was shared by even conservative religious leaders in Pakistan during the 1920s and 1930s. Indeed, one of the reasons that they were reluctant to support Muhammad 'Ali Jinnah and the Muslim League was because it was too closely aligned with the British *Raj*. The Khudai Khidmatgars led by Khan 'Abd al-Ghaffar Khan could never in good conscience bring themselves to cooperate with the Muslim League even after Pakistan was achieved.

ISLAMIC RESPONSE TO FEUDALISM IN PAKISTAN

It is significant that the indignation against the social injustice that Muslims suffered—particularly in areas like the Punjab, Sind and the Frontier—and which has been expressed in Iqbal's poetry, is substantiated by the empirical and statistical findings of British civil servants who operated in these areas. Commenting on the plight of the peasant in the districts of western Punjab during the 1920s and 1930s, Malcolm Darling wrote: "The peasantry, almost to a man, confess themselves the servants of the one true God and of Muhammad his Prophet, but in actual fact they are servants of landlord, money-lender and *pir*."[5] Darling had first-hand knowledge of the miseries and humiliations to which the peasant was constantly subject. Describing their plight in one of the subdivisions of the district of Muzaffargarh, Darling observed:

Every five miles or so is the house of a tribal or religious leader, who maintains a band of retainers to enforce his influence on his poorer neighbours, and to conduct his feuds with his equals. The poor man pays blackmail for his cattle to these local chieftains and for his soul to his *pir*, who may or may not live in the neighbourhood, but visits his followers yearly to receive his dues.[6]

Referring to the image that a typical landlord had created as a result of his rapacity and repression to districts of west Punjab, Darling reported that both in Muzaffargarh and in Dera Ghazi Khan, with the exception of about five who did not oppress their tenants, landlords were described as "all throat-stranglers."[7] In Mianwali most of the landlords were "tyrants" (*zalim*).[8] The landlords in the district of Jhang and in some parts of Multan "were more powerful than 'officers',... inspired such fears in their tenants that they could take from them what service they pleased,... eat up the lands of the smaller folk, and rarely let their tenants stay long on a well for fear that they will assert their right of occupancy."[9]

The situation in Sind was even more grim where the *haris* (tenants-at-will) numbered roughly 2 million in a population of 4.53 million in 1941. M. Masud, an Indian Civil Service officer and a member of the government Hari Enquiry Committee of 1947–8, suggested in his *Note of Dissent* that the indignities and inequities that the *haris* suffered were similar to those that serfs had been subjected to in medieval Europe.

Fear reigns supreme in the life of the *hari*—fear of imprisonment, fear of losing his land, wife or life. The Zamindar might, at any time, get annoyed with him and oust him—he might have to leave his crops half ripe, his cattle might also be snatched and he might be beaten out of the village—he might suddenly find himself in the fetters of police under an enquiry for theft, robbery or murder, or more often, under Section 110 of the Criminal Procedure Code.[10]

In the presence of his feudal lord the *hari* behaved not as a follower of a faith which preached social equality, but as an abject serf who was trying to retain the goodwill of his master through utter servility. As a mark of respect he was expected to touch the landlord's feet. The village *mullah* or the district *pir* legitimized this state of affairs by constantly preaching to the peasant what they regarded as the Islamic doctrine of *taqdir*: "It is God's will to elevate whomsoever he likes and debase whomsoever he likes. How can we interfere in the working of His divine will?"[11] Obviously the *mullahs* and the *pirs*, in order to justify or defend the existing system of inequality and apparent injustice, were biased in their interpretation of the Qur'anic verses. It would not be fair to suggest that the Qur'an advocates the extreme doctrine of fatalism as the concept of *taqdir* sometimes suggests. The Qur'anic verse which is often cited in this connection is the one from chapter 3(26) that the *mullahs* tended to use in their preachings:

O God
Lord of Power (and Rule),
Thou givest Power
To whom Thou pleasest,
And Thou strippest off Power
From whom Thou pleasest;

> Thou enduest with honour
> Whom Thou pleasest,
> And Thou bringest low
> Whom Thou pleasest;
> In Thy hand is all Good.
> Verily, over all things
> Thou hast power.

Both Islamic scholars and apologists have argued that this verse or, indeed, any other cannot be interpreted to mean that God's sovereignty over the universe is both absolute and arbitrary. God confers honor or wealth according to His will, no doubt; but His will is to promote or enhance goodness on this earth. This is clearly referred to when the verse states: "In Thy hand is all Good." One of the most well-known and influential translators and interpreters of the Qur'an, 'Abdullah Yusuf 'Ali, from whose translation we have just quoted, points out in his explanation:

The governing phrase in it all is: "In Thy hand is all Good." What is the standard by which we may judge Good?" It is God's Will. Therefore when we submit to God's Will, and real Islam illuminates us, we see the highest Good. There has been and is much controversy as to what is the Highest Good. To the Muslim there is no difficulty: it is the Will of God. He must ever strive to learn and understand that Will. But once in that fortress, he is secure. He is not troubled with the nature of Evil. Evil is the negation of God's Will. Good is conformity to God's Will. He does not cry with impatience against many things which give him pain and sorrow. He knows that "God is in His world"; and that God is Good. God's Will is another name for God's Plan. There is nothing arbitrary and haphazard. We do not see the whole Plan or Will. But we have Faith. All is, will be, must be, right in the end.[12]

This kind of explanation raises serious questions as to whether Islam as an ideology or a set of moral principles will continue to command unswerving allegiance from peasants and others who have to face the brunt of the brutalities that we have referred to above. How is it possible for a vibrant and practical religion like that of Islam to take the position that the peasant should put up with indignities ranging all the way from unjust taxation and dues to the theft of his property or kidnapping or even the rape of his female relatives because God's will, which is for the good of himself as well as of his fellow-beings, will ultimately triumph? This kind of resignation was possible in earlier times, but it is no longer possible in this day and age.

It should be noted that these fundamental questions have not arisen just in the twentieth century. From its very inception the Islamic community had to wrestle with the problem of inequality. Even during the time of the Prophet, when devotion was at its height, the faithful were not reluctant to raise questions regarding the unfair advantages of both income and piety that the affluent could enjoy. According to one of the well-known Hadith:

Some of the Companions of the Messenger of Allah said to the Prophet: O Messenger of Allah, the affluent have made off with the rewards: they pray as we pray,
they fast as we fast, and they give away in charity the superfluity of their wealth.

He said: Has not Allah made things for you to give away in charity? Truly every
tasbiha (reciting Allah has no imperfection) is a charity, every *takbira* (reciting
Allah is most great) is a charity, every *tahmida* (reciting There is no God but Allah)
is a charity; to enjoin a good action is a charity, to forbid an evil action is a charity.[13]

The essence of the Islamic social doctrine that we have just developed
is that Islam recommends co-existence between the rich and the poor
because God has created people unequal. However, Islamic doctrine also
requires that the poor should not be allowed to descend to the level of
abject poverty and distress. The preventive institution here is that of Zakat,
which ensures some measure of social harmony, even justice, but not equality.

At this stage we shall explore further how certain Islamic ideas as preached
by the *pirs* and the 'Ulama' have influenced the social and political development of Muslims in some of the areas of the Indian subcontinent which
became part of Pakistan. We have indicated above that during the 1930s
and 1940s semi-feudal conditions existed in the upper and northwestern
districts of west Punjab and in most of Sind. It has been argued that the
situation was different in the four districts which constituted the Canal
Colonies of Shahpur, Lyallpur, Jhang and Montgomery. Here the canals and
the irrigation-system set up by the British had converted these districts into
fertile tracts. It was noted by a number of British and other observers that
the influence of the *pir* had declined particularly in a district like Lyallpur,
because of growing prosperity and the emergence of a large number of
medium-sized peasant proprietors. A member of Darling's staff found in
central Punjab that the peasant was beginning to believe "that a man's
fortune depended more upon *tadbir* (effort) than *taqdir* (fate)."[14]

When we look at the situation in the post-independence period of the
1950s, we find that *tadbir* had by no means triumphed over *taqdir* insofar
as the basic attitudes of the people were concerned. There is no question
that life for the peasant in areas like Muzaffargarh, Mianwali, or Dera Ghazi
Khan had hardly changed at all. Even as late as the Ayub period, we find
Basic Democrats of the Mianwali district complaining in a petition to the
president of Pakistan that the nawab of Kalabagh was imposing taxes on the
"use of the air of the town," which in concrete terms meant that those who
were not on good terms with the nawab had to pay annual rents of "Rs. 25
per door, per window, per ventilator and per rain drain-pipe." There was
a death tax as well as a joy tax, the latter on any function of a joyful nature.
The townspeople had to find entertainment through the services of the
personal musicians and entertainers of the nawab. Other taxes were mentioned in the petition, including a shepherd tax and a hunting tax.[15] One
could understand if peasants living under such conditions displayed attitudes

of utter helplessness and despair. But even in the more advanced districts and villages surrounding Lahore some of the empirical studies found fatalism of an extreme nature to be the predominant attitude. A report on selected sociological aspects of life in six sample villages in the Lahore district reported that two-thirds of the people questioned "were of the opinion that whatever had been ordained for them would be fulfilled regardless of their wishes or efforts."[16] Another study based on findings from a village in the urban area of Lahore observed that, when the attention of the villagers had been drawn to the progress that neighboring villages had made in recent years, their response was that the people in the more fortunate villages had a *"qismat* and *risq* of their own. One must not question the will of God who may give much to some and little to others."[17] Thus, one can argue that even when feudalism of the kind that prevailed in northwestern Punjab was not present in central Punjab and particularly in the hinterlands of urban areas, fatalism as an attitude persisted because of other hardships associated with limited economic opportunities. Can one suggest further, perhaps, that the kind of values and ideas that the *pirs* and the *mullahs* propagated among the people reinforced the fatalism of the peasant and even of the urban dweller?

The elections of 1970 in which the Pakistan People's party emerged as the dominant party in Punjab and Sind demonstrated that there had taken place in Pakistan and particularly in Punjab and Sind a quite sudden and unprecedented social transformation and political awakening among the rural and urban masses. Here was a party which had openly campaigned for Islamic socialism. There stood against it not only the representatives of feudal power in Sind and Punjab but also parties with impressive Islamic credentials like the Muslim League and the Jama'at-i Islami. Did the elections lay bare a change that had been simmering at the mass level both in the rural and urban areas? Ayub's land reforms drove home to the rural masses the simple fact that there was something seriously wrong and unjust with the social system that existed in the countryside. Ayub's industrialization program had not only created monopolistic concentrations of economic power but also concentrations of industrial labor in some key urban centers such as Karachi, Hyderabad, Lahore, Lyallpur and Multan, among others. The industrial belt had spread from Karachi to central and southwestern Punjab. Thus, all the electrifying factors were present and as Nasser once said about the Arab world, there was a wandering role that sought an actor to perform it. In Bhutto, the masses of Pakistan found a superb actor. It was a monumental task to attack the fortresses of feudalism and Bhutto relied on the weaponry of land reforms, promising as much as twelve and a half to fifteen acres of land for every peasant. According to the *Pakistan Census of Agriculture 1972*, 58 percent of the farms in Pakistan were rented by tenants and owner-cum-tenants who rented all or part of the lands they cultivated. According to the same census, 34 percent of the farms were operated by tenants who did not own any land.[18] To these numbers must be added agricultural workers of ten years and above who in 1972 constituted over 12.8 million.[19] These figures give us some idea of how many millions were without any land in Pakistan.

In an interview with one of the Pakistan People's Party (PPP) leaders, Hafeez Kardar, the author was told that during the 1970 election campaign Kardar at first made no impact when he was campaigning in villages around Lahore. Peasants would often tell him that they had heard all these speeches and promises earlier but that their lot had not improved. It was only when he said that the PPP would offer twelve and a half acres of land to every landless person, that peasants would invariably ask him to come and sit down and tell them more. The author was constantly told by people in Lahore and Rawalpindi that the dynamic appeal of Bhutto lay in the fact that he often appeared as a leader who was one of them. He was seen dancing on trucks and when he was accused that he himself was a landowner and a wealthy person, he would say, "I am a believer in socialism; that is why, leaving my class and government, I have come back to workers, peasants, students, and poor people."[20] In an election meeting in Mardan he asked his audience to whom the buildings belonged. When he was told that they belonged to the nawab of Hoti, he said that after he came to power, the people would own them.

Even more serious than this rhetoric was the risk that Bhutto took in countering Islamic conservatism with the slogan of Islamic socialism. His opponents attacked his advocacy of socialism as anti-Islamic. Over a hundred 'Ulama' issued *fatwas* (religious decrees) against him. How did he react?

I respect the 'Ulama', but those who give *fatwas* after receiving money have served the *kafirs*. Islam is not in danger. Those who are in danger are the capitalists and the landlords and their puppets who cannot sleep at night and who can only sleep with the help of sleeping pills, and God willing, we shall transform the present social order. Islamic *masawat* is called socialism in English just as people's rule is called democracy. What is wrong in calling Islamic *masawat* Islamic socialism, which removes the miseries of the poor?[21]

In an interview with one of the leftists of the PPP, Shaikh Muhammad Rashid, we found that the PPP leaders in the election campaign emphasized that Islam supported socialism, that Omar Bin 'Abd al-Azis had nationalized land, and that God had made it clear in the Qur'an that land belonged to God and not to private individuals. As opposed to this, he pointed out, the Jama'at-i Islami had given a conservative interpretation of Islam and argued that Islam had recommended private property.[22] Shaikh Muhammad Rashid also published a pamphlet on the need for an agrarian revolution in Pakistan. It is significant that the pamphlet, while giving a detailed analysis of the problems that tenants, agricultural laborers, and peasants faced both in East and West Pakistan, made no mention of Islamic ideas that might help the peasants to pursue their struggle for agrarian change.[23] This omission, besides suggesting that Islam was used mainly for electioneering purposes, also indicated that a number of peasant leaders probably did not think that Islamic ideas were very relevant to or helpful in their campaign for radical agrarian changes.

It has often been pointed out that there were many loopholes in Bhutto's land reforms and that they were not fully implemented. However, it should be noted that his election campaign, his land reforms, his offer to small landowners of exemption from payment of land revenue, and his offer of five *marlas* of land for building houses to artisans, farm laborers, and tenants who did not own houses, all won for him massive support among the poorer sections in the rural areas. Perhaps even a more important result was the dramatic increase in political consciousness among the peasants. To arouse political consciousness, particularly in an area like Sind where the *Pir* of Pagaro commanded fanatical devotion of his followers, was no mean task. It was reported that in one of his meetings in Sind where both the big landowners and the peasants were present the landowners complained that they had lost control over their tenants and other small peasants who sometimes abused them when they visited their lands. Bhutto, expressing his surprise, is reported to have remarked, "Really, don't tell me I have aroused so much political consciousness among the peasants."[24]

PEASANTS STRUGGLE IN FIVE VILLAGES OF DISTRICT ATTOCK 1974–76: A CASE STUDY

So far, our analysis of the unequal struggle that the peasants and tenants have been waging against the landlords has been somewhat general. In order to appreciate the specific issues and parameters involved in such a struggle and how unequal and unjust it is as far as the tenants are concerned, we shall draw quite extensively on a case study published by Nigar Ahmad of the Department of Economics, Quaid-e-Azam University, in 1980.[25] The study makes it clear that even after a series of land reforms had been introduced by the Daultana regime in 1950, by the Ayub regime in 1959, and by the Bhutto government in 1972, landlords in the Pindigheb *tehsil* and particularly in the village of Khunda could evict tenants almost at their will. Since occupancy could only be proven through land revenue records or receipts given by landlords for their share of the produce, by denying such receipts to their tenants the landlords could evict them from their lands. The landlords involved in this struggle were Malik Allah Yar Khan, who was a provincial minister in 1967, and Malik Muhammad Iqbal Khan, who was elected as a member of the national assembly during the Ayub regime.

During the Bhutto regime, both because the tenants had voted for the

PPP and also as a result of the introduction of land reforms, the tenants became bold enough to get organized and made certain concrete demands upon their landlords. These demands centered around issues like the obtaining from the landlord the seed to which they were entitled under the reforms, receiving two-thirds of the produce as well as a receipt from the landlord for the share received by him, and refusal to give him free labor. Tenants were led by their own leaders and sometimes those tenants who had become owners, including those who had served in the army during wartime. It must be noted that Attock was one of the three districts of Punjab from which the bulk of the Pakistani army was recruited. Because of their own organization and also because of the support they received from the Bhutto government, particularly through the Land Commission chaired by Shaikh Rashid, the tenants were able to win several cases against the landlords. Every time the landlords lost, they would register false cases involving charges of abduction, stealing, keeping unlicensed firearms, among others, against the tenants. Since the local police and the bureaucracy often assisted the landlords in terrorizing their tenants, they had been successful in the past. But under the new regime, the tenants resorted to legal action and also pressured the bureaucracy through threats of public demonstrations into disclosing records which would show that the landlords were in illegal occupation of the land after the introduction of land reforms. However, in several cases, when the tenants would not surrender their produce to the landlord because they had not received the necessary receipt from the landlord, the landlords were successful in obtaining eviction decrees from the revenue courts.

In a few cases the landlords tried to enforce these decrees by demolishing the houses of their tenants and filing criminal cases against prominent tenant leaders. These situations deteriorated into law-and-order situations, particularly when the tenants and their families courageously resisted such coercive measures. Even the Bhutto government did not want such situations to deteriorate and issued instructions to the local officers to bring about reconciliation betweeen landlords and tenants. The landlords further strengthened their position by joining the PPP in 1976. The landlord, Malik Allah Yar Khan, was successful in obtaining the PPP ticket in October 1977 over the tenant leader, Bostan, who had been active in the PPP for several years.

Even though with the overthrow of the Bhutto government landlords have once again emerged ascendant, Nigar Ahmad thinks that the district and the village of Khunda have already undergone a sea-change.

The peasants have a memory now, of having successfully challenged the power of the landlords, of having won their rights through legal means at all levels of the administrative hierarchy as well as in the judiciary, of having countered the political power of the landlords by their own organization, and of enjoying the fruits of their battles on the land which belonged to the erstwhile feudal lord.[26]

This case study reveals that no systematic attempt was made either by the government or the political leaders to take a stand against the oppression of the landlords by invoking values of social justice or even Islamic socialism as the PPP under Bhutto had advocated. One wonders why this was not done. The PPP had won an election victory in 1970 on the issue of Islamic socialism. They had been attacked by the orthodox as well as other conservative Islam-oriented parties on the score that the PPP's advocacy of Islamic socialism ran counter to the tenants of fundamental Islam. The stand of the orthodox and conservative parties had been decisively rejected by the electorate. Two reasons can be suggested as to why the PPP did not invoke the concept of Islamic social justice against the kind of semi-feudal oppression which the landlords practiced against the peasants. First, Bhutto did not want to alienate the landlords altogether by taking a clear stand against them. Second, the PPP leaders and intellectuals had not done any systematic thinking in terms of how the concept of Islamic socialism could be translated into legislative or political reality. As a slogan, it had helped them in the election in that the conservative circles failed to defeat them as anti-Islamic. As political pragmatists, the PPP leadership were satisfied with that measure of success and did not have either the will or the capacity to build any intellectual or political bridges between the traditional emphasis in Islam on social justice and the PPP's advocacy of or adherence to socialism. In view of this failure on the part of the political leadership, the question arises of how long the political support of the poorer social sections like the peasants and lower income groups in the urban areas, particularly industrial labor, can be mobilized in the name of Islam. To the peasants and the poorer masses, the Islamic state has often meant the continuation of the status quo, which means an oppressive agrarian system that the 'Ulama' and the *mullahs* justify through the doctrine that such a state of inequality and poverty for the masses is decreed by God.

POSSIBILITIES OF A NEW RADICAL ISLAMIC IDEOLOGY

So far our analysis has led us to believe that Pakistan represents at this stage the very negation of Iqbal's dream that it would emerge as a social democracy. His ideas contained in his often quoted letters to Jinnah have been characterized as embodying "a clear-cut blueprint for Islamic socialism."[27] Iqbal wrote to Jinnah as early as 1937:

But it is clear to my mind that if Hinduism accepts social democracy it must necessarily cease to be Hinduism. For Islam the acceptance of social democracy in some suitable form and consistent with the legal principles of Islam is not a revolution but a return to the original purity of Islam. The modern problems, therefore, are far more easy to solve for the Muslims than for the Hindus.[28]

The diagnosis that the well-known Canadian scholar, Wilfred Cantwell Smith, made in 1943 has turned out to be much closer to the mark than Iqbal's prognosis. He described the struggle for economic power led by the corporate Muslim middle class.

They have said that Muslims and Hindus are so different that they cannot live together in one state. What they have meant is that the Muslim bourgeoisie and the "Hindu" bourgeoisie are so competitive that they cannot both own the banks and industries, run the commerce, do the professional and other jobs, in one capitalist state.[29]

If Professor Smith had pursued his Marxist analysis more rigorously instead of turning away from it, he would have foreseen that Pakistan's ruling classes would be drawn primarily from the repressive semi-feudal land-owners of West Pakistan and the rapacious merchant capitalists who had flocked to the new state from India to seek national and social outlets for their entrepreneurship.

Why has the ideal of Pakistan as an Islamic state gone awry? Why haven't the Muslim 'Ulama' been as vigorous and earnest in leading the Muslim masses for the establishment of social justice and social equality as they have been in inciting them toward sectarian goals like having the Ahmadis declared as a non-Muslim minority community? As we have suggested earlier, the religious leadership all the way from the *mullah*, the *sajjada nashin*, or the *pir* interpreted the Qur'an in such a way that Islamic ideas tended to serve the interests of the ruling class, namely, the big landowners. In historical terms the present ruling class in Pakistan which consists of a coalition between the merchant-cum-capitalists and the big landowners is a direct descendant of the kind of power structure that the British left behind in the northwest India which became Pakistan. In order to promote their imperial interests, the British created an administrative system which manipulated the religious leaders as well as the big landowners and the tribal chiefs. Similarly, just as the British were concerned about the Russians making intrusions into northwest India, their present successors, namely, the Americans, have also expressed similar concerns and persuaded and pressured Pakistan into joining military alliances or pacts.[30]

In terms of the central theme of this essay a more fundamental question would be: Is the main thrust of the Qur'an such that it supports a conservative social order? There are Qur'anic verses which call upon Muslims to fight the oppressors. This suggests that the Qur'an can be interpreted differently by people who occupy different or conflicting positions in the political spectrum. We shall deal with the conservative position first. We have already referred to a verse (*Sura* 3, 26) which was used by the *mullahs* in Sind to impress upon the *haris* that their inferior status and suffering could be explained by the fact that God in His divine wisdom elevated some people and placed others in subordination to them. There are other key verses which refer to the concept of *darajat* (ranks) and suggest that these differences are both divinely ordained and rational.

> It is He Who hath made
> You (His) agents, inheritors
> Of the earth: He hath raised
> You in ranks, some above
> Others: that He may try you:
> For the Lord is quick
> In punishment: yet He
> Is indeed Oft-forgiving,
> Most Merciful. (*Sura* 6, 165)

This verse can be defended by pointing out that God is not conferring favors or wealth on certain groups or classes so that they may use such bounties indiscriminately and disregard their social obligations. The same concept of *darajat* emerges in an earlier verse of the same *Sura* when He declares:

> We raise whom We will,
> Degree after degree:
> For thy Lord is full
> Of wisdom and knowledge. (*Sura* 6, 83)

Again, it is clearly indicated that there is purpose in the creation of these ranks and differences. This purpose is explained in the verse immediately following the above when it is declared: "Thus do We reward Those who do good."

Masud, who wrote the well-known *Note of Dissent* to the Hari Report, cites the following verse in support of his view that the Qur'an does not favor the *zamindari* system and supports equitable distribution of land among all cultivators.[31]

> For the earth is God's
> To give as a heritage
> To such of His servants
> As He pleaseth; and the end
> Is (best) for the righteous. (*Sura*, 7, 128)

Masud ignores the fact that even though land belongs to God, He gives it to such of his servants as He likes or prefers. When such differences in landownership arise, the religious leaders in a Muslim community have always been able to explain them as results of God's will and pleasure. There is no clear statement that feudalism and exploitation of the peasantry are prohibited. Indeed, the following verse enjoins the believers not to covet or claim the wealth belonging to the more affluent classes, again because such gifts have been divinely ordained.

> And in no wise covet
> Those things in which God
> Hath bestowed His gifts
> More freely on some of you
> Than on others: to men
> Is allotted what they earn,
> And to women what they earn:
> But ask God of His bounty.
> For God hath full knowledge
> Of all things. (*Sura*, 4, 32)

The translator, Abdullah Yusuf Ali, in explaining this verse, writes:

We must not be jealous if other people have more than we have—in wealth or position or strength or honour or talent or happiness. Probably things are equalized in the aggregate or in the long run, or equated to needs and merits on a scale which we cannot appraise.[32]

When there is a so-called revolution of rising expectations and above all when tenants, landless laborers, and small peasants have become conscious that the present system of land distribution has created a reign of terror and tyranny, how would it be possible for Muslim leaders to offer such interpretations of the Qur'an? All Muslims agree that Islam was not created with a view to solving the problems of a particular age and that its moral principles were supposed to hold true for all time to come. Islam is supposed to be a world system from which the Muslim community at a given time tries to extract an understanding or appreciation of the problems it faces. Thus, we see Iqbal in his two famous poems, "Shikva" (Complaint, 1909) and "Javab-i-Shikva" (Answer to the Complaint, 1913) put forward the view that the decline in Muslim power and glory had come about entirely as a result of the Muslims moving away from the correct path of Islam. Toward the end of his poem, "Answer to the Complaint," Iqbal makes God say: "If you follow steadfastly the path laid down by Muhammad, this world is nothing, you would become the masters of the entire universe." The same Iqbal in another poem, "Lenin in the Presence of God," which appeared in his collection, *Bal-i-Jibril* (Gabriel's Wing, 1935), makes God issue the following command to his angels after hearing about the inequities of the capitalist system:

> Rise, and from their slumber wake the poor ones of My world. Shake
> the walls and windows of the mansions of the great.
>
> Find the field whose harvest is no peasant's daily bread—
> Garner in the furnace every ripening ear of wheat.
>
> Rear for me another temple, build its walls with mud—
> Wearied of their columned marbles, sickened is My sight.[33]

What kind of transformation had taken place in Iqbal's thinking? Consistent with his earlier diagnosis as outlined in his poem, "Answer to the
Complaint," he should have commanded his angels to tell the strife-torn
world that the only way to restore harmony and social justice would be to
follow the precepts that had been laid down in verses dealing with non-
revolutionary situations and stable societies. God, instead of commanding
his angels to burn all those fields of the landlords which did not yield to
the peasant daily bread, should have ordered his angels to remind the peasant
of the Qur'anic precept quoted earlier, "And in no wise covet those things
in which God hath bestowed His gifts more freely on some of you than on
others."

This suggests that Iqbal was groping for a new interpretation of Islam
which would enable the Muslims to come to grips with the problem of
poverty and social justice. In his poem, "To the Saqi," he said:

> The cycle of Capitalism is done,
> The juggler has shown his tricks and gone.[34]

To Jinnah, he wrote: "The problem of bread is becoming more and more
acute."[35] He recommended a restructuring of the Muslim League so that it
would be able to respond to and solve the economic problems of the masses.
Some scholars think that Iqbal saw no difficulty in reconciling socialism
with Islam, because they equate socialism with social justice and do not
realize that the ideal of socialism is not only social justice but social and
economic equality. Conservative and moderate thinkers think that since
Islam corrects the economic inequalities of modern society through Zakat,
it automatically brings about social justice without moving excessively in
the direction of equality and thereby dampening human initiative. Socialists,
on the other hand, would argue that a slight moderation of economic inequalities through Zakat will not bring about even social equality. This
means that the notion of social justice as advanced by Islamic conservatives
is far removed from the ideal of social and economic equality that socialism
puts forward. Faced with the gross inequities of the peasant societies of
Punjab, Sind and the Frontier, Iqbal could not have believed that a conservative or moderate interpretation of Islamic principles would solve the
problem of peasant poverty. This explains his call for revolutionary change
in his poem, "Lenin in the Presence of God."

It is significant that an earlier thinker and pan-Islamicist, Jamal al-Din al-Afghani (1838–97), had also moved away from a strategy of seeking Islamic unity through governments and sultans to a strategy of liberation of the peasant masses. His clarion call to the Egyptian peasantry was:

O you poor *fellah*. You break the heart of the earth in order to draw sustenance from it and support your family. Why do you not break the heart of your oppressor? Why do you not break the heart of those who eat the fruit of your labour?[36]

A broader view of the kind of revolutionary change that lay in store for the Islamic world was put forward by the Russian Marxist Muslim, Sultan Galiyev, who wrote:

All the Muslim colonial peoples are proletarian peoples, and, since almost all classes of Muslim society were formerly oppressed by the colonialists, all have the right to the title of proletarian.[37]

Galiyev, rather simplistically but nevertheless accurately described the state of the great majority of Muslims living in the Arab world, in Iran and in Pakistan. It is true that one can apply his description to Muslims living in other parts of the world as well, but the feeling of being an exploited proletarian peoples in the Middle and Near East is greater because Muslims have been exposed to more blatant forms of Western imperialism.

The radical nature of the Iranian revolution has often been underestimated in the West. First of all, particularly in the United States, most of the policy makers have simply not appreciated how important the Islamic dimension has been in the recent upheavals in the Middle East. It is significant that Henry Kissinger, who is often regarded as one of the greatest experts on the Middle East, pays no attention to the Islamic factor in his two volumes of memoirs, *White House Years* (1979) and *Years of Upheaval* (1982). Second, it has not been realized how the Iranian 'Ulama' led by Khomaini have systematically radicalized the most fundamental concept of martyrdom in the Shi'ite doctrine. Under Khomaini's leadership, the tradition of mourning for the martyrdom of Hussein has been transformed into a dynamic doctrine. According to Khomaini and his followers, it was to prevent the establishment of monarchy and hereditary succession that Hussein revolted and became a martyr.[38] In addition, the Shi'ite doctrine of *intizar* (waiting) suggests that all secular governments are illegitimate until the twelfth imam reappears. This doctrine has given additional authority to the clergy to lead the people against secular rulers and prepare the ground for the appearance of the twelfth imam. Hamid Algar's perceptive observation on this question may be quoted:

The combination of those two themes, the rejection of *de facto* authority and the belief in the virtues of martyrdom, has given Shi'ism, particularly at certain points in its history, an attitude of militancy that has been sadly lacking in a large number of Sunni segments of the Muslim *Unmah*.[39]

It is well known that the Mujahedin-i Khalq (People's Fighters) have been the principal opposition to Khomaini's rule in Iran. The Mujahedin-i Khalq have tried to present their Marxist beliefs in an Islamic garb. They have argued:

A Marxist who is slaughtered for the cause of the people and on the gallows platform, with his mouth full of blood, or is shouting for the freedom of the people and never submits to oppression, is following exactly the advice of Ali which he gave, in his Will, to his two sons: "Be the enemy of the oppressor and the supporter of the oppressed."[40]

However, in spite of their attempts to identify themselves with Shi'ite or Islamic doctrine, the Mujahedin-i Khalq have not been able to evoke considerable grass-roots support, particularly in the rural areas. Khomaini and his supporters have challenged their commitment to Islam by pointing out that with their basic loyalty to Marxism and socialism, they have tried to tailor Islamic ideas to their Marxist philosophy.

In spite of the eclipse of some of the leftist organizations like the Mujahadin, the fact remains that a left-right conflict has emerged in Iran. It has been reported that measures such as land reforms and nationalization of foreign trade, though passed by the Majlis, have been blocked by the Council of Guardians. This indicates that the ranks of the clergy and the Revolutionary Guards subscribe to a fairly radical interpretation of the Islamic and Shi'ite doctrines, while perhaps a majority of the 'Ulama' at the higher levels and in institutions like the Council of Guardians belong to a conservative faction.

Finally, let us view Islamic resurgence and radicalism in the Muslim world from the perspective of the Western development or modernization theory. Modernization is viewed by most of the Western theorists as the process by which a citizen becomes increasingly capable of controlling his environment. To the main agents of this process in the Muslim world, namely, the educated groups including scientists, engineers and other technocrats, this process does not merely involve technical change, but an increasing ability to wrest control of their countries from Western domination. Therefore, a Muslim is struggling not only to control his environment but control it in such a way that Western influence will either be eliminated or minimized. There is a long tradition of bitterness toward the West, two of whose blunter spokesman are Khomaini and Arafat. Those of us who have interviewed the new intelligentsia in the Muslim world (the author is in the process of completing such a survey of scientists and technocrats in Iran, Pakistan and Saudi Arabia) have noticed that they may not support some of the extreme actions or policies of Khomaini. Nevertheless he is their spokesman when he says:

But when we have been bitten by a snake, we are even afraid of a piece of rope, which from afar looks like a snake. And you have bitten us too much, and too long. You only saw in us a market, and that was all. You only exported bad things to us, and that was all. The good things, such as material progress, you kept such things for yourself. Yes, we got many bad things from the West, a lot of suffering, and now we have good reasons to fear the West, to keep our youth from getting too close to the West and being influenced even more by the West.[41]

When to Khomaini's words were added the constant reiteration in the Qur'an that the enemies of Islam do not wish the Muslim world well and that if Muslims were to follow the right path, God would punish those enemies, it will be quite clear that the prospects of the West being welcome as a friend and not disliked as an imperialist are not very bright.

The Islamic world seems to be facing the cutting edges of the two blades wielded by the two superpowers. The Russians seem to be on a more open confrontation course. American pressure is more subtle but just as danger-ous. Islamic resurgence in the form of a return to or a revival of some form of Islamic fundamentalism will not be enough. What is needed is the de-velopment of a social and political ideology which will offer a social program to the masses better than any Soviet-inspired socialist program and a new political and economic order which will elicit from the intelligentsia and the technocrats a new sense of dedication and commitment strong enough to resist the blandishments of the West.

NOTES

1. The author acknowledges the research assistance received from the Social Sciences and Humanities Research Council of Canada in the writing of this article.

2. Ernst Gellner, *Muslim Society* (Cambridge: Cambridge University Press, 1981).

3. Hasan Hanafi, "Islamic Left," in *Al-Tayyar Al-Islami* (May 2, 1981).

4. V. G. Kiernan, trans., *The Poems of Iqbal* (London: John Murray, 1955).

5. Malcolm Darling, *Rusticus Loquitur* (London: Oxford University Press, 1930), p. 214.

6. Malcolm Darling, *Punjab Peasant in Prosperity and Debt* (London: Oxford University Press, 1932), p. 103.

7. Darling, *Rusticus*, p. 286.

8. Ibid., p. 291.

9. Ibid., p. 264.

10. M. Masud, *Hari Report: Note of Dissent* (Karachi: Hari Publications, 1948), p. 2.

11. Instead of relying on the English version of Masud's *Note*, I have consulted the Urdu version in which the *mullahs'* doctrine of *taqdir* seems closer to the

Qur'anic doctrine as stated in *Sura* 3, verse 26. The Urdu version is reproduced in *Al-Fatah*, annual no. 1972, p. 37.

12. Abdullah Yusuf Ali, *The Meaning of the Glorious Qur'an*, vol. 1 (Cairo: Dar Al-Kitab Al-Masri, n.d.), p. 129.

13. Ezzedin Ibrahim and Denys Johnson-Davies, trans., *An-Nawawi's Forty Hadith* (Damascus: The Holy Koran Publishing House, 1977), p. 84.

14. Darling, *Rusticus*, p. 38.

15. From Basic Democrats of Mianwali and Other Representatives of Public Opinion to President of Pakistan, Rawalpindi. Application under Article 121 of the Constitution of the Republic of Pakistan for Proceedings against Nawab Amir Muhammad Kham of Kalabagh, present Governor of West Pakistan (under sub-section (1) and sub-sections (3) and (4) of the same article 121 of the Constitution). Typescript.

16. W. L. Slocum, Jamila Akhtar and Abrar Fatima Sahi, *Village Life in Lahore District* (Lahore: Punjab University Press, 1959), p. 39.

17. Agha Sajjad Heider, *Village in an Urban Orbit* (Lahore: Punjab University Press, 1960), p. 8.

18. *Pakistan Census of Agriculture 1972* (Lahore, Government of Pakistan, 1975), p. 1, Table 3.

19. Ibid., p. 24, Table 61.

20. Zulfikar Ali Bhutto, *Let the People Judge* (Lahore: Pakistan People's Party, 1969), p. 28.

21. *Nusrat*, March 15, 1970, p. 18.

22. Interview on February 9, 1971, with Shaikh Muhammad Rashid, who later became a cabinet minister and also chairman of the Land Reform Commission under Bhutto.

23. Shaikh Muhammad Rashid, *Pakistan Main Zareei Inquilab Ki Zururat* (Lahore: Pakistan Kisan Committee, 1970), p. 20. The title may be rendered in English as "The Need for Agrarian Revolution in Pakistan."

24. *The Listener* 99 (1978), p. 624.

25. Nigar Ahmad, *Peasant Struggle in a Feudal Setting* (Islamabad: Quaid-e-Azam Resurgence, 1980).

26. Ibid., p. 66.

27. Fazlur Rahman, "The Sources and Meaning of Islamic Socialism," in Donald Eugene Smith, ed., *Religion and Political Modernization* (New Haven, Conn.: Yale University Press, 1974), p. 244.

28. Mohammed Noman, ed., *Our Struggle, 1857–1947* (Karachi: Pakistan Publications, n.d.), Appendix 2, p. 27.

29. Wilfrid Cantwell Smith, *Modern Islam in India* (Lahore: Ripon, 1943), p. 331.

30. Khalid B. Sayeed, *Politics in Pakistan: The Nature and Direction of Change* (New York: Praeger, 1980), pp. 17–18.

31. Masud, *Note of Dissent*, p. 46.

32. Yusuf Ali, *Glorious Qur'an*, 1: 189.

33. Kierman, *Iqbal*, pp. 43–44.

34. Ibid., p. 47.

35. Noman, *Our Struggle*, Appendix 2, p. 27.

36. Cited in Thomas Hodgkin, "The Revolutionary Tradition in Islam," *Race and Class* 21, no. 3 (1980): 230.

37. Ibid., p. 232.

38. Hamid Enayat, *Modern Islamic Political Thought* (London: Macmillan, 1982), pp. 190–94.

39. Hamid Alger, *The Islamic Revolution in Iran* (London: Open Press, 1980), p. 3.

40. The Statement of the People's Mujahedin Organization of Iran in Response to the Recent Accusations of the Iranian Regime (Tehran: The People's Mujahedin Organization of Iran, n.d.), p. 10.

41. *The New York Times Magazine*, October 7, 1979.

Bibliography: For Further Reading

GENERAL

Aronoff, Myron T., ed. *Religion and Politics*. New Brunswick, N.J.: Transaction Books, 1983.

Lutz, Jessie G., and El-Shakhs, Salah, eds. *Tradition and Modernity*. Washington, D.C.: University Press of America, 1982.

Merkl, Peter H., and Smart, Ninian, eds. *Religion and Politics in the Modern World*. New York: New York University Press, 1983.

Smith, Donald Eugene, ed. *Religion and Political Modernization*. New Haven, Conn.: Yale University Press, 1974.

JUDAISM

Abramov, S. Zalmon. *Perpetual Dilemma: Jewish Religion in the Jewish State*. Rutherford, N.J.: Fairleigh Dickinson University Press, 1976.

Agus, Jacob B. *Jewish Identity in an Age of Ideologies*. New York: Frederick Ungar Publishing Co., 1978.

Avineri, Shlomo. *The Making of Modern Zionism*. New York: Basic Books, 1981.

Buber, Martin. *The Kingship of God*. New York: Harper & Row, 1967.

Cohen, Steven M. *American Modernity and Jewish Identity*. New York and London: Tavistock Publishers, 1983.

Hartman, David. *Joy and Responsibility: Israel, Modernity and the Renewal of Judaism*. Jerusalem: Ben-Zvi-Posner Publishers, 1978.

Liebman, Charles S., and Don-Yehiya, Eliezer. *Religion and Politics in Israel*. Bloomington: Indiana University Press, 1984.

Schiff, Gary S. *Tradition and Politics: The Religious Parties of Israel*. Detroit, Mich.: Wayne State University Press, 1977.

Smooha, Sami. *Israel: Pluralism and Conflict*. Berkeley: University of California Press, 1981.

Waxman, M. *Judaism, Religion and Ethics*. New York: M. Yoseloff, 1960.

CHRISTIANITY

Bellah, Robert N. *The Broken Covenant: American Civil Religion in a Time of Trial*. New York: Seabury Press, 1975.

Berger, Suzanne, ed. *Religion in West European Politics*. London: Cassell, 1982.

Davis, Charles. *Theology and Political Society*. Cambridge: Cambridge University Press, 1980.

Hollenbach, David. *Claims in Conflict: Retrieving and Renewing the Catholic Human Rights Tradition*. New York: Paulist Press, 1979.

Mueller, Alois, and Greinacher, Norbert, eds. *The Church and the Rights of Man*. Concilium 124. New York: Seabury Press, 1979.

Murray, John Courtney. *The Problem of Religious Freedom*. Westminster, Md.: Newman Press, 1965.

Niebuhr, H. Richard. *Christ and Culture*. New York: Harper & Row, 1951.

Sanders, Thomas G. *Protestant Concepts of Church and State: Historical Backgrounds and Approaches for the Future*. New York: Holt, Rinehart & Winston, 1964.

Tillich, Paul. *The Protestant Era*. Chicago: University of Chicago Press, 1948.

ISLAM

Ajami, Fouad. *The Arab Predicament: Arab Political Thought and Practice since 1967*. Cambridge: Cambridge University Press, 1981.

Anderson, J.N.D. *Islamic Law in the Modern World*. New York: New York University Press, 1959.

Binder, Leonard. *Religion and Politics in Pakistan*. Berkeley: University of California Press, 1961.

Cohen, Amnon. *Jewish Life Under Islam: Jerusalem in the Sixteenth Century*. Cambridge, Mass.: Harvard University Press, 1984.

Daniel, N. A. *Islam and the West: The Making of an Image*. Edinburgh: Edinburgh University Press, 1962.

Dessouki, 'Ali E. Hillal, ed. *Islamic Resurgence in the Arab World*. New York: Praeger Publishing, 1982.

Esposito, John L. *Voices of Resurgent Islam*. New York: Oxford University Press, 1983.

Fischer, Michael J. *Iran: From Religious Dispute to Revolution*. Cambridge, Mass.: Harvard University Press, 1980.

Haddad, Yvonne Y. *Contemporary Islam and the Challenge of History*. Albany: State University of New York Press, 1982.

Keddie, Nikkie R., ed. *Religion and Politics in Iran: Shi'ism from Quietism to Revolution*. New Haven: Yale University Press, 1985.

Mortimer, Edward. *Faith and Power: The Politics of Islam*. New York: Vintage Books, 1982.

Rahman, Fazlur. *Islam and Modernity: Transformation of an Intellectual Tradition.* Chicago: University of Chicago Press, 1982.

Rosenthal, E.I.J. *Islam in the Modern National State.* Cambridge: Cambridge University Press, 1965.

About the Contributors

CHARLES J. ADAMS is Professor of Islamic Studies and former Director of the Institute of Islamic Studies at McGill University. He is the co-author of *Modern Trends in World Religions*.

MITCHELL COHEN is Assistant Professor of Political Science at Baruch College of the City University of New York. He edited and introduced a recent edition of Ber Borochov, *Class Struggle and the Jewish Nation: Selected Essays in Marxist Zionism*.

CHARLES DAVIS is Professor of Religion at Concordia University. He was President of the Canadian Society for the Study of Religion, 1971–74, and delivered the Hulsean Lectures at Cambridge University, 1977–78. His numerous publications include *Christ and World Religions* and *Theology and Political Society*.

MATTHEW L. LAMB is Associate Professor of Theology at Marquette University and is the author of *Solidarity with Victims: Toward a Theology of Social Transformation*.

JOHN P. LANGAN, S.J., is Research Fellow at Woodstock Theological Centre and lecturer in the Department of Philosophy at Georgetown University. He is co-editor of *Human Rights in the Americas*.

MARTIN E. MARTY is the Fairfax M. Cone Distinguished Service Professor and Professor of Modern Christianity at the Divinity School of the University of Chicago. He is associate editor of *Christian Century*. Among his many books and articles are *A Nation of Behavers* and *The Righteous Empire: The Protestant Experience in America*, which received the 1972 National Book Award.

JOHN T. PAWLIKOWSKI, O.S.M., is Professor of Social Ethics at the Catholic Theological Union in Chicago. He is a member of the Advisory Committee of the

Secretariat of the National Conference of Catholic Bishops for Catholic-Jewish Relations, and his recent publications include *What Are They Saying About Jewish-Christian Relations?* and *Christ in the Light of Jewish-Christian Dialogue*.

FAZLUR RAHMAN is Professor in the Department of Near Eastern Languages and Civilizations at the University of Chicago. He was the Director of the Institute of Islamic Research in Pakistan from 1962 to 1968, and is the author of *Islam and Modernity: Transformation of an Intellectual Tradition*. The best known of his works, *Islam*, has been translated into Italian and Turkish. During the Iranian crisis of 1979–80, he was engaged as a consultant on Islamic affairs to the United States State Department.

KHALID BIN SAYEED teaches Political Science at Queen's University, Kingston, Ontario, where he is Director of the Institute for Commonwealth Studies. The author of *Politics in Pakistan: The Nature and Direction of Change*, he has been twice engaged as a United Nations consultant on Iran.

ROBERT M. SELTZER is Associate Professor of History at Hunter College of the City University of New York and at the City University Graduate School. His recent writings include *Jewish People, Jewish Thought: The Jewish Experience in History*.

MANFRED H. VOGEL is Professor of the Philosophy of Religion in the Department of the History and Literature of Religions at Northwestern University. He has been President of the American Theological Society (Midwest) and has written on modern Jewish identity and on the dialogue between Judaism and Christianity.

MARVIN ZONIS is Associate Professor of Behavioral and Social Sciences at the University of Chicago, where he has served as Director of the Center for Middle Eastern Studies. He is the author of *The Political Elite of Iran*.

EDITORS

NIGEL BIGGAR is Librarian at Latimer House, Oxford. He is a doctoral candidate in Christian Theology at the Divinity School of the University of Chicago and holds degrees from Oxford University, Regent College and the University of Chicago.

WILLIAM SCHWEIKER holds degrees from Simpson College, Duke University, and the University of Chicago. He is Assistant Professor of Theology and Ethics at the School of Religion, University of Iowa.

JAMIE S. SCOTT is a doctoral candidate in Religion and Literature at the Divinity School of the University of Chicago, holds degrees from Cambridge University, Queen's University and Carleton University, and is a Lecturer in Religious Studies at York University, Toronto.

Index

'Abd al-Azis, Omar Bin, 218
'Abd al-Ghaffar Khan, Khan, 213
'Abd al-Nasser, 176, 180, 184, 217
'Abd al-Wahhab, Muhammad ibn, 180, 202, 208
'Abduh, Muhammad, 178, 212
'Abdullah Yusuf 'Ali, 164, 215, 224, 229
Abington School District v. *Schempp*, 102
Abrahannan, Ervand, 206
Abramov, S. Zalman, 52–54
Abu-Laban, Baha, 191
Adams, C. C., 208
Adams, Ruth, 97
Adler, M., 85
Agudat Israel (Union of Israel), 40–43, 45, 48, 51, 53
Agus, Jacob, 62, 64, 69
Ahmad, Nigar, 219–20, 229
Ajami, Fouad, 207
Akhtar, Jamila, 229
Albert, Michael, 96, 98
Algar, Hamid, 208, 226, 230
'Ali, 'Abdullah Yusuf, 164, 215, 224, 229
Alkalai, Yehudah, 38
Allah, Wally, 159

"American Catholic Bishop's Peace Pastoral," 66
American Civil Liberties Union, 105
American Jewish Committee, 67
Amish, 105
An-archy, 74, 82
Anderson, J. N. D., 190
Apel, Karl-Otto, 85, 97
Appiah-Kubi, Kofi, 98
Aquinas, Thomas, 107, 125
Arafat, Yasir, 199, 227
Arendt, Hanna, 79, 86, 90, 96, 98, 150
Asefat ha'Nivharim, 41–42
Assad, Hafiz al-, 183, 202
Assimilation, 56
Athanasius, St. (Bishop of Alexandria), 76
Atlas, Samuel, 26, 32
Auden, W. H., 102
Augustine, St. (Bishop of Hippo), 2, 76, 107, 144–45
Auschwitz, 64

Babhash, Shaul, 206
Baha'i, 173
Bahro, Rudolf, 98
Bakr, Abu, 156
Bar-Ilan, Meir, 52

Barnes, Timothy D., 95
Barr, James, 110, 116
Basic Laws (*Hukei yesod*), 44
Bayat, Mangol, 190
Bazargan, 194
Becker, Ernest, 98
Becker, Howard S., 99
Becker, Karl, 86
Becket, Thomas à, 125
Begin, Menachem, 43, 45, 51
Ben-Gurion, David, 39, 43, 46, 48
Benjamin, Walter, 148, 150
Ben Meir, Yehudah, 49–51
Bentham, Jeremy, 144
Berger, Suzanne, 54
Bernays, J. L., 27
Bernstein, Richard J., 86, 96–98
Berrigan, Daniel, 103
Bettelheim, Bruno, 79, 96
Betti, Emilio, 85
Bhutto, Zulfikar Ali, 217–21, 229
Bieber, Hugo, 32
Binder, Leonard, 191, 207
Black, Hugo, 112
Blake, William, 111
Blank, Irvin M., 69
Bleicher, Josef, 98
Boland, Francis J., 141
Bonhoeffer, Dietrich, 102
Bottomore, Tom, 99
Bowles, Samuel, 96
Boyers, Robert, 96
Braunthal, Alfred, 100
Brewer, A., 94
Brinker, Menachem, 61–62, 68
Brown, E. Richard, 98
Brown, Peter, 95
Brunner, Emil, 114
Buber, Martin, 14–15, 20
Bühlmann, Walbert, 98
Bultmann, Rudolf, 85
Burke, Edmund, 139, 145, 150
Butterfield, Herbert, 95

Cairo University, 190, 212
Calvin, John, 107
Capra, Fritjof, 95, 99
Carter, Jimmy, 30, 119

Catholic Worker movement, 103
Caton, Hiram, 95
Charlemagne, 77
Chelkowski, Peter, 190
Cheyney, Edward P., 95
"Christian Right" (U.S.), 81, 104
Christians, Clifford G., 117
Christiansen, Eric, 95
CIA, 193–94, 206
Clagett, M., 95
Coffin, William S., 103
Cohen, Mitchell, 7
Cohen, Steven M., 23, 32
Cohn, Werner, 32
Collins, Joseph, 99
Conlan, John, 112, 114, 116
Constantine, 76
Cormie, Lee, 94
Cox, Harvey, 110, 116
Cranston, Maurice, 121, 140
Crecelius, Daniel, 190
Cullen, Susan, 97
Currie, Gregory, 97
Cutter, William, 65, 69

Davis, Charles, 7
Darling, Malcolm, 213–14, 216, 228–29
Declaration of Independence (Israel), 35, 44–45
Declaration of Independence (U.S.), 104–5
de Clermont-Tonnerre, Stanislas, 36
Dekmejian, R. Hrair, 191
Democratic Fraction, 38
Denney, Reuel, 38
Derry, John W., 144, 150
Desroche, Henri, 101–2, 104, 116
Dessouki, 'Ali E. Hillal, 180, 190, 207–8
Dewey, John, 85, 114
Diaspora, 17–21, 26, 62, 67
Dilthey, Wilhelm, 78–79, 85
Din, Ahmad Baha' al-, 207
Din al-Afghani, Jamal al-, 160, 226
Din Khilji, 'Ala' al-, 158
Donagan, Alan, 131, 141
Donner, Frank J., 99
Don-Yehiya, Eliezer, 42–43, 53

Doran, Robert M., 98
Dreyfus, Alfred, 37
Dubnow, Simon, 28, 32
Dulong, Renaud, 54
Durkheim, Emile, 102
Duverger, Maurice, 39, 53
Dworkin, Ronald, 120, 140

Eagleson, John, 98, 100
Eccle, Chris, 208
Eccles, John C., 98
Edwards, Jonathan, 110
Ehler, Sidney, 141
Einstein, Albert, 91–92
Elbaz, Shlomo, 67, 69
Eliade, M., 94
Eliot, T. S., 22, 32
Ellenson, David, 69
Ellul, Jacques, 95, 112, 117
El-Shakhs, Salah, 190
Emancipation (Jewish), 11, 18–19, 27–28, 30, 33, 36
Enayat, Hamid, 230
Engel v. *Vitale*, 102
Enlightenment, 36, 62, 77–79, 83, 85
Epstein, F., 32
Equal Rights Amendment, 104
Eretz Israel (Land of Israel), 37, 39, 51
Eschatology, 56–58
Esposito, John, 190
Ethics: Christian, 120, 134–35, 138–39; Jewish, 13–14, 16, 24

Fackenheim, Emil, 64
Fallows, James, 99
Falwell, Jerry, 81
Fedayin-i Khalq, 194, 206
Federal Council of Churches, 107
Feinberg, Joel, 121, 140
Feuerbach, L., 84
Feyerabend, Paul, 84, 97
Fischer, Michael J., 208
Fishman, Aryei, 53
Fowler, Dean, 97
Frankfurt School, 97
Franklin, Benjamin, 114
Freeman, Michael, 150
French National Assembly, 36

French Revolution, 36, 122, 150
Freud, Sigmund, 78–79, 84

Gabai Moshe, 60, 68
Gabor, Dennis, 99
Gadamer, Hans-George, 79, 85, 96
Gaffney, Patrick, 208
Galiyev, Sultan, 226
Gandhi, Mahatma, 80, 87, 91
Gardet, L., 207
Gay, Peter, 95
Gdansk, 6
Gellner, Ernst, 105, 116, 207, 211–12, 228
George, Susan, 99
Gewirth, Alan, 121, 140–41
Ghiselin, Brewster, 99
Gibb, H.A.R., 155, 164
Gibbon, Edward, 95
Gibbons, Michael, 98
Gilby, Thomas, 116
Gilchrist, J., 95
Gilkey, Langdon, 94, 97
Ginsburg, Asher, 37
Gintis, Herbert, 96
Glazer, Nathan, 99
Gliddens, Anthony, 95
Goodman, Robert, 97
Goodman, Saul, 33
Gordon, Haim, 61, 68
Goren, Arthur A., 33
Goren, Shlomo, 43
Gorz, Andre, 95
Gouldner, Alvin W., 86, 98
Graham, Billy, 111
Greenberg, Irving, 64–66, 69
Greinacher, Norbert, 141
Gremillion, Joseph, 99
Gunkel, Herman, 20
Gush, Emunim (Bloc of the Faithful), 50–51
Gutierrez, Gustavo, 100, 105
Gutting, Gary, 97

Ha'am, Ahad, 28, 38, 43, 52
Habermas, Jürgen, 78–79, 81, 85, 96
Habib, John, 190
Haddad, Yvonne Y., 189–91

Haham, Bashi, 42, 53
Hahnel Robin, 96, 98
Halakhah, 13, 45, 48
Halakhic Judaism, 12, 15–17
Halliday, Fred, 184
Hammer, Zevulun, 49, 51
Hanaf, Hasan, 212, 228
Hanna, Mary, 103, 116
Ha'Poel Ha'Mizrahi, 40–41, 43, 53
Harris, Christina Phelps, 208
Hartmann, David, 56–58, 64, 68
Hasidic Judaism, 12
Hausaini, I. M., 208
Hegel, G.W.F., 94
Heidegger, Martin, 85
Heider, Agha Sajjad, 229
Heiler, F., 94
Heine, Heinrich, 27
Helsinki Agreement (1975), 119
Hengel, Martin, 100
Henkin, Alan, 65, 69
Hennelly, Alfred, 140–41
Herron, George, 110
Hertzberg, Arthur, 52
Herzl, Theodor, 28, 36–39, 43, 52
Heschel, Abraham, 20, 59, 61–62, 68
Heyworth-Dunne, J., 208
Hirsch, Richard, 52
Hitler, Adolf, 41
Hobbes, Thomas, 128–29
Hodges, Donald C., 96
Hodgkin, Thomas, 229
Hodgson, M.G.S., 208
Hoge, Dean, 108–9
Hollenbach, David, 135–36, 141
Holloway, David, 99
Holocaust (Jewish), 30, 55, 62, 64, 66, 79
Holy Roman Empire, 77
Hoqq, General Zia al-, 164, 172, 188, 212
Horkheimer, Max, 86, 95–96, 98
Horowitz, Irving L., 94
Humphrey, Hubert, 30
Hurewitz, J. C., 52–53
Hussein (King of Jordan), 200–201, 226

Hutcheson, Richard G., Jr., 108–9, 116
Hutterites, 105

Incarnation, 62
Ingleby, David, 96
Iqbal, Muhammad, 212–13, 221, 224–25
Iranian Revolution, 176, 184, 193
Isaacs, Stephen D., 33
Ishaq, Ibn, 164
Islamic Republican party (Iran), 172
Islamic Revival, 196, 199, 203–6
Israel (State of), 5, 13, 18, 30, 35–36, 42, 56, 58–59, 203
Iyer, Raghavan N., 96

Jacobs, L., 20
Jama 'at-i Islami, 176–83, 186, 189, 217
James, William, 85, 113
Jaspers, Karl, 80, 87, 96
Jay, Martin, 96
Jedin, Hubert, 94
Jefferson, Thomas, 114, 132
Jehovah's Witnesses, 105
Jerusalem, 58–60, 63
Jewish Worker's Bund, 29
Jihad, 154, 161, 164
Jinnah, Muhammad 'Ali, 213, 221, 225
John XXIII, 136
John Paul II, 1, 124, 141
Judea, 49–50
Jung, Carl, 85
Justification, 16

Kahane, Meir, 60
Kalischer, Zvi Hirsch, 38
Kardar, Hafeez, 218
Kasemann, Ernst, 100
Katz, Jacob, 24, 32
Kazemi, Farhad, 208
Keddie, Nikki P., 208
Kedourie, E., 207
Kemal, Namik, 160, 162
Kennedy, John F., 29
Khan, Malik Muhammad Iqbal, 219
Khan, Sayyid Ahmad, 178
Khomaini, Ayatollah Rouhollah, 5, 158,

162–64, 182, 185–86, 189, 194–95,
  198, 201, 205–7, 212, 226–28
Khudai Khidmatgars, 213
King, Martin Luther, 103
Kinley, David, 99
Kishk, Muhammad Jalal, 207
Kishk, Shaik Abdel Hamid, 201
Kissinger, Henry, 226
Kitagawa, Joseph M., 94
Kleinberger, Aharon F., 54
Kluckhohn, Clyde, 115, 117
Knesset, 43–44, 47–48
Koestler, Arthur, 98–99
Kohler, K., 99
Kohut, Heinz, 208
Kolakowski, Leszek, 96
Kook, Avraham Itzhak, 39–40, 50, 52–
  53
Kristol, Irving, 32
Kuhn, Thomas, 84
Kung, Hans, 83, 97

Labor Zionists, 39–40
Lacey, Robert, 206–7
Lakatos, Imre, 84, 97
Lamb, Matthew L., 7, 94–99
Landau, Shmuel Haim, 40
Langan, John P., 7, 140–41
Langer, William L., 95
Lappe, Francis Moore, 99
Law: covenantal, 24; *Hukei yesod,* 44;
  Islamic, 26, 159, 171; Jewish, 26;
  Rabbinic, 26; Talmudic, 26
Lebanon, 50–51, 53
Lederer-Gibel, Inge, 67, 69
Leff, Gordon, 95
Leonhard, Wolfgang, 97
Levine, Daniel H., 98
Lewis, Bernard, 207, 209
Lewis, C. S., 111
Leys, Simon, 98
Liberalism, 21, 27, 31
Liberation Theology, 105, 127
Lichter, Robert, 23, 32
Liebman, Charles, 23, 32–33, 42–43,
  53
Lincoln, Abraham, 115
Lonergan, Bernard, 94, 97, 99

Long, David Edwin, 190
Luther, Martin, 107, 109
Lutz, Jessie G., 190

McCarthy, Rockne, 113, 117
McCarthy, Thomas, 96
MacDonald, Timothy, 100
McGovern, George, 30
MacIntyre, Alasdair, 81, 86, 94–99
McMurtry, John, 98
McShane, Philip, 98
Mafdal (National Religious party), 43,
  45, 48–50, 52
Magdoff, Harry, 94
Maguire, Daniel C., 96–97
Mahdi, Imam, 187
Maimon, Yehuda Leib Hacohen, 44, 53
Maimonides, Moses, 25, 32
Makkreel, Rudolf A., 96
Manceron, Claude, 95
Mann, Horace, 104
Mannheim, Karl, 105, 116
Mapai party, 39–40, 43, 48
Marcuse, Herbert, 79–80, 96
Marginality, 24, 30
Maritain, Jacques, 107, 133, 141
Martin, Richard, 190
Marty, Martin E., 7, 20, 108
Marx, Karl, 78–79, 84, 86, 137
Masud, M., 214, 223, 228–29
Matthews, William, 99
Mawdudi, 183
Mayer, Arno J., 95
Mead, Sidney E., 114, 116
Mecca mosque incident, 206
Medhurst, Kenneth, 54
Meir, Golda, 48
Meisels, Dov Berush ben Isaac, 27
Melamed, Avraham, 52
Melden, A. I., 121, 140
Mendes-Flohr, Paul R., 32
Merchant, Carolyn, 95
Metz, Johann Baptist, 93–94, 100
Meyer, Ben F., 94
Meyer, Michael A., 27, 32
Mill, John Stuart, 44, 53, 144
Mische, Gerald, 99
Mishneh Torah, 25

Mitchell, Richard, 190
Mizrahi, 38–39, 42–43, 53–54
Moberg, David O., 108, 116
Mommsen, Wolfgang J., 94
Mon-archy, 74, 82
Mondale, Walter, 30
Monotheism, 57
Moody, Dwight L., 111
Moore, Basil, 98
Morelli, Mark, 99
Morrall, John B., 141
Mortimer, Edward, 207
Mossadegh, Mohammad, 193–94
Motzkin, Leo, 38
Moyser, George, 54
Mubarak, Mohamed Hosni, 204
Muhammad, 4, 153–56, 163, 203, 213, 224
Mujahedin-i Khalq, 194, 206, 212, 227
Mukhtar, Uman al-, 212
Muller, Alois, 141
Mumford, Lewis, 95
Munzer, Thomas, 105, 107
Murdoch, Iris, 141
Murray, John Courtney, 59, 62, 113–17
Musgrave, Alan, 97
Muslim Brothers, 174, 176, 183, 186, 190, 195, 200, 202
Muslim League, 213, 217, 225

Naipaul, V. S., 209
Nathan, Otto, 99
National Council (Israel), 41
National Council of Churches (U.S.), 103, 107
National Religious party (Israel), 38, 48–49
National Rifle Association, 104
Navon, Yitzhak, 66
New Deal, 29
Niebuhr, H. Richard, 110, 116
Niebuhr, Reinhold, 21, 32, 65, 81, 112, 114, 116
Niemoller, Martin, 125
Nisbet, Robert, 99
Nobel, Robert, 98
Noman, Mohammed, 229
Norden, Heinz, 99

Norman, Edward R., 122, 141
Nozick, Robert, 120, 129, 140–41
Nussbaum, F. L., 95

Old Order Mennonites, 105
Old Yishuv, 41–42
Oppewal, Donald, 113
Orrill, Robert, 96
Ottoman Empire, 42, 202

Pahlavi, Ashraf, 207
Pahlavi, Mohammad Reza, 207
Pakistan People's party, 217–18, 220–21
Palmer, Parker J., 98
Pannikkar, Raimundo, 94
Pawlikowski, John, 7, 68–69
Peerman, Dean G., 20
Peres, Shimon, 48
Peretz, Y. L., 29
Perrin, Norman, 92, 99
Peterson, E., 95
Peukert, Helmut, 86, 98
Philipson, Ludwig, 28
Pierce, Charles Sanders, 85
Pinson, Koppel S., 32
Pipes, Daniel, 207
Piscatori, James, 207
Pius IX, 124, 141
Plantinga, Alvin, 141
Plaut, W. Gunther, 32
Plongeron, Bernard, 122, 141
Poalei Agudat Israel (PAI-Worker of Agudat Israel), 41–43
Polish, David, 61, 68
"Political dimension," 12
Popper, Karl R., 98
Proctor, J. Harris, 207

Quandt, William B., 206
Qureishi, Regula B., 191
Qutb, Sayyid, 183

Radicalism (political), 143–45, 147–50
Radnitzky, Gerard, 84, 97
Rahman, Fazlur, 7, 165, 190, 208, 229
Rahner, Karl, 97
Rais, Mohammad Amien, 208

Rashid, Abbasid Harun al-, 159
Rauschenbusch, Walter, 110, 116
Rawls, John, 120, 140–41
Regev, Uri, 52
Reines, Itzhak Yosef, 38–39
"Religion," 16
Religious Communites Ordinance, 42
Renan, Ernest, 20
Reuther, Rosemary, 97
Ricoeur, Paul, 85–86, 98
Riesman, David, 99
Ring, Nancy, 99
Rinott, Moshe, 52
Rodinson, Maxime, 190, 208
Roman Empire, 74
Roosevelt, Franklin D., 29
Roosevelt, Kermit, 206
Rosenblatt, Samuel, 53
Rosenthal, E.I.J., 207
Roth, Guenther, 95
Rothman, Stanley, 23, 32
Rousseau, Richard W., 68, 143
Rubenstein, Aryeh, 54
Rubenstein, Richard, 64
Rubinstein, W. D., 33
Rufesien, Oswald, 47
Russian Zionists, 38
Ryan, John A., 141

Sadat Anwar al-, 1, 168, 176, 180, 186,
    195, 202, 204
Safran, Nadav, 53, 208
Sahi, Abrar Fatima, 229
Saikal, Amin, 198, 207
Samaria, 49–50
Sanctification, 16
Sa'ud, Muhammad Ben, 202, 208
Sayeed, Khalid Bin, 7, 229
Schell, Jonathan, 89–90, 94, 96, 99–
    100
Schiff, Gary S., 52–53
Schindler, Alfred, 95
Schlafly, Phyllis, 104
Schneider, Michael, 96
Scholem, Gershom, 25, 32
Schwartz-Nobel, Loretta, 99
Second Vatican Council, 59, 62, 94
Segraves v. *California*, 111

Segundo, Juan Luis, 105
Selim I, 158
Seltzer, Robert M., 7, 52
Senior, Donald, 69
Shalit, Benjamin, 48
Shamir, Yitzhak, 51
Shannon, Thomas A., 99
Shapira, Moshe Haim, 44, 53
Shapiro, Leonard, 33
Sharkansky, Ira, 54
"Shas" (Sephardic Torah Guardians),
    51
Shashar, Michael, 54
Sheri'ati, 'Ali, 212
Shi'i (Islam), 163, 185–86, 194, 196–
    97, 200–201, 205, 226
Sidorsky, David, 32
Silberg, Moshe, 47
Six Day War, 48
Slocum, W. L., 229
Smith, Al, 29
Smith, Brian H., 54
Smith, Dan, 94, 99
Smith, Donald Eugene, 229
Smith, Ronald G., 20
Smith, Wilfred Cantwell, 94, 99, 176,
    190–91, 222, 229
Smythies, J. R., 98
Sovereignty, 17–18, 35, 61, 63–65
Sperber, Manes, 65, 69
Spykman, Gordon, 113
Starski, Stanislaw, 98
Stavrianos, L. S., 99
Stern, Fritz, 96
Stevenson, Adlai, 29
Strauss, Leo, 128, 141
Stringfellow, William, 112, 117
Sunni (Islam), 163, 185, 197, 201–2,
    205
Syllabus of Errors (1864), 124
Syn-archy, 74, 82
Szasz, Thomas, 79, 96

Tahtawi, al-, 178
Taimiya, Ibn, 159
Talal, Hussein bin (King of Jordan),
    200–201, 226
Taleghani, Ayatollah Mahmud, 194

Talmon, Shemaryahu, 56–69, 64, 68
Talmud, 26, 39
Tehran, 6
Tel Aviv University, 209
Theissen, Gerd, 100
Theocracy, 26, 36, 51
Third World, 30, 80, 93
Thompson, E. P., 94, 99
Thompson, John B., 98
Thoreau, Henry David, 110
Tillich, Paul, 106–7, 110, 114, 116
Tinder, Glenn, 98
Tirosh, Yosef, 53
Tonnies, Ferdinand, 99
Torah, 24, 40, 43–44
Torcaso v. *Watkins*, 112
Torres, Sergio, 98, 100
Toulmin, Stephen, 84
Tracy, David, 86, 94, 98, 114, 117
Troeltsch, Ernst, 100
Truman, Harry S., 29

Unger, Roberto Mangabeira, 98
United Nations, 49
United Nations Universal Declaration of
    Human Rights, 119, 121, 131
United Religious Front (Israel), 42–43
Urban, G. R., 97
Utopia, 25, 57, 82

Van Herik, Judith, 96
Van Hook, Jay M., 117
Vatin, Jean-Claude, 190, 207
Voegelin, Eric, 97
Vogel, Manfred H., 7, 20, 62–64, 68–69
Voll, John Obert, 207

Wach, Joachim, 102, 104, 116
Wallace, Henry, 29
Warhaftig, Zerach, 54
Warwick, Donald P., 97
Waugh, Earle H., 191

Weber, Max, 77, 90–91, 93, 95, 99
Weber, Paul J., 107–8, 116
Weizmann, Chaim, 36, 38
Wellhausen, Julius, 22
Weltanschauung, 11
Werblowsky, R. J. Zwi, 31, 33, 60–62,
    68
Weschler, Lawrence, 98
West Bank, 49–50
"Western Wall," 49
Whitehead, Alfred North, 107, 109,
    116
Whitehead, John W., 112, 114, 116
Wiener, Max, 20
Williams, John Alden, 190
Williams, Roger, 106
Williams, William A., 94
Wilson, Edmund, 115, 117
Winograd, Philip, 32
Winter, Gibson, 110, 116
Witte, Sergei, 28
Wittich, Claus, 95
World Council of Churches, 57, 107
World Zionist Organization, 36–37, 46
Worrall, John, 97

Yaron, Zvi, 53
Yassini, Ayman al-, 190
Yazdi, Ibrahim, 194
Yazid, Caliph, 201
Yeats, William Butler, 80
Yoder, John Howard, 112, 117
Yom Kippur (Day of Atonement), 39
"Young Guard," 49–50

Zabith, Stephen, 206
Zion, 59–60
Zionism, 28–31, 35–38, 40, 43, 49, 56,
    59–60
Zionist Congress, 37–38
Zipperstein, Steve J., 52
Zonis, Marvin, 7, 208–9